# Derailed in Uncle Ho's Victory Garden

# *A note on the author*

Tim Page became a photographer almost by chance. He was working in Laos in 1964 for US Aid on agricultural programmes. He had earned enough money to buy a camera which he used to take snaps of Buddhist temples, but when a coup kicked off in the capital, Vientiane, Page realised his true potential. He captured the unfolding events for the UPI news agency and sold his pictures to the bureau offices in Bangkok.

The role of war-photographer suited Page's craving for danger and excitement, and from February 1965 to 1969 he worked as a freelancer for Associated Press, *Paris-Match*, *Look* and *Time-Life*. Page was an iconic photographer of the Vietnam War and his pictures were the visual inspiration for many films of the period. The photojournalist in *Apocalypse Now*, played by Dennis Hopper, was based on Page.

The Vietnam war was the last conflict in which the military actively encouraged press involvement and Page went everywhere, covering the Da Nang landings and the mini-Tet offensive. He was wounded four times in Vietnam. The last time was when he jumped out of a helicopter and a mine blew up in front of him. He was pronounced DOA at the hospital and, though he was brought back to life by the surgeons, this episode spelt the end of that tour of Vietnam. He suffered from hemiplegia and required extensive neurosurgery, spending the majority of the 1970s in recovery.

It was while he was away recovering in hospital in spring 1970 that he learnt that his fellow photographer and close friend Sean Flynn, son of Hollywood movie star Errol, had gone missing in Cambodia. Throughout the 1970s and 80s Page's mission was to discover the final resting place of his friend and erect a memorial to all those media people killed in the war. With his friend Horst Faas, Associated Press photographer and double Pulitzer prize winner, he originated *Requiem*. This commemorated the work of all the dead and missing war photographers, from all nations, who were lost in the thirty year struggle for liberation.

Now Page divides his time between the quiet life in Kent and frequent returns to Indo-China. He has created the Indochina Media Memorial Foundation and is involved in setting up a media studies faculty at Hué University.

*Also by Tim Page*

Tim Page's Nam
Sri Lanka
Ten Years After: Vietnam Today
Page After Page
Mid-Term Report
Requiem (With Horst Faas)

# Derailed in Uncle Ho's Victory Garden

## Return to Vietnam and Cambodia

*Tim Page*

Scribner

First published in Great Britain by Touchstone, 1995
This edition published by Scribner, 1999
An imprint of Simon & Schuster UK Ltd
A Viacom Company



1 3 5 7 9 10 8 6 4 2

Simon & Schuster UK Ltd
Africa House
64-78 Kingsway
London WC2B 6AH

Simon & Schuster Australia
Sydney

A CIP catalogue record for this book is available from the British Library

ISBN 0-684-86024-4

Printed and bound in Great Britain by
The Bath Press, Bath

For all those friends and folks who have abetted the course of these adventures and writings a massive thanks, and especially for CCP for being there.

May peace prevail for the peoples of Indochina and that same peace grace the life of our son Kit.

# *Contents*


| | |
|---|---|
| Derailed | 1 |
| A Ticket to Ride | 8 |
| Border Runs | 49 |
| The Case of the Missing F4 | 85 |
| Danger on the Edge of Town | 104 |
| Getting There Then | 134 |
| The Search | 148 |
| Getting to Know the Generals | 207 |
| Foundations | 234 |
| Glossary | 250 |
| Maps | 253 |

# 1

# *Derailed*

It was one of those dream assignments; virtual free money, a junket, a day trip at day rates, home for dinner, one's own bed at night. On top of it all, it was a story to gladden the heart of any boy, large or small. It concerned the only train running at the time in Vietnam. There should have been two trains running that day in 1968, but the commuter special from Bien Hoa 25 klicks (kilometres) north of Saigon had once again been suspended owing to enemy activity; in other words, large holes had been found in the line.

Our junket would run from the station adjacent to Phu Bai airport, south of Hue. North of Hue nothing ran. Since the Tet Offensive of early 1968, when the siege of the city had lasted a month, almost razing the whole town as US marines and airborne forces battled to retake the citadel from the North Vietnamese die-hards, no train could cross the Eiffel-built bridge spanning the Perfume (Huong) River, the only remaining overland sinew north. The station on the south side had seen vicious hand-to-hand fighting.

Eight months had now elapsed after the Tet attacks with a lull in the fighting as the Vietcong licked their wounds and the North Vietnamese units regrouped and received replacements of men and material. In the interim, some bright spark dreamed up this demonstration of the advanced state of pacification and security the 'free world' forces had brought in southern Quang Ninh province. They would run a special work train down the newly refurbished track to the railhead approximately 20 kilometres to the south, still way short of the first tunnel at Lang Co. To publicise this glorious achievement they cajoled the Saigon press corps to send some of its members north for the day in a Vietnamese air-force C-47 borrowed from their VIP flight. This was an added incentive for those members of the corps who normally never left town unless they were guaranteed to be back in their own beds that same night.

When you didn't go on the dumb junkets you couldn't be sure of getting on the specials put onto the hot spots, so I went along. The outing had a holiday ambience; the field-going regulars in the group were relieved at the chance to cover a peaceful story for a change. An army truck took us the short rumble from the strip to the forlorn, shot-up building which passed as Phu Bai's station. Here the single mainline track split into a passing line and a short siding, upon which sat our train, the propaganda work express.

For an express it was a rather miserable train, composed of eight box cars, three gondolas, a couple of tankers and a flat car. There wasn't a single passenger coach, so the forty of so members of the press and their escorts decanted onto and into the dilapidated rolling stock. The train had been put together to protect the early-1950s French-built steam locomotive placed artfully five cars in from one end of the train. The 2-6-0 configuration soot- and oil-smirched asset was one of three marooned in the northern region. Its crew had been with it since it had been imported. The engine had survived numerous attacks, as witnessed by the bullet scars; the footplate held leaking sandbags as a barrier against a mine explosion.

The train carried a few rails, track hardware and a company of regional-force troops. Hammocks had been slung in the box cars; charcoal braziers warmed large pots for the squad's communal rice and soup rations. They had been partially re-equipped, under the new Vietnamisation campaign of the war, with the new M-16 assault rifle; many, however, still clutched the older M-1 Garands and their 30-calibre machine guns were tripod-mounted on the doors of the box cars. A few sandbags had been piled in front, giving the illusion of protection; mailbox-sized slits had been carved as firing ports into the heavy planks of the box-car sides. Initially the whole caboodle would be pushed down the line, the flat car up front, weighed down with a collection of rusty rails, to take the brunt of any mines. Four of us opted for it as the best spot for photo opportunities, though we talked nervously about the obvious danger. Our presence appeared to reassure the two troopers assigned to this 'suicide wagon'.

With much tooting of whistle and puffing of oily smoke, the panama-hatted engineer shugged the train onto its southerly course. The speed never picked up beyond a clacking canter of 20 kilometres per hour, yet the whole thing swayed alarmingly, giving the sensation that we could jump the track at any moment. At rebuilt culverts and the few bridges we slowed to a crawl, enabling everyone to climb down and get ahead for a few snaps. The few peasants we passed, working the rice paddies and gardens, gazed on, bemused by our passage. Groups of small boys on foot were able to keep up with our progress, having abandoned their buffalo-watching for a more glorious escapade. The day was balmy, with a blue sky and the occasional scudding white cloud. It all felt far too peaceful, the romantic sound of the steam locomotive replacing the noise we had grown used to – air strikes, artillery or even a distant firefight. It could have been a journey in another era, the illusion spoilt only by the lads packing the M-16s and the box cars bristling with gun muzzles.

It took over two hours to get to the railhead. We stopped a couple of hundred metres back from the end of the track, in a shallow cutting blocked by a wall of dirt, across which ran a cart track. Beyond that, the cut was waterlogged, coils of old-style barbed wire pulled open to deter Mr Charles (as the Vietcong were known) from mining the next section of reconstruction. A gang of militarily ineligible men were hewing at the cart track with picks and shovels; others pushed a pair of rolling-stock wheels towards the flat car to retrieve some rusted rails for the next lay. Half a dozen dozy territorials lurked in what little shade was available, cast by chest-high bushes a few metres away from the track gang. These men represented the ever-vigilant security. There was not a machine in sight; no bulldozer, grader, hoist or crane. At this rate the war would be over before they reached Da Nang.

All work ground to a halt while the members of the press scrambled over the project, but the workers were soon goaded back into gear by our escorts for the benefit of the TV cameras. A certain futility was imparted in the desultory swing of the tools, the lethargy with which the next rails were crowbarred into position for the pickers and shovellers to down their tools, pick up sledge-hammers and perform their spike-driving duties. Everyone milled around theatrically, providing a beautiful opportunity for any VC mortar team within range. Luckily it was park time, the midday siesta when the Viets of every persuasion called a halt to all activity to creep into any available shade for lunch and a kip.

The scene had been successfully canned, the powers that be satisfied, and there was a plane waiting for us. People wanted to get back to file their stories and brag about their day out to the war over a three-course dinner. For the ride back north I opted for the lead car, latterly running as the last, which acted as the caboose, or guard's van. The lack of danger prompted a cluster of folk to ride this chest-high-sided wagon accompanying the train guard. His official status was indicated by a clutch of coloured flags on split bamboo sticks and a silver whistle; a white nylon shirt and white topi completed his uniform.

Although they must have been able to hear us coming a

kilometre away, cows and buffaloes ambled off the track only at the last possible moment to the accompaniment of the screeching corroded brakes the driver was loath to apply, for he knew only too well the amount of air that was leaking from the connector hoses between his charges. Bringing this train to a standstill would take the skill of a captain of a supertanker in the confines of the English Channel. Metre-gauge railroads are notoriously prone to derailment; an errant bovine can easily tilt the delicate balance on the narrow track span. Anything larger will cause a disaster.

We were bowling along at a goodly clip, nearing the maximum of 30 klicks along a lovingly relaid straight stretch, a matter of minutes away from the gig's end. The photographers were down to snapping each other in 'posing for Mum' pix; someone passed a joint across.

A couple of hundred metres upline was an open railroad crossing, a military dirt road heading from Route One out into the badlands, where the inhabitants lived mainly in firebases, the civilians in a free-fire zone. A small convoy of empty tankers and ammo trucks was approaching the crossing, heading in from bandit country. The lead six-by, a big two-and-a-half ton six-wheeler with a fuel bowser strapped to its rear deck, had reached the edge of the line and stalled. The two GIs in the cab, one black, one white, were staring riveted at our approaching express. They had probably stalled in surprise at the vision of an actual running train snorting black smoke and tooting its francophone whistle.

Perched in that gondola car we had a grandstand view of the accident in the offing. We could see the whites of their astonished eyes, the black dude's more pronounced. We could hear their voices crescendoing, 'Hey, man, a train! I mean, dig the train! I mean, move this truck! Shit, man, get this truck outta here!' We could almost hear the whine of the starter motor, the carburettor flooded, the boot stamping on the gas pedal. 'Shit, man, that train coming, still coming! Oh, man, move this truck!' The eyes widened, the truck fired a cloud of black fumes and started to lurch forwards. It stalled again.

We careered on, prisoners of the straight track. The guard at the front was now in a frantic state, waving his flags and blowing his whistle simultaneously, to alert whom I could not quite figure. From behind us a series of screeching noises announced that the brakes had started to bite into the pitted wheel rims. The gap narrowed frighteningly quickly, we had only seconds left to impact.

I started to climb the chest-high, smooth metal side, thinking that from the inch-wide top I could launch outwards and down the bank to safety. The ground below blurred past and I balanced precariously half on, half off the top of the metal side. The passengers in the car were milling, the whistle blowing, the brakes screeching. The truck lurched forwards again; it surely had kangaroo petrol in the tank. For a moment it appeared as though the GIs would make it; then we impacted.

I was still clinging insecurely to the top of the car's side as the whole twenty-ton coffin momentarily jack-knifed up and slewed to the right. There was a crashing, tearing sound, followed by a rumbling as we rolled bumpily, slowing, the wheels now running in the sleepers and the hard gravel of the trackside path.

Somewhere about then, I launched outwards, two cameras around my neck, as terrified of that jump as the first and only time I had exited an aircraft midair with a static line-operated parachute. My last sight of the car was a jumble of people being catapulted to the front end, collapsing on top of the flag-waving, whistle-blowing guard.

I landed, executing a bad break roll, and sat dazed for a second. The train above me was still just moving, the gondola on the point of tipping over and rolling on top of me. I scurried back a few metres and caught a breath. Everything appeared to be functioning, nothing broken; the cameras seemed to have suffered no more than an average pounding. I just couldn't make my left hand hold the lens barrel to focus on the scene around. The little finger of that hand was cocked back at a weird angle, the knuckles rapidly swelling. Feeling bruises forming where I had impacted, I pushed slowly up to survey the wreckage. The survivors were now clambering down from the derailed first two cars. No one appeared to be badly hurt. The guard looked the most dishevelled, with one flag stick broken and his whistle of authority missing in action.

A hundred metres back down the line the six-by was upside down upon its bowser, the red dirt of the underside giving it the look of a destitute crab; a cluster of people were pulling the GIs from the wreck, whose wheels were still spinning. Both seemed to have broken a leg, but they had happy grins on their faces like, 'Man, this is a stateside wound!'

Back in Saigon three hours later, the field hospital next to the Tan San Nhut airbase took one look at my distorted finger, then snapped it back straight and strapped on an aluminium construction that started at the wrist before angling up the palm to crook the finger at a rakish angle. For ten days I paraded around with this splint, looking like a Balinese dancer, collecting drinks and day rates on the strength of the story.

Years later, looking at the snaps under the loup, I noticed the stencilling on the hood of the lorry that derailed us. It said, COUNTRY POWER.

# 2

# *A Ticket to Ride*

We must have been somewhere up in Binh Dinh province when Mum shook me awake with, 'Page, have a bone.' It had taken me ages to get to sleep in a third-class couchette designed for six but holding a good double that number, the air almost solid with humidity. Why would I wish to consume a bone; why would my first waking thought be of a femur, tibia or wing of some forlorn roadrunning, grease-laden fowl? It might have been duck, but then one doesn't often think of ducks on waking. Mum's mag lite, a gift from his last gig, ushering a *National Geographic* photographer about, spiked across me and briefly round the crowded compartment, coming to rest on a mess of food on a banana leaf. The chow lady must have hopped aboard as we crawled along at under 10 kilometres an hour. At first hit, the gloop appeared to be mainly rice coagulated with poultry fat and bits of unidentifiable veg.

'Fuck off, Mum,' I said to my interpreter.

I attempted to stretch in a space akin to a VC tunnel, the earth replaced by solid unyielding wood except for a straw mat beneath my numb bum, back and shoulders. It would later emerge that this same tatami had engendered the nasty red-grey whorls on my elbows, to be diagnosed as a species of ringworm which did not take kindly to hydrocortisone cream. I itched and scratched, unfolding my legs and arms from the coffin I shared with half our luggage. Mum had coiled himself about the rest of it on the rack above. Insane to have so much gear along on a Third World category-three express. We were supposed to have been on a second-classer, but that had somehow got shunted onto another track and then our complicated staging north from Ho'ville was supposed to finish up on a steam-powered local train.

Almost twenty years earlier, when the bells rang out round the world to herald the signing of peace in the Vietnam War, I had sat there bawling my eyes out in a sudden release of pent-up emotion. In the clarity of the calm after the storm, I had vowed that I would return to my formative land and ride the train that would signal its reunification.

In the event, it took another three years after the South had been liberated to get the tracks relaid between the erstwhile warring capitals. I, as sick as Vietnam, would not get back for much longer, but I still felt its magnet lure, and the need to see the roots of my madness.

Your average GI had to be there, the career military wanted to be there, and the Vietnamese lived there. Me, I had accepted UPI's offer of $90 a week to be a staff photographer in the war zone, starting just before the first American main force units came ashore over Red Beach in Da Nang. Inexperienced, I had taken a flying dive into the deep end of the pool without really knowing how to swim. Soon enough, my naivety and the exciting flushes of the *Boy's Own* annual were replaced by the mixture of callousness and compassion of the neutral observer. My involvement escalated with the conflict. From the security of a staff position I went to the insecure realms of a freelance; my home was in Saigon, with a second bed up in Da Nang. Pretty soon I had wandered the length and breadth of the embattled state.

My Saigon home was a household of fellow souls of sundry nationalities esconced in a three-storey villa. We had the reputation of an animal-house fraternity overloaded on the risqué. Our solace had not been in the bottle, but in fine sounds over an opium pipe. Our infamous houseboy, Frankie, had also got standing orders to keep the sandalwood box on my air-conned bedroom table topped up with a stash of the finest herbs besides a good dozen ready rolls. Sam Castan, a writer for *Look*, just before he got killed in an air cavalry clash with the NVA, had snipped a clipping from his magazine which was glued to the lid. It read, 'Two seconds, you're loaded.'

The scene had lasted over two years with a continual turnover of hip hard-core buddies all in the same line of business. The Vietnamese labelled us all *bao chi* – the press. The idyll ended only after I had been hit three times; by the VC, by insurrectionist Buddhist forces, and then by the American air force, not counting a motorcycle wreck on R & R in Bangkok. I was paid to get out by my then almost full-time employers, Time-Life, with the promise that they would guarantee work out of the Paris bureau, away from this conflict. In fact, my nerve had gone and it was good to get back to the world I had not seen for five years. However, nothing had any balls back in reality; the issues were muddled, the edge was not there. Back in the war everything had been black and white, life or death.

The West had kept me for nearly a year, distracted by the Six-Day War in the Middle East on the Arab side, and a sojourn traversing the United States trying to get to the root of the folk I had been fighting alongside in my adopted home. But it had been too much watching Charlie inside the US embassy grounds live on TV, too irking to see big magazine spreads and credited front-page photos by close friends. Disillusioned, broke and confused, I bought a one-way ticket back to the Nam. The Tet Offensive, the revolution of 1968, was upon us; the place to be in the midst of the biggest rock-and-roll show on earth was Vietnam.

The Year of the Monkey had lived up to its predicted form. Old friends drifted back; soon another collective emerged, on Tu Do Street above a sleazy bar, where Grahame Greene's novel *The Quiet American* had been filmed. We dug in, two Brits and two Americans, a gourd atop the bar always full of *chau duc* flowers finely chopped, the pipeman on tap by phone with his own moped – the height of civilisation. In that first week back, the *bao chi* had been decimated in the Mini-Tet, or Saigon, offensive. Five guys in a Mini-Moke in Cholon had been ambushed, leaving one Frank Palmos to escape by sprinting away as his executioner's .45 ran out of rounds. One AK round disabled two photographers in the old French cemetery, another wound up getting greased packing a sub-machine gun. It was good to be back at the edge, and soon I was flush with five pages in *Life*, the coffers swollen.

Everything had escalated. When I had first arrived in country from Laos in February 1965, there were fewer than 20,000 US military present, mainly advisers, some helicopter crews and supporting air force. By 1968, over half a million had been tasked to shoring up the quavering regime which had been coerced into propagating the American policy of communist containment. This policy was based on the domino theory: once one country in Southeast Asia fell to communism, all would follow, until yellow hordes would be swarming ashore to throw roadblocks across the San Diego Freeway. Meanwhile, back in the heartland of capitalism, the military-aerospace industrial complex burgeoned and prospered; the products of this boom fell in spades on a nation of rice farmers. An acid nightmare of modern warfare spilled its devastating horrors across a once tranquil, outstandingly beautiful land. We should have come to learn, to liberate ourselves, rather than obstruct their liberation. 'War is not good for children and other living things,' as a poster of the period illumined, but it was very good for business. The year of sex, drugs and rock and roll was iced with the craziness of war. It felt like hanging ten on a surfboard, unable to step off until the shore is reached, the wave over. There was a certain Zen to just staying alive, enhanced by making more and more definitive images that pleased the self as well as the client.

The bubble had to burst. My stopped Rolex later read 14.32, the moment that a Vietcong pioneer trooper touched the contacts command detonating a 250-lb anti-tank mine near the Cambodian border. A routine *Time* assignment got blown away that day in April 1969, the mine exploding beneath a 25th Division master sergeant who went twenty feet in the air, losing his legs. We had exited a chopper detoured to dust off two booby-trap victims, I dutifully in the sergeant's footsteps, three paces back. Unfortunately, a device of that dimension spreads its lethality across a broad spectrum; a lieutenant on the Huey was gravely wounded, the bird itself taking fifty hits. I was right in the zone, remembering only a strange wet feeling of sitting stunned, changing lenses, then staggering back to the chopper, feeling a pain in my legs as I collapsed in the door. An attendant nurse thumped my heart back to pump mode three times, but I was logged as dead on arrival at the main medical facility at Long Binh, outside Saigon.

Strange visions pulsed by before I refocused with dim sight and one eye, paralysed on my left side and, I am told, 200 cc of strategic grey matter lighter. An enlightened neurosurgeon, another unwilling draftee, had spent hours digging a chunk of shrapnel the size of a tenpenny nail out of the back of my skull. A colleague had meanwhile been sorting through my guts for lost splinters. The resulting effect was Frankenstein's monster, with a gut like a chicken trussed and stuffed for roasting.

What a long time ago that seems, a fucking eternity! The war was a doddle compared to the aftermath. Then, to have been a veteran instantly got you labelled as a murderer, baby killer, rapist, madman. Nobody wanted to know. America's gung-ho attitude had been replaced with cynicism derived from watching loved ones blown away or maimed in living colour over breakfast. Open your paper and there was your boyfriend, husband or brother in terminal anguish sponsored by the corporations that were promoting the ball game. Peace with honour was required and deviously delivered. Come to the peace table or your cities get wiped out, your ports mined, your dykes breached. It worked, but left Vietnamese to engage brother Viet while the superpowers continued a profitable resupply of the endlessly consumed material.

Everyone who had been there tended to get overinvolved, identified with a time that now is obsolete. The war days had been the ultimate in experience, laden with a magic, a glamorous edge that none who went through it can truly deny.

Train travel allows the mind to wander, the eyes not really focusing on the passing countryside, the heady clackety rhythm becoming white noise, a mere sound tapestry to meditate upon. On a train you have a sense of actually getting somewhere, denied the traveller sealed in an aluminium tube zooming across the sky. There is an intimacy with your fellow voyager, a shared sense of the adventure rather than the common fear of being five miles high in the inexplicable. We in the West have become too comfortable to experience the realities that most of the world lives with. We are in fat city – a minimal existence in the First World is the life of a neo-bourgeois in the Third. For too long, we have consumed and preached a morality based on greed rather than concern.

The shock awakening in the fetid, overcrowded compartment brought my fragile reality up like heartburn. Bones and gloop for breakfast, or was it dinner? I craved a hot cup of tea or coffee, and normality – whatever that is supposed to be.

My oversize stirring awoke the other residents, including the infant opposite, who began to voice its disapproval, and caused legs to start unfolding over the edge of the Belsen tiers above.

Wrapped in three layers of shirting and an anorak, I still

felt clammy cold; I'd forgotten how miserable it could be at night out in the field, waking from a semblance of sleep to conditions that one never quite gets accustomed to. The deprivations hadn't stopped, only the scenario had changed, and I was back to sleeping in my shoes for security's sake, which always leaves a heavy, dirty feeling below the knees akin to a hangover mouth. Needless to say, the ablutionary facilities were rudimentary, any remote thought of sit, shit, shower or shave completely pointless.

During the three days before our departure we had gone back and forth by cyclo between the station and railway headquarters on the traffic circle by the central market a good six times. In the end I had let Mum go alone on the jaunts, each of which was gradually unravelling the bureaucracy enshrouding the mysteries of how a foreigner could purchase a ticket, let alone one that broke journey, switching from one class or category to the other.

Our first sortie out to the new *ga* in Hon Hing, three kilometres from the downtown hotel quadrant, had engaged just about the entire staff of the booking office. Women of every age, from nymphette junior teller, with painted fingers and toes and diaphanous pyjamas, to a betel-chewing crone. They were all bossed about, as we pored over maps, timetables and photographic requirements, by a hard-faced, middle-aged lady in uniform slacks and pressed blouse. It was not possible to do what we wanted; foreigners wanted things they had no right to demand. She knew; she had fought them in the tunnels, in the forests, in the . . .

She disdainfully accepted a Salem Light as Mum produced my books and babbled good party polemics reduced to a petit-bourgeois level. Five years ago, not a timetable had existed, a coveted state secret. Madame now produced a complete file containing nearly every train movement in or out of her station. The old woman was sent for tea, and the crowd swelled in the area behind the ticket windows, under the vaulted ceiling of the French-style interior. Regular business ground to a standstill as the staff leafed through the books and files, getting to grips with an itinerary that avoided the photographically unproductive conditions of night travel. Since even the fastest express took a minimum of forty-eight hours, some of the trip would have to be in the dark.

Armed with the schedules, we retreated to the railway headquarters to get it authorised, since this seemingly could not be accomplished on one of the phones that kept ringing in the background. A bribe of Western cigarettes convinced the beret-wearing deputy director of the *chemin de fer* to start pumping telexes up the line. Permission in a totalitarian state is an endless palaver of committee decisions at local level with no one personally wanting to shoulder any responsibility. Back to the station with a letter of approval, back to headquarters for a stamp, back to the station to purchase a ticket.

Outside, our faithful *cyclo pousse* drivers, ever attendant. It was five years since I had last been in Saigon, during the Western-media-sponsored tenth anniversary of liberation megabash and parade, yet on my first sortie after arriving I had heard, 'Meester Teem, I hear you come back.' A baseball-hatted, moustached, handsome and by Viet standards tall guy pushed his rig out of the line on the sidewalk opposite. In 1985 Chanh had sported an NBC-logoed duckbill, an unofficial contract having been forged by the network for the duration. Now he had on a brash yellow one emblazoned with 'Top Gun'. I declined a lift, out for an evening stroll getting that familiar whiff back in my mind. Chanh persisted. 'You want crazee smoke, dinky *dau suc*, Teem?' It is always hard to turn down an offer of precious stash and, well, back in Saigon, on the waterfront, it was irresistible. A sample would be obtained for my approval in two hours. Not a bad start, considering my arrival had not been greeted by anybody from the local Minf – the Ministry for Information.

Mrs Two Bob, the new attaché in London, had got her wires crossed, cabling Hanoi that I was arriving there on Air

France, despite the fact that the airline did not have Hanoi as a destination, only Ho'ville at the end of its flight 1 on a Thursday. It was bucketing with rain outside the terminal after the seemingly endless wait for the baggage to come two hundred metres; the air was so humid it could have been *coup-coup*ed into cubes and, in accordance with Sod's law, my tripod case had been virtually last onto the belt. It had been strange to arrive and find no one there from officialdom.

Luckily, I had one of the half-dozen existing trolleys stacked with a surplus of gear. Golf umbrella, tax-free bag with twelve cartons and four bottles, tripod case, camera bag, grip and pump vacuum bottle still in its cardboard box. A bandy-legged pensioner grabbed my barrow and set off through the melee. I succumbed to the extortionate rate of fifteen in green before I laid eyes on the modus transportati, a white Renault vanlet circa 1962. Its proud owner now proceeded to untie the back doors; one fell off its hinge and was hastily roped back on. We introduced my pile over the deck-chair front seats. My chauffeur hopped back into the rain to maul the engine's innards into life. We drove blind, the one wiper having given a desultory swipe and then ceased functioning, towards downtown at the start of the rush hour. Naturally the Cuu Long, the renamed Majestic Hotel on the waterfront, was not expecting me – no reservation – but the chief receptionist, a lady who had been there for ever, serving all political masters, produced the river-view room on the fifth floor I had always promised myself, should budgeting permit. This gig was on a glossy women's mag's expenses. The $48 for the suite *enfin* would not have bought as much as a reasonable lunch for two in the city.

It took four days for the foreign press centre in Hanoi to crank up Mum and despatch him south. Khoa, the top photo guide, had been assigned to me. Mum earned his moniker by learning to pour the ritual tea or coffee; the giant pump flask was to be his charge.

Chanh, the cyclo, had warned me about Mum, 'Him

no good communist.' Admittedly, Chanh is a re-educated ex-Ranger who fought in the heated 1972 offensive in Quang Tri province and up to the day of liberation, on 30 April 1975. Mum is one of those earnest young graduates from the system's best schools, accessed by his parents as 'devout, old hard-core party' – the equivalent of a silver spoon. Studying foreign languages, he benefited from the effects of *doi moi* – the opening of the door, the reformation that came in with Lien, the southerner now running the Politshop on the Red River. He is hot photographically, groomed to overcome the problems encountered by foreign lensmen in Indochina. The interpreters are expected to double as fixers, minders and guides. Foul or fine weather, Mum wore a Flushing Meadow veteran's sweatshirt, and I never caught him without his *Salt Lake Tribune* baseball hat. The green and white of the two easily identified him, like picking out an Irish soccer fan from a crowd.

Vietnam is only just becoming used to tourists; 1990 was actually dedicated the 'Year of Tourism'. It resembled the first stabs at opening-up that China had gone through in the early 1970s. Evidence of the opening door towered above the throng outside our compartment as the up-second prepared to leave Ga Saigon: two round-eyed backpackers, travellers in a sixties mould, struggled to sort out which car they should climb into. The train jerked to life, bouncing us around in our space, then slammed to a standstill. An accident of no consequence, causing a mere fifteen-minute delay. Foreigners magnetise each other in the Nam; in today's numbers we are still few and needed to trade tips. Investigating downcar, I found Jay and Stefan crammed in with eight folk. Mum and I had a compartment for four with a sliding door all to ourselves, so I offered our commodious space for their comfort and company. For $100 the young Texan graduate Jay, and Stefan, a printer from Sweden, had obtained tourist visas in Bangkok. Totally at liberty, they had stayed in $2-a-night guesthouses, taught some English classes, generally sinking into Vietnam more than their counterparts of two decades previously had ever been able to achieve in a tour of duty. They had been on the road for sixteen months. Our collective presence attracted, in groups and singles, the entire thirty-eight strong mixed train crew.

Somewhere north of Xuan Loc, the Terre Rouge company rubber town where the last battle before the fall of Saigon had raged, we ground to a standstill for a good hour. We were in the middle of nowhere, rubber trees as far as you could see. Hawkers, vendors and gawkers appeared mysteriously out of the woods to set up portable soup kitchens beside the track. Jay bought an entire span of finger bananas for a dollar; Mum went for some greasy soup to dunk our baguettes in.

Eventually, a third-class train came down the grade from a black storm backdrop, the semaphore dropped and the big red Russian diesel loco chugged us off. The storms were a relief in the 38°C heat; the fans of our Polish-built compartment had probably never functioned. (The other cars were solid humanity and its possessions, plus trade goods.) There was not a single spare cube of room; hammocks suspended between the luggage racks, hard bench seats either side of a central gangway, each designed for two, now occupied by at least three or four, the floor covered to seat level with bundles and bales. To move up the train was an obstacle course; the soup ladies with their kitchens slung from a bamboo pole could only just squeeze through. The bong men had an easier job, carrying only an insulated wicker basket around a teapot and, sticking out of the padding, a bamboo water pipe. A satchel provided the stash for spills and tobacco, a small oil lamp attached to the basket's handle was the fire source. Our collective blew their minds by pinching copious wads of herb into their bowls. Grinning vendors disappeared down the train, bemused by the new breed of round-eye.

In a land that produces some of the most superior smoke you can toke, the population is remarkably unhip to the weed. Ayurvedically its properties are well known, the old-fashioned apothecaries in every town having jars of it prescribed for natural childbirth, as a tisane, as a stimulant, as a relaxative, a hundred and one beneficial remedial uses. The Viets, unlike their neighbours in Cambodia and Laos, have never taken to the pleasantries of *can sa*. It is there, but considered lower class and unseemly. During the conflict with America, the VC got liberated farmers to grow sizeable crops so they could guarantee distribution to the US forces, believing that they could undermine the war effort; it was a successful ploy, as more and more troops looked for solace in the zone and dissent grew in the ranks. Wherever you went, outside any base, even out in the field, small children or mama-*sans* with betel-stained teeth appeared from nowhere hauling the goodies. You could get it loose by the key for a couple of bucks; in the cities it came ready-rolled in packs of twenty, neatly camouflaged as your favourite brand. They had ingeniously emptied every cigarette, carefully refilling each one with finely chopped grass. Should you smoke a filtered brand, then a taste of tobacco was left above the filter and a plug at the tip enabled a fire-up, without attracting attention, at the most august occasion. The packs came complete with the cellophane rip strip and tax stamp, by the sealed carton, also with its tax sticker. At a dollar a pack, ten the carton, it was a buy few could refuse. A whole generation went home converted.

The liberated zones the weed had been grown in were naturally those where ARVN or US troops only occasionally operated, denying it to the enemy with defoliants and bombs. After liberation, these inhospitable tracts had become the first re-education camps where old-regime supporters had put in time, first as human mine detectors, thereafter toiling to convert the devastation into pineapple farms or new rubber plantations. Just as the United States had been unable to get to its normal hemp suppliers in the Philippines in World War II, the navy, still needing endless rope, had turned to Midwestern farmers to bridge the deficit. It had subsidised the cultivation of thousands of acres of the weed. Postwar it had been ordered to be ploughed back in – an impossible task, leaving hedgerows and field lines with a righteous sprinkling of plants. Several US underground papers of the late sixties had published maps of where these crops had grown; naive farmers were bemused to see flocks of weirdos and hippies coming to carry it away. The farmers had found that, when scythed down, it could be fed to their hogs, producing vociferous appetites and lots of bacon.

In Vietnam the poor folk under re-education, denied any pleasures, stored up what was left over, turned on and tuned out for a moment. Those who were recycled back to the cities took a stash along, easily finding customers in a society bereft of any joy. Just about all the camps are closed now, but the habits they induced have submerged into a segment of Vietnamese society. *Can sa* is now considered a giggle, readily available from your friendly cyclo, folded up in a square of *Nhan Dan* (official army) or *Gai Phong* (liberation) newspaper, seeds, sticks, the lot for 300 dong. You are well advised to take your own skins, a commodity the people's state is, as yet, unable to produce. The bamboo bong with its built-in water filter is ideal for lower-category train travel, but hardly appropriate for a hotel lobby.

Time dragged by in our caged box. The rigid benches being too low for comfortable sitting, I was reduced to the basic Asian squat; that, or go perch in the corridor window, shoulder jammed against the raised storm shutter, bum split by the sill, two cameras round the neck tending to pull my gravity out of the rocking train. Actually making a frame was a dodgy moment of trying to pull focus and compose one-handed, at the last moment before tripping the shutter taking the security hand from inside to the button. The sleepers and roadbed blurred by three metres below, and I had to keep alert to onrushing shrubbery of a spiked or thorny nature which encroached upon the single line. The rains were just about over, leaving the whole place in a verdant tangle. A ripple of heads up ahead disappeared on the bushier sections, giving warning to duck back inside. The people with their feet propped out of the window got their soles whipped like pilgrims. An alternative to these positions was to sit on the steps which gave onto the end of the car, though here reverie was subject to interruption as illegal riders and vendors came and went. The real disadvantage was the proximity of the steps to the communal toilet, which, after a short time, oozed a swamp from under its door until the water ran out, then it was just undiluted organic sewage.

At the intermediate stations, basins of water lined the entire length of the platform and for 50 dong, a lick-and-promise wash was achieved. The bowl minders also hocked half-cooked sections of fowl carcass and whatever speciality their locale could cook up. A seething mass of folk did a roaring trade between the stationary trains awaiting clearance to proceed up or down the line. A word of caution to anyone making the trip: do not leave either end without a large supply of small-denomination bills. Notes of two and five G are often unchangeable, obliging travellers to have wads of totally tatty torn paper – 10s, 20s, 50s, 100s – which could also be used in the car-end bog.

We got to the coastal resort city of Nha Trang at half past midnight; our scheduled time had been four hours earlier. Sheer fatigue had set in and it would have been tempting to stay aboard with our fellow travellers, but we were expected by the local committee, who supposedly had a lightning city tour put together, before we caught the next daylight up in the morning. After all, I was supposed to be shooting and writing a tourist-travel piece to boost new-found interest in Third World trekkie tripping. Nha Trang has always had a lot to offer, serving as an R & R centre for GIs during the war.

The Minf lads were still at the *ga*, not surprised by the time of our arrival. They claimed that security in town was bad, so had hung out with their staff car at the deserted station. The few other descending passengers flitted off into the shadows.

Only a few of our smaller items would fit in the boot of the Minf Lada out in the car park beneath the only streetlight, a pale 100-watter behind a filthy glass. The rest of the space was taken up with a selection of threadbare tyres and sundry parts for trading. We were all obliged to squeeze in together with our duffels and camera bags, while the driver busied himself with the loose wires dangling from beneath the dash. Nothing but a click emanated from the engine as a dead battery did little to abet a dead starter motor. We had to extricate ourselves from the baggage and get out to perform a jump start.

We spent the night at the Khach San Nha Trang, a hotel built in the 1960s by an enterprisingly corrupt Viet official who had somehow got enough material to construct his dream complex. During the war it had housed those dudes lucky enough to get a few R & R days out of the field as well as the privileged with townside postings, the remfs – the rear-echelon motherfuckers. At that time it had not only hot and cold running water, but hot and cold running women complete with hot and cold running diseases.

This central part of Vietnam had at one stage in 1966 boasted a unique malady called, in a column of the *Saigon Daily News*, a case of the shrinking chicken. Apparently it had been spotted only in members of the Indian ethnic group. These were a residue of the French colonial era when thousands of Indians from France's outpost in the south of India at Pondicherry had been imported to help with their administrative skills; their families still ran many of the better shops dealing heavily in the black-market money business. A half-dozen of these had been unfortunate enough to contract an infection which caused the male members gradually to reduce in size. No American medical authority ever really tagged it, and the local press never published any photos. The story shrank to its own death.

At nine each morning, the lobster-fishing boats come into Nha Trang from offshore Hon Tre island to dock under the spans of the bridge. There had been an almighty stink in 1968 incriminating full colonels in the green berets after someone had blabbed about dumping double agents, well chained, into the rocky channel these boats now plied. Like most bridges in this country, it runs parallel to the remains of at least one other. There are anti-sapper mining screens around the supports.

Guarding the north side of the bridge are an archaeological progression of bunkers dating from US and French colonial times, giving onto a rocky hill topped by a Cham ruin. The Po Nagar temples at the heart of Khan Tara princedom of the Cham empire were first sacked in the late seventh century by Malay sea raiders, again in the late ninth century by Chinese, and were finally restored in the twelfth century as the empire shrunk back to Angkor from its original glory, having stretched from the Andaman to the South China Seas. The central brick stele building still contains an Indian-influenced Buddha effigy in the style of Jaya Indravarman, who actually sacked the then Cambodian capital. The last restorations were probably happening as Marco Polo passed by on his way to China. The Chams then simply evaporated as Viet dominance gained. The glory of their civilisation was echoed in China, where gunpowder had been used aggressively for the first time. Back here in Britlag, we were just peeping from under the shrouds of our ages: Robin Hood about to go into his woods, virtually your first Vietcong, your original guerrilla; while in Canterbury Thomas à Becket was being stabbed at the altar, martyred for the dogma that would eventually rape Indochina.

Po Nagar now offers another, more modern, historical connection, gathered in the hands of photographers who hover by the kiosk which dispenses snacks and sodas to the pilgrims. Just about every model of camera available in either a PX or an oriental duty-free airport store is poised to snap the visitors. The flash clipped to the rig is often powered from a motorcycle battery housed in an old canteen cover.

Ingenuity is the forte of the Vietnamese survival techniques. Here, Nha Trang's photo elite ran a school of Petriflex Mirandablats Rokkor Rokkormats, a gamut of Instamatics through Chinese Seagull chic. The advent of colour film, the infiltration of Kodak and Fuji, was doing more to bridge the gap between capitalism and communism than any psy-war team winning hearts and minds. In the early-morning drizzle, the lads and ladies of the photo corps were barely busy; even the beggars, normally present along the meandering stepped climb, were only just beginning to crawl and creep to their positions. A leprous lot by the gate held the concession to be the principal vendors of the *huong* – incense sticks – that every self-respecting visitor will buy and light as a gesture to the *cuong* 'spirits'.

On the way back to the station, we stopped to admire a beelike swarm of youths busy stripping and rebuilding three burned-out Russian turbo-jet aircraft engines. Mum organised our luggage into the station master's office, our official presence notified upline by the super conductor in Saigon. In the light of day, Ga Nha Trang does not qualify as a tourist attraction. The platforms are low, continental-style, almost level with the tracks, the difference levelled by a sea of garbage and sewage. The waste and effluent was mostly organic and biodegradable, food for a flock of mainly pregnant nanny goats that scavenged for coconut husks and the banana leaves used for plates or wrapping pâté. The layout of the station is a railway modeller's dream, the up and down track being one, which passes the main building in a giant loop and back out on platform two. Another track held a mixed freight-and-passenger local that looked as if it had not moved in days; people were living in the box cars and carriages. In the loop were old loco sheds with a turntable and a small switching yard. At the end of the platform a giant water tower, once used to resupply the steamers, now leaked showers onto a group of waiting passengers and a few delighted goats.

The train was, naturally, late. Time to squat outside a café at the north end of the station and drink large glasses of the freakily strong Ban Me Thuot coffee grown in the hills inland from here, and roll a couple of spliffs for the journey. Mum stocked up on the little green parcels of pâté, cloves of garlic and French rolls, forewarned of the delays upline from the typhoon damage and flooding.

The coastal plain as far as the jungled hills three klicks away was a sea, the rice bowl of central Vietnam having been inundated by three successive typhoons that were only now passing out of the area. Bamboo clumps tufted above the waters, hamlets clustered on islands, the train running along dykes above the paddies fed from the overflowing rivers. All the bridges were crept across, washed-out sections taken at walking speed; boats poled by, faster, in the fields. Everywhere people piled sandbags, shovelled mud and hard-core fill, and it was still soaking down in a Scottish mist. Long lines of brown and white ducks perched contentedly on the little berms between the brown paddy waters. Buffalo idled about in seventh heaven. The fruit vendors hardly bothered with the slowed train in the pouring rain. The whole atmosphere was leaden damp, our compartment fellows resenting our shoehorning into their already overcrowded space.

My backside, which had recovered overnight, soon felt as sore as when I used to ride atop tanks back in the 1960s. Dusk, then darkness, happened two hours earlier than their tropical norm. Black clouds blotted the horizon. Reaching for the medical bag, I accelerated my fatigue to fetal oblivion for a while.

The next downtime was only interrupted by Mum's need to feed me bones. Thereafter, I begrudged every jolt and rattle until we reached Da Nang, two days late. The station was dead, save for the signalman passing the loop, the key that unlocked the next section of line to the one-way traffic. Eventually, a couple of cyclos appeared on the forecourt and we piled aboard perched atop the baggage, not bothering to haggle a firm rate to Mum's frugal disgust.

Da Nang has always been spooky at night. In 1975, a good half a million ARVN military ended up abandoned there to the fast-encroaching liberation forces. A lot of hatred and resentment got bottled up, partially re-educated and put back into the town. When I was there in 1980, and again in 1984–85, it was wise not to wander about the back streets after dark. Too many Soviet sailors and personnel from the air base were getting abused, occasionally knifed and robbed.

The old French building on the riverfront, next to the post office, had housed successively the governor; the French navy (when the city was known as Tourane); an advisers' barracks, shared as a hostel for the press corps; the navy; and, finally, the American consulate before the last US citizen was evacuated in disreputable scenes of panicky flight. The new regime had converted it into a museum of imperialistic crimes. Virtually anti-American, it was a propaganda tool rather than an exhibition. The forecourt in the 1980s had housed a gutted Huey helicopter, a horrendous Soviet-style statue and a rusting collection of weapons. Water had dripped onto dioramas and sand tables of local campaigns from the gutted rooms above, once our *bao chi* suites. Spotty black and white photos peeled from the damp walls; they came from the archives of the agencies, the files abandoned in 1975. A couple of bored ladies had sat knitting thin wool, perched on a relief-sculpted room-sized map of the city's liberation.

Now this edifice was closed, two rooms at the front advertising *pho* noodles and video; a sideshow in the ruins. In the courtyard only the statue's plinth and an American jeep remained, its hubs sitting on the ground. The whole anti-US thing had been detoxed. The arrival a few months previously of a group of ex-marines, with funds provided by the film director Oliver Stone of *Platoon* fame to build a clinic in a village just south of the city, may have warmed the local committees to the winds of change. A new generation of folk were now running the shop here, obliged to help, eager to please, unencumbered with the old hardcore old line histories the original liberators continually wanted to play.

Trucking through the cool night, I thought the streets now did not bear the same threat, the town had a mellower feel. We pedalled past the old war museum towards the mouth of the Song Giang along the waterfront, past the *Cercle Sportif* (the original French club), the port authority, the dock entrance, finally pulling onto the forecourt of a newish-looking, but apparently closed, hotel. Our clamourings finally aroused a sleepy desk clerk, who checked us in efficiently in fluent English while Mum placated the cyclos with wads of dong. The chattering clerk helped schlep our chattels up to the top floor. Why, I ask, am I always assigned a room farthest from the lobby, with no lift and a neckful of cameras? As we struggled upwards, the young man was throwing detailed questions, wanting to know what the state of play was at Kensington Palace, which teams would make it to the Cup Final. He had graduated from Hue university where all the faculties put great stress on the teaching of English, even benefiting from occasional courses given by a Brit working on the restorations for UNICEF or from their Oz teacher-training programme. A three-week-old *Newsweek* almost put the guy into orbit; the paucity of the printed word in Vietnam is pathetic. There is a shortage of paper, ink and the freedom to publish. Any book is a revered object sold and resold, the selection either pap or heavy didactic party shit. The only stuff in ample supply is turgid volumes of Marx and Hegel or dissertations lifted from a party plenum.

All ports have a mysterious air, redolent of foreign, the window to the outside. With the new spirit of *doi moi* the flags of the ships tied up now at Da Nang are as varied as before, though the Stars and Stripes is conspicuously absent, aced out of the trade race by its Asian surrogates.

I was first despatched here in February 1965 before the marines had landed, and then through their build-up, as a staff photographer for UPI. Later on, as a freelance, I had always found a story up in I Corps, and we could move about by bike or jeep at our own risk. Besides the war, there was the beach, China Beach, which curved from the foreland of Monkey Mountain overlooking the bay down to the outcrop nearby known as Marble Mountain. Network US television has now converted the antics of the beach into a sitcom, but can never convey the freshness and freedom the surf could bring. The beach is a ten-minute ride from downtown. Today only a part is accessible, for the Nhan Dan – People's Army – have taken over the marine base that used to back onto the beach. The base is now a ghost city, the old hangars agape and empty, weeds pushing through the hard pads, water and control towers sticking up like dead trees. Large areas are given over to vast heaps of scrap awaiting recycling at mills down south at Long Binh. The paranoia of the military prevents lingering on their beachfront, although you can stroll its length under the watchful glare of the sentries, to arrive at the new resort which has been thrown together in the lee of the sacred Marble Mountain.

It had been a long day, climaxing in the cool of the caves and a hot walk down to the resort. Mum and I couldn't wait to hit the water. The whole sweep of surf, sand and coconut fringe was deserted, except for two Russian MiG pilots doing push-ups by a coracle while two nymphettes in pyjamas pestered them to buy some naff marble objects. The freshness was numbing, the two-metre waves pummelling; our tiredness evaporated. We swam out and floated, surfed in.

That should have been the time to quit. Like a junkie wanting more thrill, I plunged back out, Mum screaming unheard cautions from the shallows. The riptide caught me and I was going nowhere, my paddling providing no progress; Mum, receding, could be seen frantically waving his arms, the beach behind now totally empty. I was going backwards through a slow-motion, wide-screen nightmare. In panic, I went under, sucking in draughts of salt water. I knew I was drowning.

Suddenly I could feel the chi spread through my body like a decision: to coordinate every nerve, to concentrate as in meditation the feeling of every muscle, to put together a move. Using the next onshore swell, I gained four spluttered strokes. The brain spin eased, and my progress picked up with the following waves. It was still upstream, like climbing a powder-snow dune, but there was motion in the right direction, the down-coast drift inevitable. Mum splashed along on a converging course. I crawled out, like a shipwrecked survivor cast ashore. Mum made me walk it off until I spewed saline bile, contentedly voiding body and soul. Freaky as a bad acid trip.

The US coastguard had maintained a small mission in Vietnam during the war, several of their 'point'-class cutters based at the facility in the lee of Monkey Mountain, the promontory opposite Da Nang, still topped by bulbous US-installed radar domes. The guard is a separate service of volunteers, all professionals addicted to the craft of boating; charged mainly with drug interdiction and safeguarding the nation's beaches, lakes and ports. Their task during the war was to intercept hostile gunrunners infiltrating south and keeping water traffic moving in the overcrowded harbours. They were unsung and unglamorous, rarely covered by the hacks that hung out at the press centre.

Back in the good old days perhaps forty mainly young *bao chi* had been continually on station up north. The marines had set up the press centre for us on the river upstream of the docks, in a former nightclub. It had a bar with river view, and the restaurant menu had been lifted out of Howard Johnson's turnpike fast-fooder. The frozen steaks had been airlifted and the milkshakes were thick as snow. They kept on the same flirtatious local waitresses, attempting to police them up with pinafores over a smocked uniform. Nightly we were regaled with the latest stateside movies projected outdoors accompanied by a long 'happy hour' of drinks at half-price

– was it a dime? For this our bureaux in Saigon coughed up a few dollars in MPC, the military payment certificates, the monopoly money brought in supposedly to contest the black market, creating yet another layer of trading. The military had a captive audience to feed its line to. To abet this, they kept on site a staff of press information officers (PIOs), assigned to hold our hands out in the field and pump us for titbits on our return. When we were not out doing the war, there was often a fierce volleyball game between them, superfit, and us, in every shade of body consciousness, in the courtyard.

The summer of 1966 had been a hot one politically; the government in Saigon had changed like a yo-yo and the Buddhist minority had fermented into open revolt in Da Nang, necessitating the despatch of ARVN airborne and marine units from the central reserve to quell the insurrection. It had been a bloody fight, the rebel units gradually retreating into an enclave around the Thinh Hoi pagoda while the civilian population bore the brunt of the casualties. It was good dangerous high-adrenalin street fighting: moving a couple of doorways before a machine gunner could zero in, dashing over intersections in between bursts. We had summary executions of prisoners, massacres of schoolkids and downtown airstrikes. Everyone had a fierce tale on their return to the inviolate press centre.

One evening, the third of the counterattack, the rebels lured a platoon of pressmen to their temple as hostages to their waning cause. Hearing the crack of loyal ARVN troops' M-16s ever closer, a dozen of us dared to walk out. When we had got almost to the safety of government lines we were sprayed with fire from behind. Bursting in on a terrified family, we went to ground in their front room. The incoming ceased, so, with two others, I ventured out of the back door. As we stood deliberating the best route, over back fences and walls, an M-79 fragmentation grenade exploded three metres up in a kapok tree. Those little barbed hooks of shrapnel wrapping the 40-mm mortarlike round that a thumper throws off are designed to maim rather than kill – it is more incapacitating for an army to deal with its wounded than its dead. The three of us were lucky: we only took relatively light wounds. My worst one was caused by a piece of shrapnel that drove just in front of my right ear, while a chunk snapped my nose. The blood coursed into my eyes, freaking me to believe I was blinded. We missed the rest of the action and the mopping-up in the city.

To recover from the mental shock, I went to Hong Kong, blowing the accumulated wealth of months of shooting on duty-free goodies topped with a stack of records and books. To get back into the swing again, I thought I'd go with the coastguard on a routine 'market-time' patrol up to the DMZ, a rehab cruise with fishing and swimming calls.

Three days out, the routine changed to nightmare. As the watch was about to change just before 4.00 a.m., with only two of the nine crew on duty, we were fired on by an air-force B57 Canberra maritime reconnaissance bomber. It had come to check out suspicious radar blobs that we on the *Point Welcome* were steaming towards. The B-57 had dropped an illumination flare and with little further ado had launched into an attack on us with its 20-mm cannon, presuming we were a North Vietnamese vessel. The first burst came in a stem-to-stern riddling the boat's length, the explosive rounds cooking off the jerry cans of petrol stored aft. Much of the communications gear was also knocked out. In accordance with the rules, to identify ourselves the riding lights and deck floods were switched on, but the attack continued.

No one could have slept through that lot. I grabbed a couple of Leicas and stumbled out, to be greeted by a sheet of red flame against which silhouettes danced to extinguish the blaze. Then in came the supporting F-4s. At water level above the hull, seen but unheard, the muzzle flashes of a supersonic Phantom winked a tiny strobe, the shells exploding as the aircraft roared above and beyond. Then came a ripping, tearing sensation and pain. Two of the rounds had blown into the aft end of the flying bridge where all the hydraulic and electrical cabling was housed, sending porcupine quivers of metal shards and rubber into my left side. I had been framing a crew member against the red glow as one of the shells, one of 6,000 that a Phantom can fire in a minute, detonated on a guy wire a seaman was grasping. It looked as though the fire extinguisher I thought he held had exploded in his hands. He disappeared in a flash and I crumpled sideways into another crew member, emerging from the below-deck companionway.

I felt like a pin cushion, clusters of steel spines through the left side of my face and eye, more in the hand that had held the camera and another in the gut just above my shorts. The Rolex on my wrist had gone, replaced by a large hole through the arm where the shrapnel had cut the bracelet and gone on its oblique way. Time froze and I heard the din of the attack reverberate through a foggy deafness. Hot and sharp all over, I was bundled below decks as the surviving crew fought to organise the insanity, while, overhead, two Phantoms wheeled to put in more strikes. My view was circumscribed by the mattresses and the mess table which had been tossed over us, to afford us some protection. A bale of dirty laundry materialised as dressings, a towel to wrap around the shredded hand stumps of the guy I had just photographed. Deep in agony, I triggered mindless blurred frames of table legs and cabin corners, near-abstract monochromes of a condensed, frightened world.

The whole craft shuddered as the air force pressed home their mission. The next run got the skipper, who had bravely climbed out on the wing of the flying bridge with a signal lamp, cutting him in half and destroying what remained of the commo gear. The whole inferno was taking place in the South China Sea just off the DMZ, half a klick from the beach, where both the enemy and friendly Viet navy junk forces were now plying our vicinity with their own harassing fire.

Up above me a seaman and the chief petty officer struggled to save the boat, pulling the wheel with one hand, prone on the floor to avoid the incoming fire. At one point, the chief later told me, he heard a voice telling him to get up and go look out over the side, at which moment a bomblet from a cluster-bomb unit plunged through the opposite side of the wheelhouse to explode below.

We abandoned ship as the stern settled, the fires still burning, and spent an agonising hour in the water until our sister vessel, the *Point Comfort*, had come up. Once I had been fished out, Sister Morphine took over and the long series of stages back to the med facility in Phu Bai began.

The beauty of Vietnam was not discovered by many foreigners; it is locked inland, only occasionally spilling onto the coast. From Da Nang to Hue, where a spur of the Annamitic Cordillera runs into the tropical blue of the ocean, the scenery would pride a Club Med catalogue. Like the first glimpse of the Mediterranean along the Côte d'Azur, like Big Sur or the Norwegian fjords, the landscape is one to retire into. Though I have travelled this ninety-odd-kilometre stretch dozens of times – by bike, boat, jeep, chopper, plane, but never before by train – the unfolding vistas of the Hai Van Pass, Pass of Clouds, will never cease to blow my mind.

The commandant of the train was a happy fellow with a peaked officer's hat, the cardboard of which was disintegrating, leaving it plopped over his round visage. Loaded with railroad lore, he had crewed on the first train to make it south after liberation, in 1978, and was chuffed to be given a book in which I had written about this. Mum and I were ushered into a compartment where two honeymooners billed and cooed, and immediately taken off to the dining car and told that anything on the menu was ours.

Riding over the Hai Van by jeep or bike takes you up to the almost perpetual clouds which give the col its name. They swirl around the layers of fortifications going back to the Nguyen dynasty, below which lie the posters the French put up and the American-era bunkers and guardhouses made from culvert sections. Next to the main French bunker, truckers who must ply Route Seven, and the convoys through to Laos, have maintained the *cuong*, the spirit house inside which offerings of fruit, rice and flowers are continually freshened. On the lintel a Hue blue vase with white sand inside acts as the holder for dozens of sticks of huong, the incense made by the roadside in the village at the foot of the col. Look back and there is the beautiful sweep of Da Nang Bay, the flat paddies and the exciting hills; look north and the road snakes and hairpins to the hills cascading into the sea, backed by the straight coastline and white-capped surf. Everyone gets down to look; it is stunning – the swirling mist, the smell of the mesquite, even the clattering roar of overtaxed trucks struggling to the top, provides a romantic throb. I had flashes of climbing passes in Nepal, of cresting the St Bernard in the Alps, of dropping below the rim into Yosemite Park Valley in California.

The Vietcong never really had to do much to close Route One over the pass; a few rocks and a couple of dudes with burp guns could seal it off, so it had been almost left alone, the fortifications seeing service as toilets more than barracks. Whoever manned them was in for a lonely vigil. During the war I had gunned a Honda bike or other dubious vehicle through here a dozen times, never encountering Charlie, and only occasionally meeting an ARVN squad desultorily patrolling the highway. They preferred to stay holed up in the half-dozen *postes* strung over the thirty klicks, extracting whatever 'taxes' they could get out of the trucks and buses. Charlie did the same, with a little political indoctrination thrown in. This was a Pax Britannicus that the arrival of the US forces in the area had wanted to alter, making it dodgy for the gas tankers to get the short distance to the tank farm in the lee of the southern end of the range. These were operated by Shell, a company owned by a country not militarily or directly involved in the conflict and never suffered a serious attack. The liberation forces also required petrol, oil and lubricants, though not on the same scale as those who believed their mission was in freedom's democratic capitalist cause. Esso had to put up a farm closer to town, which often took incoming.

Back in 1985 travelling north from Ho'ville to Hanoi, we had stopped for the customary look-see, pee and radiator check, to find that a group of entrepreneurial soldiers condemned to this lonely outpost had opened a café in the erstwhile toilet bunker by installing a scrounged ex-US Conex shipping container at its front portals. The seven-man squad with junior lieutenant in charge, all from Hanoi, had served fifteen months in Cambodia. Their reward, this easy-duty checkpoint posting counting the Laos-bound trucks grinding by. The sergeant of the outfit had imported his girlfriend to make coffee and *pho* when not hooking the drivers. It had been chilly in the mist that day, the *café filtré* made with condensed milk (a *café sua*) hitting the spot, the perfect time to consume a couple of spliffs. The lads with Cambodia under the belt were only too pleased to pour more coffee and then an endless pot of tea for a return toke. It ended up with me taping up their tattered plastic grips on their liberated 16s with lurex grey gaffer tape before the Blue Max – our Soviet Gaz three-quarter tonner – rolled off down towards Hue.

The railway had not been left inviolate. The simple expediency of blowing the tracks north of the massif had ensured that no train ventured onto the tracks that twist, loop, tunnel and turn, one moment on a precipice above the shore, the next perched on a saddle overlooking rolling crags and hills. Now the track has been repaired, and the up category-one was scheduled to make the run in less time than a bus. The only drawback of taking the train to Hue from Da Nang is that you do not get to stop in Lang Co, crab capital of Vietnam, at the north end of the hills. It is also the site of the Viet Minh's first blowing-up of a major bridge back in the 1940s in its anti-French campaign. The original pilings still march across the Dan Cau Nai laboon, paralleled by another blown set and a new concrete span. Along the causeway peasants heap piles of oyster shells from the bay to be used for nacre inlay.

Hue, the old imperial capital, is where, traditionally, the women are the prettiest, the food the most delicious, the temples most interesting. Gone are the days when a sampan on the Perfume River could be rented for the night with female company included; now they can be hired only for a desultory punt around the houseboats in the shallows between the market and the Huong Giang hotel on the south bank. The riverside is a gardened walk with floating restaurant too expensive for those not in a tour group or members of the local Mafia. It almost allowed me to float back to the orgasmic nostalgia that Hue had always provided in the relief from wartime.

War had blitzed into Hue during the Tet Offensive of 1968, the Vietcong and North Vietnamese forces taking the entire city except for a couple of US adviser compounds. What followed was a Stalingrad set-piece battle, which they lost after nearly a month's horrendous fighting pitted against the best part of a marine division and two regiments of air cavalry. One must not discount that the ARVN forces were also involved, but they had been on stand-down for the New Year holidays, leaving their units little cohesion to resist or retaliate. Much of Hue was turned into rubble, the firepower used by both sides awesome. It was rare that the Vietcong should attempt to hold a provincial capital for an extended period, but, having taken thirty-nine major towns countrywide, the government was stretched thin.

The Vietcong had stockpiled enough for a short offensive, then taken advantage of the inability of the US and ARVN forces to seal off their supply routes to the city's west through the area where the royal tombs are located. Eventually the fighting had swung out to this area, leaving much of the classical heritage shredded by shrapnel and bullet-pockmarked. Neither side respected the sanctity of the temples, leaving the archaeological department with enormous restoration problems. Hue itself was almost totally flattened; the streets around the citadel on the north bank were reduced to piles of rubble by the increasing frustration of the marines, unused to house-to-house combat, who called in close support from the *New Jersey* 15 kilometres away in the gulf, and airstrikes round the clock. The battleship was sending in shells the size of Volkswagens, while the land-based artillery delivered rounds from 60-mm to eight-inch. Anything that did not burn in the town was blown to fragments. Vietcong sappers even managed to drop the central span of the elegant Eiffel-built bridge in the centre of the city. The seventeenth-century citadel, with its 15-metre-thick walls, dominated most of the central part of town, the flagpole atop the ramparts tauntingly sporting the yellow-starred NVA banner. Irate marines had run up the Stars and Stripes when they had retaken it, only to be reprimanded to substitute the southern republic's flag. The graceful colonial quarter, with the university campus, schools and hospitals, is on the south side, laid out like a provincial town, tree-lined streets, villas and buildings set back in lush flowering walled gardens: beautiful to behold, hell to fight through, ambush heaven.

Casualties among the populace and combatants topped 10,000, including those deliberately executed whom the liberation forces considered subversive. Later they admitted that this was a mistake.

Today, it is hard to tell what was then the ultimate in modern warfare raged down the leafy boulevards. Hard to find a wall with still unpatched shrap and bullet pocks. New stucco is everywhere, a welcome sight in a country where most buildings are peeling apart. The broad streets hum with a jam of bicycles, Hondas and cyclos, the bicycles a rentable commodity and still the best way to get around or travel the 12 klicks out to the tombs. At midday and 4.00 p.m. the lycée lets out hundreds of beauties who take to their cycles, their lustrous long black hair streaming behind them, going home on their wheels. They wear the *ao dai* national costume of diaphanous tunic over pantaloons. Walk along riverside Le Loi and groups of these demure innocents will detach from the throng to grill you with the objective of perfecting their English. It is possible for a tourist to end up here, rented bicycle, government guesthouse and a gig teaching private graduate classes. Hue wants to know, every second face, bobbing up beside you asking impeccably polite, thought-provoking questions, with no fear of repression. You will leave your hotel next time to find a delegation of maths and chemical students with their leader, who had approached you on the earlier sortie, to conduct a discourse on logic.

Jay and Stefan appeared at the Hoang Giang hotel disco one evening, on rented bicycles, having bussed up fro Da Nang for a few thousand dong. A guesthouse by the station was three bucks a night, the bikes the same, initially hired from one of the myriad unemployed who run themselves as taxis, the passenger perching on the baggage rack. They were teaching English in two high schools, conducting al fresco lessons, wandering the tombs and temples with the same *ao dai*ed darlings I was snapping for an *Elle* piece. They had the freedom to go just about anywhere and do just about anything. Theoretically permissions and papers were required, but no one in authority seemed to take the slightest interest in them, save for the opportunity to brush up on linguistic skills and deflect the occasional dollar.

On the bandstand that night was a group that reflected the Viet ability to take influences on board and turn them around as their own. In the 1960s, the voice of protest had been a young Hue resident called Trinh Con Son, the Dylan/Lennon laureate poet of the Nam, born of the

Buddhist protest movement against the Catholic Diem family clique's despotic repression of the country. He had been in and out of detention before and after liberation; his music was now considered radical chic. That spirit was belting out now through hi-tech imported gear, with some touches derived from the few cassettes of Boney M and Abba available in the market. An oriental twang, the odd beat synthed in with middle-of-the-road Third World, nonaligned pop. It was foot-tapping, finger-popping, yet smacked of revolution as only art can do in a succinct way. The yuppies, the Mafia with attached dollies, the Lao smugglers all loved it, throwing themselves about in an approximation of videos of smuggled Travolta tapes. All were put to shame by a little young student in tight stonewash and T-shirt, barefooted strutting an act good enough for a slot on *Top of the Pops* or MTV. Subversion in today's Vietnam is conducted with a knowing wink, the purity of the People's Democratic Socialism diluted by the unstoppable beat that started the whole revolution in the sixties.

When travelling in Vietnam, always carry a large stock of 555s (export-brand Brit cigarettes by State Express). The poorer the nation, the more the populace seems to have the nicotine habit. In Vietnam most provinces make their own brands, with names such as Jet, Hero, Cuu Long and Sport, from the sun-dried local weed. A filter, export-quality, Vietnamese cigarette, even when classed as 'Virginia', has all the carburettive powers of a Gauloise butt. 555s are virtually an alternative currency, a *laissez passer* into the world of round-table negotiations. They are the conversation opener and smoother of difficult situations, the polite pause indicating respect. Whenever you sit down for the first parley, the hosts will decant a fresh pot of green or black tea, with hot water from the ever-present Chinese Thermos, floral-decorated with original stopper missing, burnt-out light bulb as replacement; then tear the rip seal of a pack of their smokes. One is then supposed to produce one's own pack and proffer that. Business is under way.

Two months in Vietnam may require a supply of thirty cartons. Ironically, they are cheaper on the open market in Hanoi or Ho'ville, by a few hundred dong, than at the duty-free at Don Muang or even in the official dollar shops in the major hotels. No self-respecting *fonctionnaire* about to embark on a mission to higher echelons would think of leaving home without a pack, be he smoker or non. Thousands of cartons destined for the ports of Haiphong, Da Nang or Saigon never officially cross the docks. The same devious supply lines that were used during the war exist in today's liberated Nam. Back then it was possible to pre-order a fridge, jeep or TV; once, I even heard of a crated helicopter, from a selection of Korean, Filipino or Chinese middlemen, which could be delivered to the place of your choice, with all papers ostensibly in order.

Both Mum and I had, by now, become unwilling to face the discomfort of third-, fourth- and finally fifth-category trains on which we were booked for the rest of the northerly progression. With amply applied State Express and a 38,000-dong supplement for us both, we got transferred to the overnight first train a day later. All we had left was $160 worth of uncashable Thomas Cook sterling traveller's cheques which no one was interested in, black market included, and our stock of 555s. We paid the cyclos for their last day's work in smokes and pedalled to the *ga*.

Our compartment was equipped with a washbasin in a folding commode – unfortunately not working, as evidenced by a five-gallon jerrycan of water left in front of the marvellous piece of Indian engineering. The other occupants were a young lady and her five-year-old son. Mum knew her, she worked at the embassy in Hanoi part time and they had had a fling in the foreign-language school. The train commander arrived and was prevailed upon, having been issued his 555 ration, to let me ride on the locomotive front over the bridge that had divided North from South Vietnam.

It would take us two hours to parallel the road up to Dong Ha along the stretch that Bernard Fall had christened *la rue san joie* – the Street Without Joy. His book of the same title, on operations here in the 1950s, had been required reading during the war, as had his *Hell in a Small Place*, the story of the battle of Dien Bien Phu, which was likened to the offensive then going on around the marine base at Khe Sanh. His history lessons were not so distant mirrors of the blunderings of the new campaigns being waged. Fall was to become a victim of the conflict, blown away on a mine while accompanying a marine patrol in this very sector in 1966.

To the east of the tracks to the coast it is sandy, arid, with very little population; to the west up to the hills, a fertile rolling plain given to paddies and small villages. The hills had always been a liberated zone, the Vietminh, the Vietcong and then the North Vietnamese Army foraging down to the lowlands for supplies and to interdict the major north–south artery. By the late sixties, a corridor nearly 40 kilometres long had been turned into a series of fortified base camps surrounded by interlocking firebases, each with its own integral artillery support. As the American presence drew down, the entire structure was turned over to the AVRN.

Vietnamisation, as it was euphemistically called, was put to the test during the Easter offensive of 1972. The North had unleashed its largest attack under the cover of drenching rain and low cloud, which denied the embattled ARVN the air support needed to deal with the unprecedented enemy artillery and, more worryingly for the last US advisers, battalions of new T-54 main battle tanks backed by troops that really wanted to win this time. The new Vietnamised army, save for isolated marine battalions, took to its trucks, abandoning its invaluable artillery tubes and causing a collapse of the entire front.

Eventually, after three weeks of some of the most intense

fighting of the whole war, and not without the recommitment of US firepower – including an endless rain of B-52 arc-light strikes, the new TOW (target on wire) missile-equipped chopper gunships and round-the-clock offshore naval gunfire from half a dozen warships – a halt line was called on the Song My Chanh. The once thriving cities of Quang Tri and Dong Ha had ceased to exist. Firebases though impregnable, known by their call signs borrowed from their COs' loved ones – Mary Jane, Nancy – and even the largest Con Thien, fell like ninepins. They were encircled and then rolled up. Forgotten coordinates on military maps where a good chunk of American youth had perished for nothing had been finally liberated.

It was also totally wasted. The chief business up here is scrap recycling, though the pickings are thinning. There is probably no accurate total of how many pieces of ordnance, how many rounds were fired in these fields. What goes up has to come down. The earth is impregnated with chunks of expended firepower. Ten years after liberation, the road- and railside were still littered with carcasses of armoured fighting vehicles, T-34 and -54 turrets plopped down in paddies and on dunes. These were the rich and easy pickings, high-grade recyclable metals, destined for smelting to ingots in the mills in Long Binh, to be shipped to Japan and Korea, only to return as Sapporo six-pack beer cans, Toyotas and Hondas. Some of the wreckage may have been deliberately left to give the populace a continuing awareness of the great patriotic fight that had taken place, lest their situation did not remind them enough. Some of the lucky ones had become millionaires from the pickings, while most folk were reduced to subsistence farming and sifting through the trash.

A great piece of American ingenuity that never quite worked, proving more fatal in its disassembly than during its operational days, was the McNamara Line, named after the secretary of Defense who had conjured it up. He went on to run the World Bank. Stretching from the coast to 30 kilometres inland, it was an electrified barbed fence with blockhouses, minefields, fields of fire – any number of mean devices interlaced with electrical detection aids which, in turn, turned on the whole gamut of aerial fire and artillery. To clear up the 17 million live pieces of ordnance had cost nearly 2,000 casualties.

The poor folk who drew this lot came from the ranks of the old, so-called puppet, regime of civil and military administration. Called to inhabit the new economic zones as part of their re-education programme, their job had been that of human mine detectors. Downtown Dong Ha, the first town of note on the river Cam Lo, has a high percentage of amputees hobbling along the stretch of Route One lined with Café Com Pho and black-market gas stations. Outcasts, usually ID-less, the lowest in this new society, they are reduced pathetically to begging. Their cases for prosthesis are only just on the agenda at some bureaucratically top-heavy ministry in out-of-mind, faraway Hanoi. However, their patch is not infertile; Route Nine, the main thoroughfare for supplies to southern Laos, hooks a sharp left before snaking back up through Cam Lo to Khe Sanh and the border. The town is rife with goodies rolling off the back of lorries, and superstitious long-haul travellers are always good for an alms hit to appease the spirits of the road. The roadside joints are open round the clock in a capitalistic celebration, making it one of the busiest towns in the country.

The environment is blemished; from the raised carriage of the train, you can look down gullies and from embankments, a view the street does not afford. The whole place is pockmarked with craters. Scrub pines struggle to grow in the poisoned sandy soil. All common land is spotted with unemployed youth and penniless pensioners burrowing in the dirt with long-handled hoes, unearthing rusted shell casings, ammo boxes and shell shards. They are like *Star Wars* Jawas, only here clad in remnants of old military garb and tatty black pyjamas. The pickings are piled on two-wheeled, hand-drawn carts to be dumped by the roadside for the weekly truck pick-up. When the mist descends you think of the bleakness that the fields of Flanders must have instilled in the levies thrown into the maw of World War I. A feeling of desolation, mourning. You almost hear the keening, the eerie whine-whistle of incoming, the chatter of machine guns. The cloak of war hangs like a shroud across northern Thua Thien province.

The locomotive was a big Russian reversible, at this time pulling the train in the normal mode, though it often runs backwards. Getting there through seven cars was an obstacle race with much face loss for stepping on toes, in mango baskets or in live-fish boxes, complicated by the oncoming contingent heading for the tail-end chow wagon. The final section of the obstacle race would have challenged the train surfers at São Paulo, because the locomotive was four feet away and two feet higher than the first carriage. Straight down rattled a buckeye coupler and a bundle of swaying hoses. The track sleepers flashed mesmerically underneath as I stood contemplating the gap. The train commander nimbled across first, then Mum with the gear, before I used that Western advantage – the long leg – to good effect, finding myself half hung up with the loco-side part of the team hauling me in like a spinnaker, an amused crew member meanwhile keeping hold of my other arm for balance. Now all I had to do was edge around the motor housing, guardrail-less, burglar-style into the cab. Every small boy wants to ride the footplate, and here I was allowed to toot the overhead cord-operated horn, to the giggles of the five-strong driving contingent: a driver, assistant driver, assistant to him, a gofer, who spent most of his time hanging out of the door, and a spotter-cum-gauge-watcher. The last-named task did not require much work, there being a mere three gauges. The speedometer had a large red line on 80, and another, more observed, at 50. Descending into the old DMZ down a newly laid, dead-straight track, we hit 55 kilometres an hour, that velocity somewhat daunting as the train swayed and jolted out of sync with the track joins, the track itself undulating to the pattern of the craters it covered. The crew just giggled, a group of small boys daring providence. Their revenge on the system.

I led Mum from the train compartment out along the narrow catwalk running along the side of the thudding diesel the forty feet to the cutting edge of the cowcatcher. The rush was the same as being in the door of a chopper contour-flying, the speed somewhat slower, though the diesel din emanating from the greasy vent plates flat against my back was as awesome as the vibrating thud transmitted from the rotors and turbine in a Huey. At least no one was taking potshots at us; friendly farmers waved at the apparition of a white man hanging on for dear life while his two white-knuckled companions kept him from falling off sidewards. It was hard for Mum to drag me back in; the exhilaration and cool rush of perching like a figurehead on the thundering up express was really tripping. As we rolled over the Ben Hai I launched a ceremonial gob into the waters between the flashing girders while one-handedly trying a frame of the unification span. The return to the normality of our compartment was anticlimatic.

The first-class sleeper conductress, wearing a cardboard-badged, peaked cap, appeared with our overnight bedding; a sheet for below, a hairy blanket of indeterminate cleanliness and a minuscule square, solid, white-cased pillow. She then returned to her flip-down seat in the corridor to preen in a pocket mirror. One of the lipsticks my sponsoring magazine's cosmetics department had provided me with gained me access to the car-end pukka sit loo, normally reserved only for women or officers. The conductress even made a point of coming to tuck me in, earning a licentious wink from Mum, who then proceeded to snog the night away with our travelling companion, curled up on the opposite top bunk with her son.

The compartment was sticky, made worse by the howling tannoy admonishments to keep the steel shutters down. In the panhandle of Vietnam the local sport for working out your aggression is hurling rocks at passing passenger trains, the more enterprising of the peasants vaulting through open windows to steal what they can lay hands on whenever the train slowed down or at stations. Needless to say, the ceiling fans were not turning and the corridor light not extinguished, presumably so our conductress could continue to preen and flirt with the rotating crews.

At 50 kilometres an hour it took us all night to crawl up to Vinh, which registered only as a cacophony of vendors' sounds backed by the huff and puff of the first steam locos shunting outside. Originally we were scheduled to change here for an up local, so it was a pleasure to drift off to sticky sleep again. Next, we ground to an unscheduled halt in Thanh Hoa, where the commotion outside precluded further sleep, the loudspeakers barking caution. Armed guards scuttled down the corridor as I groped loose-bowelled to the *cabinet des officiers*. Any rules about its use while standing in stations went straight down the hole, propelled by the greased swill from the gastronomic last car. Outside the door a scrum of traders were launching an attack on the steps, now guarded by crew members with solid truncheons, and pistols. I struggled to raise a shutter and popped off a couple of flashes, which kind of cooled out and simultaneously agitated the clamouring rag-shrouded mob. Careful scrutiny would subsequently reveal a couple of folk flashing peace signs at the compact's lens.

North of Thanh Hoa lies the Ham Rong, the Dragon's Jaw, so called from the shape of the mountains that tumble to a gorge carved by the Dap Bai Thuong or Songchu River flowing from Laos. The railroad and Route One cross the jaw on a single span, a bridge that cost more American plane losses than any other single target in the north. Seventy-two jets were downed trying to take out the most important link in North–South communications. Anything heading down the Ho Chi Minh Trail crossed this span. It was hit on numerous occasions but always patched back into operation, until finally succumbing to a TV-guided smart bomb in 1972. The once elegant double span still has a ragged profile. It is still strategic, so it is forbidden to photograph it, though we had got grudging permission to shoot from the northern karst outcrop.

Five years earlier, my minder Tien and I had walked the bridge snapping happily, only to go directly to arrest as we sauntered off, causing two hours of kerfuffle in the guard post under the southside buttress. That had been the last of nine infringements in five months; so far on this trip we had avoided any military or police confrontations. The whole atmosphere had lightened up.

With the need to make use of the privileges extended by the conductress, and the chill early-morning mist seeping into the dawdling cars, sleep was impossible. I rolled a large jay, wrenched up a shutter and assumed the perch, window frame soon numbly bisecting my bum. Occasional lights flickered and passed, bamboo clumps and houses took on more distinction as dawn gradually turned the grey to shadow white.

Our express status now appeared to have been downgraded, for at nearly every town we ground to a standstill. No one got on or off the train, but their bundles did. Virtually the entire contents of every compartment and the obstacles from the corridors were systematically heaved out to the prearranged eager hands. Those with no prior agreement were passing up flapping wads of dongs, getting Hero cigarettes and Thai-made socks in exchange. Sometimes we slowed in the now pouring rain and a bale would plummet into a cottage wall or plop into a trackside puddle. Looking back, I would see a scrabbling crowd resembling the food handout in a refugee camp.

The vista from the window was not encouraging; as far

as the horizon, the typhoons had dumped the Tonkin Gulf over the almost grown rice crop, flattening it, flooding the landscape in a densely populated area normally blessed with abundance. The grey light, the rain, the disaster outside and, in addition, the disaster inside my guts signalled a timely end to the trip. The southern suburbs clacked by, the views familiar from previous road travel; Route One here ran in tandem with the still single track.

The train pulled slowly into Ga Hanoi a mere three hours overdue; Mum and I were late by three days. Porters official and freelance fought the groggy descending passengers for their baggage; beyond the ticket barrier was a melee of cyclos in the downpour. Mum had to parley our ride downtown with a packet of crumpled minor denomination bog-paper bills and our last pack of 555s. Five bags, Thermos, brolly and the two of us were stacked aboard one of the low-slung, unpadded vehicles that were the capital's taxis. Getting to the glum foyer of the Than Nhut hotel had the feeling of a homecoming. The downstairs rat sat unmoved by the still not functioning lift, the same glum staff presided over the reception and the same PLO – or were they Algerian Liberation? – delegation lurked at the bar. I prayed for one of the first-floor rooms with hot water – some hope.

# 3

# *Border Runs*

Three months later, in 1990, I returned to Hanoi. Our incoming flight arrived at the same moment as an Aeroflot Iluyshin, which disgorged a batch of returning *Gastarbeiter* wearing their entire multiseasonal wardrobe. The Thai flight I was on had diplomatic priority, leaving the bundled natives and gesticulating E-bloc tourists milling behind a screen of AK-toting immigration police. Their collective mass emitted a rancid smell of garlic and borscht from the cramped cigar tube in which they had spent the last twenty-four hours. They were most irate to be elbowed by the duty-free perfumed diplomats and aid types fat from their Bangkok R & Rs. We all had plastic bags bulging with goodies, velcroed carry-ons and fibreglass suitcases; their luggage was lumpen bundles holding the things they had needed to survive their indenture in an alien land. They had taken their chance to help repay the massive debt the socialist dream had run up. As the comrade tourists eyed our opulence, I felt, for once, like one of the affluent: at least I wasn't wearing plastic fifties-style sandals and a rayon shirt!

My main man was waiting just beyond the officials' dilapidated plywood sentry box. Tien had been my minder and interpreter five years earlier. We whooped a greeting and ignited my Chiang Mai flowers before we even cleared the baggage.

I had, as usual, misjudged Tonkin's climatic vagaries and

was dressed like my entourage in a collection of vestments that would have done a Mothers' Union bring-and-buy sale proud. It had been warmer back at Heathrow than it was in Hanoi. The 'three-star' Thang Nhat had no heating, and the temperature was hovering between 2 and 6°C at night. Everything had a dark, damp ambience to it, heightened by the drabness that characterises Hanoi on occluded days.

Tien did not want to get out of whatever cocooned heat he had managed to store beneath the mosquito net and the grubby, heavy, damp and lumpy quilt. He had peeled off two layers the night before, leaving a full set of street clothes to sack out in; Dinh, the driver, hadn't taken off a thing, save his thin shoes and army anorak. Like a foolish officer, trying to set a good example to his troops, I had slipped into my Lankan *longyi* and a fresh T-shirt, only to awake freezing in the wee hours, hips numb from the bare boards, to grope for sock and sweatshirt. The three of us were sharing a four-bed cell in the guesthouse of the People's Committee, a series of one-storey barracks connected by verandas in downtown Cam Duong. It overlooked the Olympic-size stadium, in the middle of which was the football pitch – also serving as the local common for buffalo grazing. It had taken us all day to creep up Song Hong valley from Tuyen Quang, a mere 200 kilometres downstream, not even stopping for lunch, subsisting on bananas and coffee. We drank the coffee black after Tien failed to wedge the condensed-milk can securely back, leaving the rear end of the Land Cruiser and all our gear coated with slowly solidifying caramel.

Except for the odd phosphate-extraction adviser at the mines five kilometres outside this completely rebuilt town, I was the first foreigner the man from Minf had had the opportunity to greet in two years. To this end, he had put on shoes and his best coat, once part of a summer suit, giving the result of an overstuffed scarecrow, the jacket only just containing the sundry layers beneath. The outfit was topped by a jaunty black French beret. We wanted some hot food and I would have given hard currency for a hot shower. The hot meal was obtained – at our expense – at a shack backing onto an open sewer next to the phosphate railroad's marshalling yards. Our local man tried to assure us it was the best in town over the ghetto blaster pulsing Boney M. The meat must have been the entrails of the relatives of the scraggy beasts browsing in the sewer out back, the *pho* noodles were dehydrated, the rice broken and bearing traces of the local mining industry. My team guzzled canned Bino beer fresh up the track from Ho Chi Minh, anaesthetising themselves for the night. The hot shower never materialised – in the whole cantonment where we lodged there was not a single bathroom – in lieu, two large Chinese Thermoses awaited me pre-dawn at half past five. None of the other barrack occupants was performing ablutions beyond hawking and spitting, but foolishly officerlike again, I proceeded to shave and wash out of an enamel bowl with my allotted hot water. Tien emerged grumpily, pulling on layers, claiming that washing in this weather caused pneumonia. Dinh brushed his teeth and left to play with his beloved truck. Tien's water was used for coffee.

Flashlight in one hand, I groped to the end of our veranda and fell down three rough steps to the lavatory facilities. Probably it had been originally intended as a cookhouse, two tiny square rooms with a door apiece, at the back two bricks removed at floor level as drains. Somehow, in the rush to rebuild the town after a month's Chinese occupation in 1979, they had forgotten the roof, the toilet bowls or the squatters. To perform, one balanced on the 10-centimetre sill overhang into the room, which, on torch sweep, was a seething, lumpy slime with geomorphological striations towards the missing bricks. Running water was a dripping tap into two cisterns, whose surface was a thick meniscus harbouring a perfect zoological cross-section of the evolution of the mosquito.

On the way out of town we stopped by party headquarters,

housed in a soulless ferrocement building, to pick up two more permanent committee members. The new delegates also needed the obligatory working breakfast on us, that is. I fretted about the passing of optimum sunrise light as we made yet another stop, this time to pick up the commander of the nearest army border-guard post.

The township of Lao Cai probably had a population of upwards of 20,000 in French colonial days when this was the main crossing point for the railway into China, and then on into the Soviet Union via the Trans-Siberian express. During the height of the Vietnam War, it was possible to get important shipments from Moscow in ten days, but even then, everything had to be transshipped onto Vietnam's metre gauge. The town had escaped attention from the American air wings owing to its proximity to the Chinese border, so had thrived on the cross-border traffic. After liberation, relations with the tiger next door had soured, aid had been severed, with the Vietnamese left in isolation to bask in their victory while the hardline party types who had led them stole the country into an agricultural bankruptcy. The massive flow of fuel and supplies from the Comecon states now had laboriously to arrive by sea at the country's woeful port facilities.

Lao Cai could no longer be called a town, merely a dot on the map with a name. Not a building stood in the grid of overgrown streets; where the main boulevard had run to the water, giant bamboo 15 metres high grew from the road divide, rubble peeked from beneath a jungle entanglement which was gradually covering the entire street. A machete was necessary to explore the erstwhile two-storey buildings. The odd soldier in hybrid bits of uniform sauntered by, dragging recyclable remains from the ruins. Caution was proffered to not poke about too much: not all the mines, either theirs or Chinese, had been cleared. I loathe mines, on the basis of personal experience. This was an archaeological site with no digging; that awaited a further thaw in relations with Beijing, which was still going through the whiplash of the Tiananmen Square massacre. My local party lads assured me they had long ago drawn up plans for the town's restoration to its past glory; right now, it was better not to provoke the dormant tiger, only stroke it by allowing consumer goods to flow in either direction by discreet means.

The Red River isn't really very red up at Lao Cai, more a dysentery brown, an unappealing colour tinged with nasty white froth blobs where the current eddies the waters around the low-season snags and stumps. Strung across the half-klick width between the steep bambooed banks, like a set of broken teeth, were the remains of the bridge the Chinese had blown up as they retreated back in 1979. Even uglier swirls and haystacks had accumulated around the now grass-topped piers, from which broken girders hung into the current. The spans slumped in broken Vs beneath the constricted streams. The rail and road link to their erstwhile allies had been truly professionally trashed, as a rap on the knuckles for Vietnam's intervention in Pol Pot's genocidal Kampuchea.

We squatted down at the top of the abutments which had originally locked the jagged tangle below to the top of the bank. There was no way that we could scramble across.

We slithered down, guided by dangling lianas, to a small cove created by the current swirl upstream of the wrecked pier, a small sampan was preparing to pole out across to the other side. It was hailed, but blithely continued on its voyage, rowing upstream for 400 metres before letting the six-knot current carry it across. The other bank was still in Vietnam, our Minf men said, but only the military could cross over. What of the traders? I asked. Farther upriver, they said. Japanese TV had filmed from here two years previously, and now they would like to extend an invitation to me to visit the frontier. We were going across.

Through the eddying mist, 800 metres away on the other side upstream, the sampan poled into a floating raft where a group of soldiers lounged around some sort of powerboat. Our delegation started to hop about and wave its arms frantically, vainly shouting into the current. Eventually somebody twigged and jumped about in reply. Three lads got into the motorboat and cast off, with one of them balanced on the foredeck like a high-wire artiste complete with eight-foot bamboo pole. In the stern, another struggled to crank over what appeared to be a 10-hp Seagull outboard motor. We could see him wind the cord up around the recoil starter atop the motor, step back into the boat and pull. He did this three times before a puff of smoke appeared, followed by a burst of noise, dying after ten seconds. On the middle thwart, the third member of the team sat trying to counterbalance the pole man and the ever more urgent cord puller. He was nervously cradling a light machine gun with a drum magazine. The boat slid downstream at a quickening speed, the pole artist vaguely dabbing ahead to slow progress. They were perilously close to the bridge wreckage by the time there was a sustained burst of power which, at full power, only just chugged the craft towards our small harbour.

One of the things about being alone in a strange land is that one starts to muse aloud, more for reassurance than to elicit a response. 'Why did they not start the engine before they cast off? You know, before they left the other side?' A group of blank stares turned my way and there were oriental shrugs. In the Indian subcontinent, when in doubt, or on the point of loss of face, people will waggle their heads in a cross between an affirmative and a negative gesture. The gods may know, ours is not to question; who's worrying?

As the boat drew closer, we could discern its lopsided lowness in the water. The machine gunner was now baling with an old basin. At first I thought it was one of the cast-iron speedboats-cum-tugs that the Viets had used to keep open their ferries and floating bridges during the war. The quarterdecking had a hole for an automatic weapon; the aluminium hull plates were gaping where popped rivet holes were unplugged. The engine on the back would have graced a 1940s Sears catalogue and was lacking its entire casing, and I doubted whether there was an original part to it.

They ground the nose into our cove and I was levered aboard after the party secretary had scrambled in to take command. The first lieutenant from the border post stood back, offering contradictory orders. Tien was, meanwhile, trying to communicate my photographic requirements and cover the event at the same time. Only Dinh stayed behind, making the expedition now eight strong. In the quiet of the cove we drew about 10 centimetres of freeboard; given no radical shift of passengers we were just afloat. I perched facing aft on the quarterdeck, trying to keep my Nike Wind Airs from the water slopping in the bare bottom of the aluminium hull. There is nothing worse than plodding about squelching in wet running shoes; too akin to wet jungle boots in rice paddies in the war, feet for ever damp, prey to rot, immersion disease, blistering and Agent Orange. So far, I was dry.

Now, more than ever, was a case for starting the engine before takeoff; our covelet was only metres upstream from a tangle of girders and swept-down tree snags; a metre out the current had a brisk pace. Not until the ever more delicately balanced pole man had edged offshore did Motorhead deign to wind his cord round his charge. Would it start? First time, second time, third time? No. Each rewinding cost precious seconds, while we rapidly drifted towards a narrow gap between piers. More ominously, we were being swirled towards the bank. All along the gunwales knuckles whitened; Poleman started jabbering and probing with sharp stabs just off the prow. We swept on, bumping the detritus; the whole caboodle listed as everyone shifted balance, blown froth washing in. We were in the gap and the current caught us full, propelling the overloaded wreck into the chute. In seconds we were spinning and then dropping two metres in twenty. Those who had bits of my gear were holding their arms aloft.

All I could think of was how far it would be to the nearest place where I could touch bottom with my feet, the next bend being a half mile downstream. Snags and rocks were submerged just under the surface. Dressed to sink in my countless layers, topped with a shoot vest loaded with film and lenses, I had flashbacks to watching marines in full combat gear with flak vests stagger and drown from a broached landing craft in an amphibious assault at Chu Lai in 1966. I also remembered the painful experience of abandoning the sinking and burning *Point Welcome* coastguard vessel the same year. Then, I had had to swim for it shredded with shrapnel wounds, initially encumbered with a Leica and a Nikon, which I reluctantly surrendered to the South China Sea. Neither now, nor then, were there any life jackets.

The river calmed. We spun lazily out of the turmoil of the wreckage, righted the boat and hung on while Motorhead removed the carburettor, shook it and taped it back on. A hank of old electrical cable was lashed about it, and then the motor fired, coughed and caught. Flat out, the dying Seagull could make about 1,500 rpm, and with that we chugged back upriver, back into a scene that should have been the set for *A Bridge on the River Kwai* after it had been blown. I felt as though I should be trying to push harder, willing it upstream against the surge we had just schussed down. Nosing into the mid-current buttress, Poleman kept us just off the debris, the Politburo lads reaching and almost tipping the lot in.

The Vietnamese have never been noisy rejoicers in their victories, so often have these only been minor ones in a longer struggle. There was just an audible swell of chatter of relief above the water's rush; the motor's pulse strained less; Poleman sat down; I went back to trying to compose a frame from a fish's point of view.

The bamboo-raft dock was designed to take the weight of an average Viet, so my twelve stone put it right under the egress to the sandbank. Dry feet in the Nam have always been a luxury; the Vietnamese are among the sockless of the Third World; a misery in the urban chill of Hanoi or Haiphong, where imported pantyhose donated to strategic room maids can bring virtual Western-standard service. Their sisters, meanwhile, labour up to their crotches in the alluvial tilth of the paddy field, liberally fertilising it with buckets from the household privies. They do this clad in an extra pair of cotton pyjama trousers to ward off the agues, stooped over for ten hours a day. During the war it was not uncommon for this to be done by moonlight, war work and reparations occupying the daylight.

Since *détente* has seeped to the border, the troops stationed on the Song Hong northern bank have started to tidy things up. They are based at the old crossing point, Ho Kieu, where a tributary of the Red River was once spanned by another elegant bridge. A platoon was busy rearranging the forest on the outskirts of the wrecked village, cutting down wild bamboo before artfully creating a two-poled fence at the back of the ruins which had once fronted the road and rail tracks. Part of the squad was picking through the rubble, carefully stacking bricks, tiles and slates into reusable heaps. A new customs-cum-immigration building down the street had just had its crowning construction-year sign painted; the barrier was still a makeshift bamboo pole with rocks as a counterbalance. The occupants did not appear overworked, though on our somewhat unexpected appearance, one of them rushed outside to raise his barrier as our party sauntered into town.

The Hotel de Douane must have been a truly romantic place to idle the time awaiting or enduring formalities or a train. A long building with tall rooms, balconies on the front, a terrace with veranda at the back. The garden next to the station which it abutted must have been lawned under the giant mango and mahogany trees, a perfect place to sip pastis. Now it was overgrown, trees, bushes and undergrowth having taken over the grass and the shell of the building in an Angkorian fashion. The way the roots straggled down the façade and afforested the stairs, verandas and walltops was almost beautiful. In the one-time bar, the army, quartered across the street in another wreck, stored its bicycles. The main street climbed steeply up to where the remaining track lay on the embankment to the bridge's approach.

It was at this illogical moment after arriving that I was ordered to refrain from shooting pictures until clearance had been given, until the commanding officer of Ho Kieu and his committee gave their personal nod of approval. No problem since I had already canned five rolls since we started the venture.

Vietnam is a place of endless inexplicable sit-and-waits, of endless palavers with local bodies who believe they are more important than they actually are. They all have to justify their authority and, in reality, although the powers that be in Hanoi have already cabled ahead to clear any programme with the local committee, they still get sticky when you turn up and can thwart the best laid plans. Minf Central can order something, but the local Minfs still, in a strange democratic way, have a power of veto. It makes for more employment and total confusion, and your guide has to sort it all out.

We were parked for negotiation in the old frontier post at a long table beneath the gaze of Unclo Ho. Two township committee lads with bad teeth busied themselves pouring hot water into a chipped and filthy teapot, having pinched some leaves from a rusty army-issue caddy. Outside, a Simpson motorcycle burst into life as a noncommissioned minion was despatched to retrieve the local military bigwigs. The building's stepped veranda ended at the overgrown rails; in the middle a 50-foot flagpole flew an enormous Vietnamese flag. Beyond that, a group of border guards played miniature snooker. Seldom is this played on a level footing, and most of the cues are barely straight, much less tapered. Four other folk perched on a shell-shot balustrade gawking into China over the dropped Viet spar. Beyond that, the Chinese one was intact, and they had an equally giant flagpole topped by their banner. The water churgling below was a translucent jade green overhung with arched royal bamboo fronds, but I was not allowed to photograph it.

The customary fags and tea had been exchanged three times before the Simpson returned with another, mounting the commanding officer, his executive and the political commissar. More pleasantries, more tea, more 555s, much passing of my previous books on the country at war and at shaky peace in 1984–85, and then my party was given the freedom of the township, accompanied by their swollen entourage.

We slithered down to the water's edge and gawped at the erstwhile enemy, who gawped back at us. Occasional sampans scuttled across, powered by leg rowers at the stern; they appeared to be ferrying an endless supply of bottled Chinese Emeishan *piju* lager to the Viet side. The bottle bears a beautiful blue and white label of a waterfall, easy to spot throughout the country, down to the southern delta and in Cambodia. It is available at nearly every train station, market and café, its frothy head not discouraged by the normal Vietnamese practice of adding ice. It has spelled the demise of the old French beer, La Rue, brewed in Saigon and said to contain a large percentage of formaldehyde – guaranteeing the drinker perfect preservation should his untimely death be away from his home village. It was only quaffable poured from its litre bottle over large lumps of ice, generally of dubious origin. Rumours abounded during the war that VC soft-drink hawkers had infiltrated the ice works, booby-trapping the lumps that found their devious routes to the battlefields with slivers of glass or razor blades. Like a lot of information at that time, it was hard to substantiate, though to the unaccustomed there was always a good chance of a case of the runs. An adviser worth his salt marked his map overlay with all the spots where either beer or ice was available. Today, even the remotest *ville* can come up with a home-brewed or imported can or bottle of the amber, but up north in the hills of Tonkin ice is still a luxury. *Nuoc da*, solid water, does not travel well over the road infrastructure hardly improved since the 1960s.

My long lens was getting the Chinese all antsy. The traders started to disappear, the bonhomie between the banks subsided, my cohorts scuttled back to their *poste* with my gear, suggesting a diplomatic cuppa. Anyway, the programme had to be completed; that is, everyone was looking forward to feeding. After much handshaking and political nothings translated over the final thimbles of tea, the Politburo mounted three up on its Simpson and headed out of town.

We still had the leaking speedboat to renavigate. I spotted Tien sorting out bundles of 5,000-dong bills to tip the crew. One more Motorhead refusing to fire his charge before Poleman had us adrift, but we had an uneventful crossing.

Our next hot date meant cramming twelve into our Land Cruiser, the white whale. We were going shopping, en route picking up some of the lieutenant's cohorts from the base nestled half at the back of a scrub-covered hill, the forward slope facing the river, zigzag trenches just traceable from the huts up to the crests. Back in 1979 the militia had been caught napping; overpowered with a massive onslaught of armour, they had retreated, scorching the countryside, for over 60 kilometres downstream before sufficient weaponry reinforcement of regulars could be pushed up the only access road. There was now a real defence in depth, the trip flares provided by the presence of the local indigenous people.

Nowhere in the entire country is there complete harmony between the thirty-seven ethnic minorities and the Vietnamese, who had arbitrarily carved up their turf into districts and provinces alien to their wandering souls. No one has ever got an accurate head count; those living on national boundaries know no frontier. The mountain folk always had a better rapport with foreigners than with their neighbours. Insurrection, rebellion and mercenary behaviour are an inbuilt part of their culture.

It was too late by now to shoot the market in full frenzy. The heat of the day was creeping up, the *crachin*, mist, was rolling back, leaving the road dusty and rutted. We dodged around what had been enormous craters caused by land mines; the bridges we scuttled across were composed of disparate planks on recycled girders. In the marketplace four remaining women of the Thay ethnic group sat on plastic sheets beneath other plastic sheets surrounded by a poor residue of trade goods which they had humped over from their relatives in China that morning. The lads from the border-guard base were crestfallen and set about trying to pose the betel-chewing crones and their filthy children into line for my benefit. The prettier, younger ones caught chicken fever and split in every direction, hands over embarrassed, giggling mouths.

Midday feeding had inevitably to come next. There is nowhere in Indochina where life does not grind to a standstill at lunchtime. Officially invited, en masse, by the border lieutenant, we bumped back to the border camp. Tien's ID card was MIA for the third time, so he disappeared on the back of a Minsk motorbike to the ruins of Lai Cao. It was a perfect pause to roll up a big fat one, sit on the brick steps leading up to the team house and await the food while the camp muddled about in a vague manner, awed by our presence, setting the table while shooing impressed women with enamelled wash bowls about. Below me, two off-duty soldiers sauntered by with a chair to find some shade under the lemon trees down behind the well on a spit near a stream shrouded in bamboo. They became the barber shop. Someone brought me a glass of tea.

I was rolling another twist when luckless Tien turned up. He had already left the giant vacuum flask behind in a coffee shop. That had been a 60-klick round-trip retrieval. The golf umbrella had twice gone MIA, and before the journey was done, passport, lenses, bodies, official papers and the ubiquitous ID card would all go missing and arrest our progress. Every traveller to the Orient must allot considerable contingency time for such hiccoughs. In any trip, it is advisable to say a ten-day programme will take fourteen. This will include untoward parleys, permissions unceded, idiotic bureaucracy and the inevitable mechanical breakdown, a summary of Third World snakes and ladders. Turning around became second nature; going back was another chance to snap something that a stoned reflex had caught on the fly out of the corner of the peripheral eye, yet hadn't quite been able to put together as a frame the first time.

Probably Dinh, the driver, had been caught behind some lopsided, overloaded lorry. The Ho trail is a series of diabolical potholes verging on craterdom. Thrown about, I had to develop a loose-framed attitude. I was simultaneously scanning for a photo opportunity and checking the feasibility of calling a halt. After a month everyone finally got a handle on my hand signals, backed up by a rudimentary 300-word vocabulary. Eventually both Dinh and Tien took pride in bringing scapes, vistas, objects to my notice for photographic approval.

The Co Lap Xuong officers' and NCOs' mess served the worst meal of a gut-wrenching week. The wash bowls the harried camp followers had been occupied with contained the swill now set before us. The party secretary in beret played mum with a large ladle. The executive officer started popping beer bottles open with his black teeth. Everyone was issued with a bent aluminium spoon. An animal free-for-all ensued. The soup had some stringy greens and weeds added to the stock of splintered chicken bones and offal, with chillies as an afterthought. The pork was thickly sliced in two-inch chunks, undercooked and with bristles sprouting out of the fat. Some grey shreds were so tough that they would have distanced themselves from being discussed as buffalo, their accompanying decorations were green of the same texture though, I suppose, vegetable, all in a thin grey greasy sauce. To be polite, I pretended to eat.

It is basically difficult to screw up boiled rice. This camp must have gone out to sieve for extra gravel to put in the rations. Owing to a lack of decent milling machinery, Vietnamese rice ends up broken, of a quality Westerners would normally feed to animals. After harvesting it is often spread on the roadside to dry before winnowing, which probably accounts for the high rock content. Chickens love it; humans, in a land with a low density of toothbrushes and fewer dentists, have the highest rotten-tooth rate you can find anywhere. The Indochinese dental surgery in extent is the toothpick, the only countrywide object not affected by the paucity of production. Post-meal ceremony is a ritual picking with more thimbles of tea to wash down the remaining sinews.

Border Post Number 253 prolonged our departure with an emotional farewell in the guardroom with a presentation of the droll Viet army girlie calendar off the wall. It had made a great backdrop to the portraits I had been shooting of the assembled dignitaries as well as being a macho flip-through point of conversation. My photographic interest had been misinterpreted and it was ceremoniously taken down and handed to me. The lieutenant had disappeared, returning with a gift to aid me on my travels: a sample-sized tube of smuggled Chinese toothpaste and a handkerchief-sized square of cotton, a dual-purpose wash cloth and towel. He also insisted that I take the oval-framed snap of himself holding his baby daughter, flanked by his wife, to give to mine. Their poverty and generosity was so sadly touching; it is hard to picture this happening to a Chinese photographer on the Scottish or Canadian border.

* * *

The Chinese border has been off limits as long as I can remember, which is why one of the most vicious battles in military history was fought out with hardly any coverage by anybody. Almost total censorship was drawn across the border zone stretching from the Tonkin Gulf at Ha Long Bay, with its 3,000 dolomitic stack islands, all the way to Pa Tan, just about on the Lao border. During six weeks in the autumn of 1979, probably 70,000 soldiers and untold numbers of civilians perished as China made its displeasure felt over Cambodia. Little news leaked out; both sides played the miniwar, the cards held chest-tight, releasing only tales of atrocity to court international sympathy. The odd foreigner had been allowed up to the front, but the overall picture was hard to come by, the enormity, ferocity and depth of the incursions minimised at a time when the young government of unified Vietnam struggled to deal with an inept economy beset with misguided cooperatives in the south, typhoon damage in the centre and a two-front war. The country was still a key pawn in a devastating international chess game between the superpowers.

By 1985, permission to get into the zones wasted six years earlier was just being granted. A new lot occupied the Politburo, it was the tenth anniversary of liberation and the whole country was to be turned into a giant party for the international media. Places and battle sites never visited since the war were suddenly vying for television attention. Select bunches of us were allowed to travel due northeast from Hanoi to what was once Friendship Pass. At a distance of 165 kilometres, the frontier at Dong Dang is the closest to the capital; the important provincial centre of Lang Son is 12 kilometres from the pass on the Ky Lung River. As at Lao Cai and Cao Bang, in between these were once important French garrisons which had been taken in the first campaigns by General Giap, the Vietminh commander, as his troops tested their mettle in picking off the outlying colonial posts. All these cities lay over tortuous one-lane highways climbing over rugged hills and along valleys prime for ambush. The thinly spread fledgling national army could pick its spot against the thinly spread occupiers, most of whom were made up of local colonial levies or Foreign Legion mercenaries. Many of the ex-Nazis and refugees had fought to the last, believing relief convoys would break through, but most bugged out, their faith in the empire evaporating with the dedicated human wave attacks paved across their redoubts. Like their later counterparts in Washington, the politicians in Paris inhibited the men on the ground from doing things their way. Both actions were to spell the beginning of the end of their countries' respective neocolonial aspirations.

The last French troops had vacated the area thirty-five years before and now it was almost impossible to spot the last vestiges of their presence. Virtually every building over one storey high had been razed when the latest occupants pulled out in 1979, every culvert and bridge blown, anything of use carted across the border. Invading battalions had brought with them threshing machines to reap the rice harvest they believed they would see out. Right up to the moment of attack, the element of surprise had been maintained. At Lao Cai a train had run on schedule six hours before the jump-off, at Dong Dang the mixed passenger and freight down express was caught in a no-man's-land. It was still sitting there rusting, cratered and overgrown tracks stretching into each country, six years later when they let us loose in the pass. French TV and I had signed flimsy papers in Vietnamese absolving them from responsibility before allowing their Russian minibus and my Volga to enter the restricted area. The odd skirmish still took place way back up in the hills; minefields still littered the countryside which nobody had accurately mapped. Dong Dang, itself shadowed by the hill inside China, was a ghost town; not a house in the once thriving town boasted a roof, though the occasional rag-clad inhabitant could be glimpsed tending small patches of tobacco. They appeared to be living a troglodytic existence in the ruins, kibbutzim in the first line of defence. Fighting positions beside the green patches were the only works in good condition. Somewhere in the folded foothills up the valley loudspeakers blared propaganda, didactic nonsense that the squatters totally ignored.

The place had a spooky feeling of lull before the storm, of going down a road where eventually a sniper will open up, an ambush be sprung. Living under the gun induces a sullenness at the obligation to put on the bravest visage, to try to carry off a more cheerful demeanour, allowing your buddies and comrades to have a sense of stoic humour about the situation. Any moment could be the last.

That day the light was pallid and foreboding, the greenness appeared to have gone grey. Philippe Duceaua and the French TV crew went off to interview the ruin dwellers to try and get an accurate picture of what was actually happening. That is when I saw the train and went hot and cold. The end of the line between Hanoi and Saigon would provide the first chapter, 'Unification Express', of my new book. I wanted it stacked up long-lens with the saddle of China as a backdrop, from the vantage point of a knoll that looked down on the old switching yards and *ga*. I ploughed off through the undergrowth up the steep slope, conscious only of the limited time we had on station. Not even the province Minf lads – our designated local hitters – wanted to hang about; besides, there was no place to get a bowl of *pho* or a cup of tea. The trogs who appeared from the ruins were unfriendly; I suspect they thought our presence might incur the wrath of the Chinese mortar crews, creating another round of bad news incoming. I didn't get to the top; frantic calls and then Tien beating a path towards me made me hold up. Unable to hear what he was screaming, I backed up to meet him. Mines! I was in the middle of a fucking minefield, ploughing along like a buffalo. Our descent retraced the ascent exactly.

During the war US air pilots left Vietnam's frontier strip with China inviolate, fearing the possibility of Chinese hordes descending as they had across the Yalu in the Korean conflict. Instead, the navy and air-force fighter-bombers had ferociously worked the transport corridor over where it emerges from the karst-stack mountains south of Dong Mo. To accommodate the normal gauge of Chinese tracks, two sets of rails run parallel inside each other all the way to Hanoi and at the rail and road bridges at Bac Ninh Giang, the whole deck is still made up of rails. At one time spluttering Chinese-built 2-8-0 steam locomotives pulled the line; a few examples still exist for the avid train twitcher, though their demise has been spelled by new Czech and Russian diesels.

Five years on, a superficial skim of poorly mixed asphalt and chippings had been decanted by hand over the same road. The bomb crater potholes have sucked up the skim, making for an undulating ride; farther up in the hills things are the same as before. Gangs of women were strategically hacking up the entire highway with picks and shovels in the ongoing construction programme. Maybe in another five years a reasonable road would run to the frontier. The only machinery around was in a woeful rusting state, often cannibalised, more than likely dating from before the liberation. It can be hard to exhort peasants to quit their profitable rice fields to labour on the public works for less than $10 per month, but somehow, the work got done, leaving me to marvel at their dogged tenacity.

However, we found our parallel railway line had undergone total *perestroika*. There was a new trackbed with twin-gauge rails affixed to concrete ties; even the Cuban girders had had the blessing of an oxide-paint coating. Where the red stuff had come from is unfathomable, for paint is possibly the scarcest item around – the whole country needs a coat. In Tonkin, the buildings' last peeling flakes are of French heritage; only privileged ministries get in on the maintenance rations. The reason for this reconstruction was that the rails were going to run to China. Trading was proving more profitable than warring. The border had become porous, permitting market goods to flow south in quantities not seen since 1976 when relations originally soured. Thermos bottles and tea sets loaded the stalls in Dong Mo's intersection market. Spiked around with sharp karst forest-shrouded hills, this insignificant, dirty district town had been the last stopline for the Chinese invaders in 1979; back in 1985 tank transporters had lined the main drag awaiting their charges out on exercise. Down the road, a detachment of 175-mm-long Tom howitzers, captured from the ARVN in the 1972 Quang Tri offensive, had stalled on their overwarm Detroit engines.

Now in 1989, two moth-eaten mountain ponies wandered from the empty sole side street across to the steps of the post office while in the middle of the intersection two pigs frolicked in a puddle. Another ran out squealing from behind a roadside teashop, hotly pursued by its owner. This causes all the other stalls and party HQ to help try to catch the beast. It was cornered dangerously close to the stalls selling the imported crockery. This zoo was completed by a rainbow assortment of ragged curs, some tethered and in somewhat better shape, destined for the truck drivers' soup at the *pho* stands. *Pho* literally means 'noodle soup', but the sign habitually stands for 'Eats'.

Having just completed the official troop withdrawal from Kampuchea (which had renamed itself Cambodia again), Vietnam was finding itself with a surplus of troops in an army already the third or fourth largest in Asia or the world – depending on whose count. Beyond Dong Mo, in hills once used as minefields or tank tracks, this peasant army had been harnessed to reterrace the steep slopes into paddies. The harvest was abundant and coming in; beside the foot-pedalled threshers hung the *bo doiś* pith helmets, their AKs neatly stacked to hand. A once dead stretch of land now bustled with productivity, the province's contribution to the swelling rice coffers quintupled in as many years. Before, ownership of a buffalo had the drawback that it would end up as hamburger from the uncharted mines; the whimsical beasts now wallowed in families in old craters or grazed in herds in the harvested fields. Extended families had been enticed out of the overcrowded delta to resettle with their newly returned military husbands, sons or fathers. A district once devoid of people had been repopulated, serving once more as an in-depth kibbutz-fashion line of defence.

In 1990, Lang Son was still a dump. The local Minf, dumb, to pay him a compliment. When we stopped off at province HQ to pick him up to accompany us to the free-trade market in the border zone, he wasn't even there. The zone is his turf, and he was warranted a day trip. It is not as though he had a lot of PR to deal with up there. Ensconced in the guardhouse with two uniformed provincial police, with a pot of the bitter army tea and three packs of 555s, we awaited Monsieur Huong, who was summoned by the despatch of an underling on a bicycle. He arrived to say he had confused days and permission must be resought at party and military levels. I stormed out, knowing any market hereabouts would have traded off its best stuff by midmorning. Minf suggested we lunch first while he gets his act together. Around the block, opposite the ruins of the hospital, we entered a *com pho* – a rice-and-soup dive. The squadrons of flies were undeterred by the smoke generated by the wood fire where a prison-thin soup was cooked for us.

To impress us, the scabrous owner shuffled out from the rear sleeping area, making to switch on his imported fan. A spaghetti of frayed wiring descended from the roof beams where the sky was clearly visible through the missing tiles, the building a reclaimed, burnt-out ruin. It had been raining, the odd drip still hitting the floor, which was covered in a slime of food spittings, chicken droppings and grease. The junction box consisted of two exposed wires, which the owner grabbed and wound around those trailed by the fan. There was a lovely blue acrid flash, which plunged the dank room into further gloom. Judging by the kerfuffle outside, the whole block had been blown. We left the filthy family enterprise rapidly, leaving most of our order in a halo of flies. Minf had come looking for us, now all ascrape and abow, having checked out our delegation's priority. His mind was also definitely set on a good spot of shopping.

The Minsk is your basic East-bloc two-stroke technology applied to a rugged practical 125-cc scrambler. No frills, little chrome, no fancy electrics, available with custom-made luggage racks designed to tote loads better suited to a buffalo cart. In November 1989 you could buy one for 700,000 dong, say $175 at the best rate; four months later the price all along these northern fringes had doubled. Its value as a pack pony and motocross machine is considered the ultimate. Normally they are ridden with three up, squidged between tank and bundles. Most of the drivers of the little red Russian machines are young studs from the border garrison partially in mufti, who have been issued Minsks as one of their perks, to run the trade into China. Chinese ethnic Thay and Thai run it the other way. They know that anybody on a Minsk is a bona fide trafficker; the Viets similarly accept the ethnics, whose relatives south of the border have the most up-to-date intelligence. Any attack would be forecast in the market.

To get that far, the army has artfully installed a checkpoint on the last hill before you drop down to Dong Dang. It is more of a supermarket checkout line with diligent border guards walking around with pocket calculators. The local Minf cautioned me, 'No photos', monkey business afoot. Slabs of dong passing around, not even discreetly. The bikers wheeled on by previous arrangement while buses and lorries were backed up on both sides of a flimsy bamboo-pole barrier balanced with a shell casing and an old wheel tub. The jam made it easy to shoot, until the camera was spotted by a zealous NCO who took us for rich Hanoi traders up for a day's loot in a private rental truck. His fantasy of a blue 5G Ho bill was shattered by our delegation status. Cautioned, we crawled on.

Dong Dang was doing its best to be a new town; the open-topped houses were being reroofed, not just thatched. Antiquated roadmaking machines were carving kerbed boulevards between rubbled buildings, creating a reverse archaeological progression. A new bridge spanned the small river I had waded through before. In what could be thought of as downtown, a barber had set up shop; a kitchen chair, a mirror propped on a ruined window, with a poncho lean-to roof supported by bamboo poles. The wrap around clients' shoulders was made of the camouflage nylon of a US parachute flare. The route out of town is deliberately car-proof, a Minsk delight, to discourage traffic beyond the trackside markets save for those who have tipped the lads back at the Checkpoint Charlie for the privilege to progress.

The goods for sale at the stalls were hardly what would attract your average Western customer – a panoply of wares of Woolworth's quality, the bare essentials of a market economy. Every stall, whatever its trade, carried a stock of Thermoses. The stalls selling medicines displayed them in clear plastic bags in the bright sun alongside batteries whose juice must have long seeped back into the ozone. Plastic sandals, children's clothes and cheap toys clamoured in piles. Among assorted hardware we noticed a box of double-sided razor blades. My lads disappeared in a schoolboy orgy of consumption while I sauntered about, eyed suspiciously, cursing our late arrival and trying to make a meaningful snap from the residue of the morning's action.

At a crossroads squatted clusters of female porters clad in black sarongs and blue blouses, counting wads of dong before trekking back across the hills to their homes. Periodically, one of these porters will take a short cut to avoid a profiteering army patrol and will set off yet another of the forgotten mines. Business is too booming to be deterred by the odd death or amputee. An army truck pulled up to disgorge their return loads; circular bowls of hardwood.

Rather strangely, the Vietnamese export chopping blocks to the Chinese, as well as brass ingots and dried abalone. The volume of trade probably tops only a few million dollars a month but with the improvement in relations, a floodgate could soon be opened, letting in more goods than those flowing in via Cambodia from Thailand or those coming across the docks legally.

An old adage has it that given spoons, a million Chinese can build a dam; how many it takes to haul and hack a 40-ton T-59 tank up a 45-degree 1,200-metre mountainside covered in triple-canopy forest and down the other side in relative quiet is conjecture. Make that a squadron of four behemoths and the mind boggles at the task. The sheer audacity of it, the logistical nightmare it presents, and the ensuing surprise it produces, should enter the hall of fame in the annals of warfare. The tactic was lifted almost straight out of Giap's field manual.

Nguyen Van Giap was the architect of the Vietminh victory which sealed the fate of the French empire at the battle Dien Bien Phu. Totally without logic, the French had created a large base 320 kilometres west of Hanoi, deep in the mountains near the Lao border. It lay in a verdant valley encircled by dominating hills; one tenuous road linked it with the rear in the Red River Valley. De Castries, the French supremo, could not conceive that, antlike, the Vietnamese nationalist forces would drag field artillery as well as anti-aircraft weapons over apparently impassable terrain, much less keep the tubes supplied with sufficient shells. The peasantry had been drafted as mules: hundreds of peons on minimum rations slaving each piece up and down scarps and through dense jungles. They had surrounded the base and prohibited air supply; then they pinched off the outposts before storming the command bunker in a human wave. That was in May of 1954, and from then on, the remaining French citadels had lost their spirit to continue, the will to fight *pour la gloire de la France.* By the autumn of the same year, Ho's troops had entered Hanoi under the cease-fire agreed at the convention in Geneva. French Indochina was broken up into North and South Vietnam, Laos and Cambodia, wide open to the influence the United States was attempting to establish in the vacuum created by the Korean conflict.

Although the Chinese invasion had been somewhat heralded by cross-border incidents, the onslaught in early February 1979 took the local Viet militias all along the 800-kilometre common border by surprise. No regular units had been moved to forward positions. Central command had forgotten their own feats, leaving the levees north of Cao Bang, 60 kilometres up the Song Lan Boun valley to the border, to face that dreaded clank which heralds an armoured fighting vehicle's arrival. Without the appropriate arms, the infantryman with his rifle is like an ant beneath a boot; a tank sows terror in its deliberate, unstoppable advance. It will roll right over you and it takes an incredibly brave, or foolish, man to expose himself to pop a Molotov cocktail up its engine or crew vents. This attack had rolled on right over the province capital of Cao Bang, 200 kilometres due north of Hanoi, and had not been contained until reinforcements had fought over the same single-lane mountain road the French had relied on in the 1950s. Ironically, the towns that were now being taken in reprisal for the Cambodian invasion were the same outposts of colonial rule Giap had decided to pick off before going for set-piece battles in the lowlands.

The garrisons had fought desperately to survive at the end of logistic lines completely exposed to infiltration and ambush. Their future was sealed before the cement of the blockhouses, in their Maginot-line majesty, had set. The *ésprit de corps*, the camaraderie existing in these isolated forts, outposts of colonial rule, was rife with romantic deeds. Foreign legionnaires, drafted Frenchmen, African and

Indochinese mercenary levies sometimes had their families stationed alongside them, as remote from Paris as they were from command in Hanoi. The legionnaires were the backbone of the *poste* system, their ranks swelled by the military residue of World War II: German prisoners of war who had accepted an offer of French nationality or death in the ranks of its new expansionism. The other side of their lives was one of tedium, boredom and deprivation, the border towns offering few diversions and the populace often rebellious. The French, unlike their later American counterparts in the southern republic, intermarried or took a concubine for the duration, many settling after their tour was up, opening a bistro, entering the civil lists or the planters' world.

Cao Bang town has less to offer than it did back then. The Chinese hordes levelled the place on their retreat, taking with them the rice which their support troops had harvested in the six-week occupation. Cunningly, they had carried improved threshing machines just behind the advance elements. In February the rains were draping damp shrouds over the drab burgers who had survived, their numbers swollen by a large garrison still quartered in the dilapidated colonial barracks on a crag up above the market. Bullet-chipped, blackened bunkers looked down on the new People's Committee Guesthouse (translate as government-run transient officers' quarters and mess). The building was still under construction and clung precipitously half on the neighbouring crag. It was typical of the socialist central plan for a modern hotel in every provincial town or major resort area. It had an air of being Cuban-designed and built, not quite finished, much less planned.

In communist countries there is always a shortage of everything, and the construction industry is probably the most beset. Half of what is allocated ends up hot in the private sector or on party officials' pet projects; that is, their homes. Cement is a commodity that falls off the back of lorries faster than the half-dozen antiquated mills can bag it. What reaches the building site is a small percentage of the amount required, necessitating the thinning of the aggregate mixture. It is fortunate that Vietnam is not prone to earthquakes, for the whole lot would crumble down, as happened in Yerevan, Armenia, 1988.

The Kach San Cao Bang had a perennially unfinished atmosphere. There were only two other vehicles – a party official's Volga and a Gaz staff-car jeep – in the parking lot in front of the huge entrance steps leading to a cabaret and restaurant, which had never yet opened. No one was about. Dinh went off to explore a line of what were either barracks or military storage sheds.

My A-team was pooped after bumping up from Hanoi, our only requirements a wash, food and a rack. It was the end of another normal day on the road in the Third World, surviving the endless jolts and jars, swerves and braking on a track that had twice switchbacked up to an altitude of 2,500 metres. Except for a midmorning *pho* before the cols, we had existed on a diet of thick, sweet coffee, Salem Lights and Fisherman's Friends. The lads were practically addicted to these lozenges, especially in conjunction with a 555, only surpassed by a Strepsil with a Salem. The Salem has clung on as a second favourite despite having been the preferred toke of the South's last president, Thieu. It maintains a sissy image but can gain maximum Brownie points with women café or *pho*-shop owners. A strategic winner of hearts and minds, or imperialism's ugly head still unsevered.

Dinh reappeared with a giggling, pyjama-clad teenage girl. Her ring of keys indicated her position as a jailer or concierge. Tien turned on his effervescent charm. The boy is profligate with women, his reputation tailing back as far as Bangkok and Tokyo. Officially the place was full. No, the telex had not arrived about the reservations. But we were lucky, we could be squeezed in. Only for one night, mind.

As the honoured guest I would get the downstairs room with a view over the long-distance bus station backdropped by the grey-green hills rising towards the Chinese border. On the nearest ridge beyond the river, a Mark II standard monolith marked the *liet si* (cemetery), home to 5,000 souls who had not survived the six-week occupation. The boys had been relegated to one of the sheds down the hill but in likelihood would use my crib as theirs; they were already feeling the quality of the damp cotton quilts, one top and one bottom, that my queen-sized cot bed had. I was wondering what to do with two wardrobes when the giggling girl heaved open the ill-fitting bathroom door. Not one piece of joinery appeared plumb true. Doors hung off kilter; triangular slots beneath the window frames admitted a northern draught and drizzle. Wiring sprouted near a panel box in the hall; throwing the attached switches achieved a flicker in the bedroom. Any ablutions after dark, which it now was, would be battery-illuminated. Closer inspection revealed a toilet lower than a milking stool, a wash basin without plumbing, a pipe two and a half metres high, live with water – the unfinished shower, I presumed – and a wooden tripod with an enormous bowl. Attention to detail was not missing; a towel rail had been nailed into a crack, and two greyish handkerchief-sized flannel towels were thoughtfully provided. The partly tiled floor was awash, the toilet bowl brimmed with unflushable turds.

The girl left, still giggling, her air suggestive of her lust for anything outside of her dismal world. We were the characters she dreamed of, fresh from the Czech or Russian movie magazines that occasionally reached her, or straight off the screen of the cinema with the shell holes in the roof, next to the bus station. A 500-dong ticket would probably transport her further than she would physically ever achieve. Even Hanoi was virtually another planet, the bus fare the equivalent of her monthly wages.

The man from Minf chose that moment to make his appearance. He was a jolly older cadre in a shabby suit jacket, rakish beret, and shoes without socks. Under the jacket, layers of shirt and pyjama poked from beneath the cowl of a threadbare turtleneck pullover. He accepted a 555 before introductions were even performed, then a whole pack, and took the proffered jay with my card. The ensuing babble sounded in high spirits, so I assumed that our mission programme for the morrow was in order. The spliff drifted to Tien, Minf coughing out that dinner was ready. Our presence had automatically triggered behind-the-scenes mess activity, a chance for Minf to show status with a banquet plus untold beers, to which he would be invited and for which I would no doubt pay.

The economics of this trip were fathomable only in a Vietnamese way. I had surrendered just about my entire stash of money to the foreign press centre on my first working day, a Monday, in country, keeping enough to pay the hard-currency chits at the hotels, and the dollar stores for cigarettes and strategic *pourboire* spirits (preferably Johnnie Walker Black). For my dong supply I merely had to ask Tien, who would produce a brick of blue 5,000-dong notes, the largest bill in existence.

Having Tien carry all the petty cash, I had no need to worry about losing it or getting ripped off in Vietnamese haggling. I could go marketing with two hands and eyes for the camera. Viet rates were guaranteed at any hostelry. The system suited me and them, keeping an eight-week budgetary nightmare to a minimum. Hell, at the final tally, Director Quang of the press centre was worried I would be short of pocket money in bestial Bangkok and returned two of the tattier C bills.

The official exchange rate was then around 7000 dong for one imperialist dollar. Strangely, the highest rate was not down south in boomtown Ho'ville, but on the Tonkin Gulf at the port of Haiphong, where 9,500 to the dollar was paid for bills of twenty denomination or over – Washington being the preferred portrait. The exodus of boat people is no longer from the southern provinces; now it is the economically deprived fisher- and city folk of Tonkin craving the goodies they glimpse on imported videos. A boat ticket is paid for in gold, a now liberated commodity, revered by all Asians. Local committees advise the Mafia bullion dealers of the leeway they have in the exchange rates. The bone of contention is still the question of who will get closest to the seat of corruption, who will hold the political reins. *Plus ça change*.

Vietnam has been reduced to a 40-watt existence. Two bulbs, examples of Hungarian economic aid, glimmered in the barn-sized mess. We descended there, a trail of bobbing flashlights, and sat ourselves at one of the three grandly laid tables. One was a banquet for a gang of local party philanderers, with a folding screen in readiness to keep them secure in their conspiracy. The other two tables were already stacked with an unappetising selection of dishes on dirty, greasy plates. Waterfall beer, at 4,000 dong a bottle, clustered already decapped as the centrepiece. My not drinking alcohol provided a stumbler, since the tea was habitually served only after meals, but the dignitaries' table behind the screen was raided to relieve it of its pot. The dishes were barely distinguishable; everything was grey and sinewy or green and stringy, red colour provided by tomato skins. The stock would have made a gulag inhabitant's Christmas. Last came a lot of cold fried eggs with a dollop of sweet and sour sauce on top in a soup bowl.

The tannoys down at the bus stand announced the first departure of the day for Hanoi. It was 3.00 a.m. and other vehicles were to be despatched to far-flung provinces every half-hour. Just as it had been out in the field during operations and patrols in the war, dawn was a welcome relief. The mess was unable to provide coffee or food, so we repaired to a *pho* shop disgorging the ethnic trading ladies – swathed in black embroidered blankets and footless woven leggings – which from its raised position gave a market vista encompassing most of the root-vegetable section. The root traders also seemed to have cornered the sugar sales: bowl-shaped mounds of brown buzzing with flies intermingled with the tubers. Pairs of prowling pigs rooted on the periphery.

The hope of an easy day's ride vanished with the end of the paved highway, 200 metres beyond the last house of the town. The main road was still under construction, all the difficult bits of culvert digging, bridge building and roadbedding having been abandoned at various stages. At some sites, draftee soldiers picked disconsolately over large rocks. A chill mist clung to the hills on either side of the valley. Covered wooden bridges reminiscent of picture-postcard New England or Virginia spanned the tumbling, ice-cold tributaries. Fording was preferable to using the bridges since the decking was often loose planks or just parallel girders. On the outside of river bends an ingenious network of sluices and channels fed Heath Robinson–constructions, wheels pounding or grinding rice to flour for *pho*.

Cresting a rise on a graded, gravelled section approaching some roadside dwellings, I realised that the neat hedges on either side were moving. We were in the middle of a military exercise. The bushes transformed themselves into troopers, the back of their packs sprouting foliage from holders like rattan table mats; the helmets were similarly adorned. Dinh slid to a standstill, springing me into action. Tien headed for the officers clutching my tomes to placate them so that I could start snapping. Half the attacking company were bootless and a lot of the shod were in shower thongs, the barefooted lads coping better with the viscous red mud, oblivious to sharp stones as they leaped across trench lines and scrambled through dense undergrowth.

Near the border zone, Minf had us stop at the local agricultural department at Don Duong; hidden in the lee of a dolomite karst, it also doubled as the advanced military command post. Two more subministers climbed aboard after a quick exchange of tea and State Express. Our potholed progress ended at a partially restored bridge, the Song Le

Nin, a twisted I-beam across a gushing torrent in a tight V-shaped chasm.

During the war, rather than submit to the embarrassment of falling off the monkey bridges in the delta, I had ignominiously plunged through the slurping canal or streambed. My vertigo was not alleviated here by the sight of a four-metre drop onto icy black rocks, but a chain of outstretched Minfers and Tien passed me safely across the chasm. Upstream, limpid pools of green water gave way to constrictions of tumbled boulders with miniature cascades. Coming upon a fly fisherman would not have been surprising; instead, a half-naked tonsure-clipped Mung boy tickled for fish, spotty like trout with catfish faces.

Our goal was an hour's hike away at the river's source, the former headquarters of Ho Chi Minh in the struggle against the Japanese. The first and last American advisory mission to the communist nationalists was played out in 1944 from the deep caves of Pac Bo. Almost inaccessible, virtually invisible from the air, with a tunnel that egressed from the complex into Chinese territory, the site was impeccably chosen. Under the command of Lieutenant Colonel Patti, the liaison team was dropped in with weapon pods to organise Ho's insurgent Vietminh forces to harass and sabotage the enemy and rescue downed Allied fliers. The same team was at his side when he proclaimed independence in Bach Dong Square on 2 September 1945. Ho's opening address liberally quoted from the American Declaration of Independence (in turn borrowed from the French), hoping that he would attract their recognition for the emergent republic. It was not to be; British ineptitude and French vanity were to subdue the Vietnamese dream, leaving the OSS officers (Office of Strategic Services, precursor to the CIA) to bug out of the north, though not before organising fifth-column groups and trying to wreck any mechanical or industrial assets. The general in charge of these efforts had then turned up in Saigon as one of the first commanders in charge of MAG

(Military Action Group), drafted in to bolster the collapsing southern regime of the despot Ngo Dinh Diem. Designated 'Cold War combat team', the CIA-sponsored mission began the United States' fatal involvement which was to last for the next two decades.

At Pac Bo the Americans lived in the gloomy fortress side by side with their future foe. Ho liked and respected them, and acquired a taste for Luckies, later Marlboro. Below the complex, in a tall clump of king bamboo, a spring gurgles into a round pond serving the erstwhile kitchen. As part of the tourist lure, gravel paths have been laid between the attractions of the place where the glorious leader sat, shat, scribbled poetry or just gazed into the future. Perched at the poetry spot in the Y-branch of a kapok tree, a militia guard sniped occasionally at the spotted fish with a well-oiled folding-stock AK. The backdrop was the scarp the T-59s had slithered down.

Minf assured us that we would all be boosted up a category at the *kach san*, meaning running water at a minimum, the apparatchiks' black Volga having disappeared. My new chambers were directly above the last ones, explaining the swamp below. The swamp upstairs simply seeped down through what was the intended waste outlet for toilet, basin and standpipe. The latter dripped hugely, continuously; the cistern dribbled in harmony. Let's hear it for the running water, the cat wash with doily washcloth towel.

The chicken we had been unable to dissect without the benefit of an electric saw the previous evening, reappeared in a different guise, chopped through, each segment featuring a collar of bone splinters. It was enhanced with a dash of *nuoc nam* (fish sauce) and green chili accompanied by the same rocky rice and green string in gravy. Hunger overcoming valour, I consumed some noodle soup, bananas and, for a change, more condensed-milk coffee.

The same buses left monotonously at the same hours throughout the night, though my new bed was dry, the stains not worth thinking about. At dawn the bus-stand tannoy began playing patriotic songs, Viet disco synth rock in a discordant traditional overtone. The dim bulb threw amber shadows around my swamp, revealing a roll of loo paper on a bit of wire. Vietnamese bumpf is an unappetising grey-brown with the consistency of crepe paper made of cardboard – emery paper to a haemorrhoid. Still, there was a seat, though, somewhat alarmingly, unattached.

As I reached for the crepe roll, I froze in mid-grasp. Less than a foot from the toilet bowl, decorously spreading across the cubicle corner, lounged an arachnid of unknown species. It was one of those that you instinctively distrust; it was wearing fur coats on its legs with an ugly body at the centre the size of a Zippo. Probably it had no interest in me whatsoever, lurking in the fecund corner to prey on other life forms emerging from my swamp. I was not comforted by this insight, having once had a similar critter drop on my arm at a motel in Santiago de Cuba. I had finally trapped it in an upside-down wastepaper basket, where it went berserk. A Cuban TV guy had appeared, hearing my cries, and condemned the beast as *muy peligroso* before stomping it to death. Ants were still hauling carcass trimmings away a day later.

My furtive movements for the loo roll caused the Vietnamese specimen to scuttle up the corner wall. I shuffled – proverbially caught with my pants down – to the relative security of the entrance hall. Getting out of Cao Bang would constitute a strategic retreat.

I found Tien and Dinh wolfing down their breakfast *pho* at a shop on the outskirts of town. The owner's sideline was brand-new Minsks in a choice of black or red at 106 million dong apiece. With 230 per cent inflation in three months smuggling from Lang Son was a growth industry. Dinh got the whale leaping up the col towards Na Fac; we broke out at 2,000 metres from the clammy mist of the valleys. The rolling mountains were almost denuded of their forest cover. The nascent paper industry, the traditional use by the Vietnamese of charcoal and wood for cooking, even in cities, and then the devastating war years have stripped massive areas of northern Tonkin. The erosion tracks are already evident, though, with UN assistance, a number of replanting programmes have got under way, using settlers from the overcrowded delta and contingents of soldiers no longer needed to fight the two-front war.

Where the road comes out of the mountains, the Song Cau River was once bridged by a multi-spanner. Only partially replaced since the US bombing campaigns, it was impassable. Three lads washing their green Simpsons at the ramp responded to Dinh's crossing enquiries with elaborate gestures downstream to an emergency ford. Selecting every lever and knob on the shift case, we managed to get across up a 45-degree sandbank. The water came halfway up the doors, the current discernible while the wheels slipped and gripped on the rough bottom. Sundry vehicles watched our progress.

We had devoured lunch at a transport café and were standing outside yawning, taking in the drab village and its one through street. A long-distance lorry thundered down the dusty road at high speed, just as a black and white cur took it upon itself to cross the road. There was a thump and an unearthly squeal. The trucker drove on, probably imagining the damage yet another rock or hole had done to his Wartburg-built suspension; the dog dragged itself to the steps of the café and lay writhing. A dozen shabby villagers clustered round, indifferently watching the body in its last spasms. My First World impulse to be some sort of saviour surfaced and subsided, and I raised the camera and started hitting the shutter, pulling zoom to perfect the frame. It is always impossible to drag the eyes away from the moment of death. The crowd started to drift away, leaving the carcass at the ditchside, interest lost. I caught the eye of one lad and made chopstick motions, but he shook his head. A watery-eyed Tien beside me said, 'No good, burst insides, not in head.'

A dog seller on the road to Tran Tao – birthplace of the Vietminh army – with a dozen fluffy puppies in a chicken-wire cage on the carrier of his bicycle was quoting 200 dong a kilo.

# 4

# *The Case of the Missing F4*

Tuan Giao is a road junction in the Annamitic mountains of Tonkin. From Hanoi, you approach it over Thud Ridge, so named from the large numbers of F-105 fighter-bombers that were shot down during the war on their approach to the Red River delta area in their unsuccessful attempts to bomb the north to submission. So many of these planes went down that they got monikered 'Thuds'. This spine of mountains then bristled with anti-aircraft and flak weaponry which poured a volume of fire upwards, causing the US air force to divert missions just to suppress it. The USAF had not thought it possible that the Viets could be so aggressive in defence. Later on, the Vietnamese installed SAMS – surface-to-air missiles – the cylindrical shipping cases of which have now been erected to form classical arches at the approach to all northern villages.

Dien Bien Phu lies to the west, Lai Chau to the north. We had tortuously snaked the 120 klicks from the latter in five hours, frequently stopping to document the ethnic folk who inhabit these high regions. Here in the farthest northwesterly corner of Vietnam, hemmed in by Laos and China, there has never been a real census. Estimates vary, but the indigenous peoples outnumber their lowland governors three to one. Black Thai, Blue Thai Meo, Man and Tho predominate, grouped in the family-clan villages either strung along the scarce roads or perched precariously on steep hillsides above spectacular raging river ravines. Except for the grassy uplands, the whole countryside is clad in triple-canopy primal jungle forest. Huge hardwoods rise to a height of 60 metres from the V-shaped valleys. Beneath the trees a dense undergrowth struggles for space. Ferns, vines, bamboos and draping orchids prevent you penetrating more than a few metres off the trail. The locals disappear up or down tiny paths leading to distant slash-and-burn fields or dwellings on stilts. It is *National Geographic* or picture-postcard stuff. Unvisited, unspoilt frontier country. Ideal for the guide book I had been commissioned to shoot.

There are few places on this planet where you can get a feeling of virgin turf. The hills in the northwest quadrant of Vietnam may have seen no more than a few hundred white people since the French were hoofed out; the only ones to make it to this remote area have been East-Block advisers or downed pilots. This is definitely not tourist country, though I suspect groups of yuppies and trekkers will be buzzing here before too long; this whole zone could become a new golden triangle. It would destroy the lingering atmosphere of the twenties and thirties, the heyday of the French era. The solid stuccoed villas, now occupied by party hierarchy, bear testimony to the opulence that the colonialists once lived in. The ethnic population, who were indentured, virtual slaves to the French system, working the plantations, live a lifestyle centuries old, a large minority still flamboyantly dressed in their native costumes. The menfolk are for ever on the lookout for any game, big or small, sparrow to deer, to feed their communal pots. They do this with antiquated black-powder flintlocks, blunderbusses, rifles – a gun collector's dream – apparently with great success, for wildlife is a rarity to behold. With a macho style befitting the Italians or the Maltese, they gun down anything that takes to wing or foot.

The infrastructure of roads has barely been improved since colonial times, though the war with the United States brought some widening of the tortuous tracks, enabling trucks to pass down from China to the Ho Chi Minh Trail. The Chinese assumed responsibility for their upkeep, maintaining an engineering corps of 200,000. The utilitarian chasm-spanning bridges are now rapidly passing into obsolescence. On many of the roads closer to the border, where the Chinese swept in with tanks in their ill-fated punitive war, they were obliged to destroy their own handiwork, so recently fraternally forged, for they left a scorched earth in their wake. Much of the way, the road is wide enough for a truck passing, though it is a rutted and boulder-strewn surface; between towns there is not a single gas station or place to fix anything. In Vietnam the driver is also expected to be a mechanic and any truck leaving town has at least one assistant driver, as well as a helper who does the monkey work on flats and dropped shafts. All vehicles double as buses, and are consequently overloaded, belching smoke from decrepit engines running on dirty, low-grade Russian petrol or diesel. The cheap, putrid smell of the imported commodity hangs as a pall over Indochina, until their own wells can come on line.

Dinh had last come this way back in the seventies and was for ever marvelling at the improvements he spotted. I was bemused by the roadworks. Miles from anywhere, we would come upon a band of locals armed with hammers for fragmenting large rocks, a few barrels of tar, an assemblage of odd wheelbarrows and, possibly, an ageing Romanian road roller. Most of the chippies and shovellers were quaintly dressed local women pulled straight from the fields. The menfolk are usually off strolling around with their flintlocks, or sitting by the roadside sucking on pipes; the kids look after each other in droves.

We had left Lai Chau at daybreak, Tien and Dinh breakfasting on *pho* in a café next to a primitive workshop where our blown spare was being fixed with ruinous tools. I was served five bantam eggs, yolks mashed, hyped as an omelette;

the bread man had still to pass, so sticky rice acted as a mop to the oil. After yesterday's rain, the guesthouse was awash to the veranda steps, though there was no water in the pipes to the eight washbasins just about hanging to the wall at the end of the building.

We had all ended up going out to the cistern in the pissing rain, rousing the guard pig to furious oinks from its post inside the communal toilet. A slew of frogs peevedly left their position on one cistern's rim when we dipped our enamel basins for our bath water.

We were climbing up to 2,000 metres above the valley as the mists dissolved below. Dinh was enthusiastic about getting to Tuan Giao, because his buddy from his wartime motorpool days down the Ho trail had married an up-country lass and resettled there from his native Haiphong. Binh, his friend, had somehow got the Honda spares concession for this neck of the woods, necessitating periodic trips to the coast. He was also the agent for two Viet pharmaceutical companies, so the living room of his substantial two-storey ferrocement house on the main street was littered with boxes of ampoules and three spotty youths aimlessly going through piles of sprockets, tail lamps and chromium trim parts for the parallel enterprise. There was much rejoicing as the two army brothers reunited after nearly two decades. The customary green tea was produced by Binh's betel-chewing wife, but it was evident that lunch should be our treat; the VIPs in town had to show power and face.

The chosen venue lay opposite Binh's emporium across Tuan Giao's dusty main drag. Heavily jewelled and besilvered ethnic Thai women passed by in knots, smothered with red powder kicked up by the blue Gzil trucks, usually tankers topped with a frame of logs acting as drop sides to barrels, bales, baskets, fowls and beasts with their keepers. The woman stopped and hovered at the woefully poor stalls lining the street. Only the dross end of a car-boot sale was on display, and the usual shoddily-made Vietnamese goods.

There were few goods representing the vast smuggling industry we were used to seeing in other towns, and Laos, a mere 100 kilometres away, held no sway upon the market.

The blue and white *pho* sign hung suspended from a gallowslike pole this side of the monsoon drain. The bamboo shed with corrugated-metal roof was reached by rickety planking thrown across the sewer ditch. Bamboo bead curtains attempted to keep the local winged wildlife out of the dirt-floored interior. Binh was obivously a regular, bantering with the fortyish proprietress who installed us at the best table, where we could be glimpsed from the street. The only other customers were a middle-aged ex-officer and his toddler son tucking into a communal bowl of noodles.

Large bottles of Chinese beer magically appeared upon the table for the Viets, a pot of tea for me. The proprietress retreated to the three-hole-range kitchen overlooking the shop floor. A spotty youth of draft age swiped at the dirty tables with a filthier rag, and replenished the beer. Madame kept barking orders at him whenever he appeared taskless, while she chopped, stirred and strained.

The ploy was for the crew to consume as much beer on my tab as possible. The empties were stacked meaningfully on an adjacent table, making our tab easier to calculate. There were no nibbles to quench our raging hunger, not even the usual saucerette of peanuts one is supposed to get mouthwards artfully with chopsticks. I rolled a jay of Thai, killing time, building the munchies syndrome even higher. The tea did not quench my thirst, and the *citron pressé* I had ordered was still in the boiling-water stage of construction. It wasn't on the menu, but then there wasn't a menu, nor a chalked-up price list.

Large bowls of *pho* finally arrived, to be consumed with the etiquette of animals. By road-fare Indochinese standards that place would not get even a quarter of a star. We sat back on the benches to pick at our teeth with split bamboo. The end-game teapot had not yet appeared; the lads sat back rapping. Considering that our next stage was at least to Son La, perhaps farther, it was a propitious moment to roll a couple for the coming slog over two 20-kilometre passes. I knew the road, and combat rolling in the Land Cruiser front seat meant risking that the stash would end up anywhere but on the creased skins. The stash was in the tuck across the road. Dinh passed me the keys and I flailed through the fly curtain. I hadn't got back to the café when I saw the others leaving across the ditch bridge into a crowd of curious ethnics; my plan thwarted.

Farewells were bid and we set off down the street to check in at the police post at the junction to get the latest local security update. Banditry is still rife in the hills. Many people from the ethnic minorities join the forces to get their basic training, get issued with a weapon before going AWOL into the remote mountains to prey upon passing transport. They see themselves as Robin Hoods, though there is a new breed called Jawas after the 350-cc twin Czech bikes they ride.

The previous day, cutting across cordillera from an old French summer hill-station retreat to Lai Chau, most of the way had been a succession of blind breakneck bends opening to view of the road snaking above or below us. It was the only way to become aware of an oncoming vehicle, unless the horn of the other vehicle was functioning. On the descent from one harrowing section, the charred chassis of trucks littered the roadside with a horrific regularity. Lower down had been a fresh wreck, that acrid, burnt-out smell still lingering. Nearby were two freshly made graves of hard earth edged with stones. Joss sticks had burned down at the head end. Tien and Dinh stood embarrassed, their hands at prayer, for a protracted silence. Dinh returned to the truck and dug about in the dash to find some more incense to light. The spirits of the road badly needed appeasing. Probably one day a small shrine would be set up here.

Five minutes later, as the road emptied out onto a plateau from behind a high bluff, a primitive roadblock of boulders had been rolled across the highway. We slid to a standstill, only then noticing the green and tan rag-clad *bo doi.* One was recumbent, his head on a boulder, his machine gun across his gut; another squatted, toying with his weapon, beside a huge rock; while the third shambled towards us on the other side.

We all read the same moves; the set-up, the stick-up, the possible army check point, the bribe, the ambush. There was a rush of intercommunicated adrenalin vibes. As we skidded towards them I was already out of the door, Leica raised, framing the whole scene wide-angled. The dude ambling our way, AK at combat slope, was not sure whether to pose for the picture or act aggressively; effectively disarmed, he hovered between grin and grimace. He changed tack and headed for Dinh, who put on his most perfect Uncle Ho. 'Now look here, children, brethren' act. The others resumed relaxed postures, defused by our counteroffensive. I made two more snaps before they could roll a couple of rocks apart.

Therefore, it pays to check in with the edge-of-town post just so they know you have passed into their control zone. It could be hours or days before they reacted, but the system would eventually crank into gear. We all went into the station, causing the Thermos of hot water to be produced, the onset to a pot of tea, and out came the 555s and Salems. Tien and I left Dinh wittering on, telling road tales. Back out in the bright light a human caravan was passing, back baskets stacked with firewood, ethnic Sunday finery put on for the market.

Wanting to make a long shot, I reached for my F4 and its monster autozoom, but it was not in its accustomed spot on the front seat. My troops had breached the cardinal rule: last to leave makes the sweep for the rest. In the flurry to leave the *pho* shop, $4,000 worth of gear had been left next to the empty beer bottles.

We hightailed it back to the lunch zone, disgorging as one, to be met by a blank expression from the proprietor, disclaiming any knowledge of the missing equipment. A sense of panic set in, for without this unit I would have no long lens to finish the shoot for the commissioned guide book. Such a hi-tech piece of equipment could never be found in country, and getting a replacement from Bangkok would be a nightmare, to say nothing of the cost. There was no insurance, either.

A large crowd had gathered, the woman spitting forth at them at the accusations we brought. Dinh came across and added to the kerfuffle. We sped back to the police post, a funk at the loss seeping in. The lad tackled the cops inside while I chain-smoked on the steps in front of a growing cluster of locals and their offspring; we were still the only show in town, now the news had got around. The boys popped out like a cork with a gaggle of gendarmerie, Tien calling, 'Wait here', with which they all bundled into the truck, U-turned, spitting gravel, and sped off in the direction of Dien Bien Phu.

I sloped back into the near-deserted station, tired of smoking cigarettes and getting irritated by the encroaching school's-out populace of Tuan Giao. A fresh Thermos appeared, another pack of Salem Lights was handed over. I settled back in the committee room with not even a notebook to scribble in, all my gear having disappeared off on the chase for what now emerged to be two known local bad boys on a Jawa who had left town in a hurry after being spotted with a black bundle. This information got through in a mix of five languages plus meaningful pantomime.

As the hands on my watch snailed round the clock, a feeling of abandonment crept in. The afternoon got longer; Son La receded as a destination. How far had they gone? I had seen two buses head that way while still on the stoop. How long does it take to overhaul and search a bus? Would the Jawas get away? Glumly, I blamed myself, and the glamour of the adventure deflated.

A dustier truck eventually returned – not a bright face

inside. We were cajoled to go across the junction to the compound housing the people's committee, the criminal-investigation department and, above a knoll, the army barracks. One room in a long building doubled as bedroom and office for the senior lieutenant in charge of the base; his army cot and mosquito net stood under a barred window. The only other furnishing was a scarred wooden desk and a couple of wooden chairs (one was instantly changed from a clothes stand for my benefit). The following act could have been a scene from 'Alice's Restaurant'. The lieutenant laboriously took down the whole story, continually interrupted by a flow of deputies reporting in and being despatched. More chairs were produced for the accumulating officialdom, all of whom needed filling in on the events. We had to move to an adjoining mess hall to accommodate the assembly. Tien was overwhelmed, attempting to feed me enough translation from the kaleidoscope of opinion. A lot of diligent-looking uniformed lads with weapons turned up in the barrack square, half a dozen mounted on upmarket Hondas. They sped off on missions that were not interpreted.

We sent Dinh back up to alibi his buddy, still on the suspect list. The shadows outside lengthened. We were guaranteed to be spending a long night in beautiful down-town Tuan Giao. I had taken the stance of announcing in no uncertain terms, threatening virtual international intervention and party-political turmoil, that we would *not* be leaving until the missing F4 was safely back in our possession.

Binh was eliminated. His local reputation could not bear the loss of face, and his interest in photography was confined to four Pronto Prints tacked to the mirror in his foyer. There was the ex-soldier and toddler who had slurped up and left before us. There was the alleged possibility of a long-armed thief reaching through a side window. He or she would have had to play forward for a basketball team to reach the table, yet certain members of the local plod force started enquiries along that line. Realistically, that left the soup lady and the serving boy. They had both been pulled in, looking the worse for wear, and stuck in different cells. Their stories conflicted and did not add up. The woman's histrionics of protest were audible across the compound.

More officers and heavies turned up at the compound; it had become a province-wide event, judging by the out-of-town plates now ranked in front of the mess. We were shown our quarters as the sun went down: a barracks with four slatted wooden beds and a large cupboard with a padlock, for which we were ceremoniously given the key to stash the rest of the unimaginably expensive equipment. The bedding was dank, the only clean item in the room a handkerchief-sized towel of thin cotton. Mosquito nets in tangled dirty rolls hung over each cot.

Dinh was back up the street reassuring poor Binh, whose status now precariously dangled wide open, a loss of face as a suspect tantamount to being obliged to leave town. Besides, Binh clearly had an inside track to the burg's underbelly. Not all his Honda parts were of kosher import, and in a country where most people still only consume the bare basic caloric intake, he was downright overweight, the rolls bulging under a white T-shirt.

Periodically, there would be a discreet knock on the bolted double wooden doors and another batch of province officials would come in to view us as though we were a zoo act; ostensibly they were reporting in. By now, I was holding court from inside my fat sack, a viyella-sheet sleeping bag heaped over with two damp quilts. When Dinh returned with a clean bill for his mate, he reported a flurry of police activity in town. Known bad boys were being rounded up and grilled. Should this have been a Hollywood drama, a group of FBI agents could have been expected to appear in a silenced black helicopter.

The naked light overhead flashed on and woke me. It must have been past midnight; not a sound bestirred the post. Three local cadre, now familiar faces, stood grinning inside our room. The camera had been found, they announced. By now, the relief was a mere watercolour wash on my hazy brain. A comatose sleep swept away an awareness that we would be out of town on the morrow. My last fading thought was to wonder why the latest delegation had not actually got the missing machine in their hands right then.

When morning arrived, the barracks, which we had only seen in the dark, was as gloomy as that at Cam Duong. Lined up on the veranda were four giant Chinese Thermoses and a tripod affair balancing an enamel basin. Two thin small handtowels were draped from the chipped rim. My lads skipped the wash and brush-up, just replacing one extra layer of clothing, while I used up all the hot water, stripped to a Sri Lankan sarong, to the titters of the emerging bedraggled garrison. Travelling with the lads was getting a bit pongy, now six days out, without them indulging from the cat-lick's Thermos. It never would happen in southern Cochin, where the populace deem it necessary to immerse themselves at least twice daily. Tonkin is clammily chilly, then boiling hot; near to freezing in the morning, peaking up to 30°C by midday up in these hills.

After breakfast in the mess (the bread had weevils, the tea was bitter), all we needed to blow the burg was the recovered gear, but things are never that simple in Vietnam. On our return to the committee's HQ at the quadrangle, the crowd that had gathered parted for the Land Cruiser to let us descend to a virtual Cup Final winners' reception. All manner of officialdom and party flacks milled for position. Somebody was organising a performance, in which we were the star turn. The local press and television were there en masse, wielding a totally uncoordinated, obsolete collection of photographic equipment: Russian, Chinese, Japanese and DDR-made gear at least a decade old, held together with an ingenuity of brackets, bolts and elastic bands that only the Vietnamese would create in their efforts to circumvent the lack of spare parts. Although the morning light was stunning, flashbulbs and a strobe winked our way. The local TV station made to capture the event with a film cameraman as well as a guy with a video camera. Providing portable illumination for these two was a lighting engineer with a hand-held high-wattage inspection lamp powered from an assemblage of a once-dead motorcycle and a car battery, the whole carried in two baskets hung on a bamboo pole in the timeless oriental fashion. With the one central power source, they were inextricably linked. They reminded me of the poor network circus covering the war in the South in the 1960s.

The whole assembly headed for the committee's meeting room, furnished with a row of tables end to end for 10 metres. We poured in and engaged in a form of Eton wall game crossed with musical chairs to grab the exactly lined wooden classroom seats. Someone switched on the two overhead 40-watters and started to hose us down with blasts from their prize possession, a newly acquired oscillating Chinese Great Wall brand stand fan. We got the centre of the table, opposite the top cop. A statue of Ho Chi Minh oversaw our gathering at the north end. At the other sat a cardboard box, flipped open so I could glimpse my state-of-the-industry black Japanese technology. The F4 looked in one piece. I was dying to get my hands on it, in an anti-climactic way. Would the exposed film be intact? Were the batteries dead? Had it been dropped?

Tien bothered to translate only a modicum of the proceedings, which concerned the glories of the system of state efficiency; democratic, pluralistic international fraternity; the whole obligatory gamut of opening exchanges with foreigners in this people's paradise. Then, Tien warned me the chief policeman would say a few words, the party chairman would chime in, then the CID dude, followed by my speech and acceptance of the recovered equipment. The speeches dragged by, my mind working overtime on how to address this assembly satisfactorily in a way that would hasten our departure. The chairman and I were positioned beneath the metre-high bust of Ho, where he delved into the box and grappled with the correct method to place the three-kilo lump of evidence back in my hands. We had to run it three times to satisfy the whims and ineptitudes of the diverse media needs.

Nor was this all: the little scene of the presentation was a mere warm-up for a morning's cinematic efforts at re-enacting the crime at the scene for a local party-political TV propaganda. It would probably fill a slot akin to the evening news crossed with *Crime Watch* and a dash of *Perry Mason*. The whole cast trooped back up to the scene of the crime, where the culprits were conspicuous in their absence – the *pho* shop lady and her assistant. We ran the whole lunchtime scenario in slo-mo, backing up whenever Lai Chau TV hadn't quite captured the moment. The main road was totally blocked with the assembled populace of the burg, splashed colourfully with the ethnics in their best clothes, loaded with silver necklaces proclaiming their autonomy and wealth. The F4 had been located in an empty export-quality beer carton in a pile under the table upon which were displayed the shop's potable wares. A ferret-faced CID man re-enacted how he had unearthed it with the diligence of a well-trained party man. The whole performance dragged on for three hours, the day burning off to a mountain-clear, hot day.

The story came together like a jigsaw puzzle. Tien was barely bothering to translate any more, the play explaining itself; though the end game, the trial and sentencing, was not to feature our live testimony. The *pho* woman had caught the young lad, now her shop slave, in flagrante with her eighteen-year-old daughter. Massive amounts of face loss all round, so, committed to silence, he had become her toy boy, serving clientele and mistress, for ever strapped; for had he run, the army draft would have nabbed him. He weakly admitted to a fantasy where he was a photographer in Hanoi, so the Nikon had triggered a hope of escape. His mistress, not knowing of the fantasy, but seeing quick money, had covered the theft. Not a frame had been exposed.

We left town, burning dust, the CID man who had discovered the camera riding shotgun in the back to Son La.

There were no rooms at the inn when we got back to Hanoi. There appeared to be no rooms at any other inn in town, either. The whole infrastructure had been swamped by delegations. Most annoying, especially considering that I had been greasing the skids at the Thanh Nhut now for some five years. The receptionist was a real cutie, who used the foreign perks she received to pretty herself up rather than flogging the stuff on the black market. She always looked chic with an artful touch of make-up, a Western clothing item setting off just so the drab uniformity available on the streets. Long ago, Tien, one of the state's leading womanisers, had briefed me to keep Ms Ha sweet, especially since her father was, or had been, Hanoi's chief of police, an important post in this police state. And nothing ever got nicked from any of the dozen rooms I had graced, be they suites, garret, ground floor or baggage holds. I had had fewer of the rats that had been bothering the German ambassador's baby in his quasi-permanent first-floor suite. I had not even minded being bumped down to one of the rooms where washing meant dodging down a tall, cold, draughty, tiled hallway to the common facilities. These quarters had obviously been the lot of junior officers and minor functionaries in town from the sticks, back in the colonial days when the hostelry was still La Metropole.

It is still a remarkable building, a period piece from the *belle époque* when Hanoi was the de facto capital of all Indochina. The ballroom, now used as the dining room, more like a canteen with its glum serving staff and short, awful menu, had hosted soirees that would not have been out of place in Paris. Now occasionally, a fraternal folkloric troupe would pound indigenous instruments and go mechanically through resuscitated native dances. These entertainments reverberated through the otherwise cathedral-quiet three storeys on wholly unpredictable nights, the only clue a surging mass of unwashed E-blocers in ill-fitting clothes eddying through the long bar and lobby area. The rooms are of massive proportions, the ceilings four and a half metres high. Three-bladed suspended fans spasmodically work according to the vagaries of an antiquated switch panel with odd trails of wire drooling down behind. A good slap of paint would not go amiss anywhere; the last lot probably got applied in the fifties – once white, now a smoky buff. There is probably enough mahogany in the floors to keep a whole flock of yuppy builders in south London busy for a year. It has not seen wax since liberation, but is swept daily by the dogged force of harridans who inhabit a suite next to the common bathrooms near the stairwell. Their function is also to spot guests' movements and purvey Thermoses with boiling water for tea. They rate a lipstick and a pair of tights apiece, which guarantees same-day laundry return and that roaches left on ashtrays are replaced after cleaning. None of their efforts at housekeeping could keep each room's pet family of cockroaches at bay; but then you have to look at cockroaches from the point of view that they actually consume dirt and filth, recycling it into their own body protein. You learn to cover all consumables or stick them in the fridge – there is one in about half the rooms.

The place is funky with a heavy hint of bygone times, easy to imagine as a 1930s film set, a comfortable place to get into nostalgia. Anyway, I had got used to being there, reservations or no. My track record, and the efforts of one of the lads from the foreign press centre who were for ever chatting up Ms Ha, were usually enough to get me a room ahead of some poor UNDP forestry adviser fresh in from Bangkok. E-bloc visitors lacking hard currency got shunted into the Hoa Binh (Peace) barracks down the road or to a billet in the suburbs.

Tonight, definitely, there were no rooms. Clumps of Japanese business delegates, or were they filmmakers, with giant suitcases on trundle wheels and stacks of hi-tech boxes, fretted at Ms Ha and the other behind-the-scenes personnel, and waved Rising Sun red and gold passports and indecipherable documents. The chief assistant to Ha – a ferret in a beret, who chain-smoked 555s – told me in an aside that I should hang loose in the 40-watt lobby on one of the uncomfortable carved seats. After eight days of splash baths and indifferent accommodation in the high northwest country, eight days of Land Cruiser, all I wanted was a hot shower or, better still, a long soak in one of the giant claw-footed iron tubs, followed by ten solid horizontal hours.

Tien had gone off on his new Honda 90, trying to find me somewhere to crash. I never saw him again that night, and his sometime girlfriend behind reception disappeared, leaving it to Ferret-face to inform me that there were no rooms available in or out of town.

By now I was in a 'prop me up' state, keeping awake with occasional infusions of *café sua*. The early-evening flow of traffic through the lobby to the cavernous, bleak restaurant had ebbed, those residents desperate enough to dine out had already gone, and I still had not spotted a familiar face. In a matter of minutes I would just flake out in their decadent lobby. The threadbare night shift finally despatched their token French speaker to my hardwood nest with a key. We shouldered my scattered chattels and slugged up the tatty lino stairs to the first floor, then all the way down to the right, right again and to the end of the corridor. The hallway had dankened, the coir runner ended, the ceiling lighting blown before we were halfway its length. Our footsteps echoed on the chequered tiling.

Room 117 had a musty emanation before the key went in the lock. The door took a shoulder to force its swollen jamb; the faint light from the hallway lit a puddle just inside. A regular drip fell from the ceiling, plishing into a spread of water. The desk boy groped to the right for a light switch and toggled, creating odd sparks. Another downstairs help arrived, hopped the puddle into the room and eventually located a lamp which cast a glimmer in the main room over in one corner. It illuminated a sturdy desk pushed up against a wall with peeling stuccoed plaster. Two beds and an upright chair made up the rest of the furnishings. One of the beds was sodden wet, the other marginally damp. I turned to point this out to the deskies but they had beaten a retreat quietly, having put my bags across the threshold.

The room, they explained, had been held for a high-ranking up-country party delegate who was a no-show. On pain of demotion they were letting me be accommodated for a night; there was still an outside chance, *peut-être*, that I would have to get up in a bit, pack up and move. 'Where?' I had wanted to ask. Possession being nine tenths of the law, I felt secure for the moment; it would be possible to create a dry space to collapse. First the longed for in-tub steeping in hot water. Having undressed, I found the room decidedly chilly; the heating had extended about the same distance down this wing as the carpeting.

The switchboard cluster in the entrance hall was still gently arcing, spasmodic sparks of blue and white. The drip plopping in the spreading puddle appeared to come from directly overhead, though a tributary was trickling down the wall towards the electrical fireworks.

The bathroom was ominously dank; beyond the small sill the floor was a sheet of water. A sweep of flashlight revealed the bath; not a claw-footed iron job, more of an oblong broken porcelain-tiled reservoir, gently overflowing. Two large brass spiggots dripped, one at dribble, one at plip-plop speed. Neither would budge further shut. On one side of the reservoir sat the seatless toilet bowl, also full and lapping over, mercifully with clean water. The standard-issue duck-egg-blue crepe loo-paper roll sat on the end edge of the bath, limply unusable in its primary role.

I turned my attention to the washbasin. It was a handsome thirties artefact of scalloped-shell design with beautiful high-rise taps, *robinets* with four spoked china capstan handles. Lille was once a thriving town turning out fixtures like this for the dominions. A cracked mirror in the last stages of fungal encroachment dimly reflected my shivering, paddling image. One tap spun any which way to no avail; the other, after a Stilson-effect grip was applied, budged from a steady drip to a tepid trickle of blood-rust water. Naturally there was no plug on the frayed string tied to the plug-uplifter lever. In bending over the basin to execute this test, I was struck by a large plop on the back; an upward sweep of the torch beam revealed a large crack in the plaster exposing the lath of an upstairs bathroom, known to be derelict.

Half moored to the creeping wet zone above had been a stucco rosette from which a brass ferrule introduced the wire for the bathroom lighting. The stucco detail had detached from the crack running behind it, the brass attachment now a mere loose washer; the black-cracked, insulated wire terminated at the brass bulb fixture just above head height. Reaching round the door, I tried toggling the switches again. A series of sparks and flashes started popping from the switchboard and somewhere up near the half-suspended ceiling rosette. The slight jolt I caught made me realise I was barefooted in a puddle. The power supply here was below 110 volts at best, but still capable of putting out a jolt.

Closer inspection revealed a light bulb in the socket above my head, surprisingly intact. Light bulbs are still a luxury item, not that easy to find even today, and their quality reminiscent of the last Hungarian ones that appeared years ago on British supermarket shelves. Probably the obsolete plant for their manufacture had been shipped to Haiphong as part of a socialist aid package. I reached tentatively for the bulb, hoping that it would at least shed light on the flood. I froze, stunned by the sight of the glass globe half full of water, the filament still intact, partly submerged. A snail trail of damp down the disintegrating flex was keeping it topped up. Presumably a certain amount was electrolysing away.

Despondent, dirty and pissed off, I beat a retreat, too tired to descend to the lobby, too pooped to stagger downwing to the communal head. To make a passable rack was like seals nesting. The blankets, sheets and pillows were all heavy with damp; the driest went underneath, the East German anorak, too short to wear, acted as a cover. Shivering, I woke with the first light, body heat drawing up condensation from the mattress. I got dressed, spooned condensed milk into a glass of hot water from the Thermos and flopped back till seven, when the day shift would come on.

In the breakfast café I was to learn the whole exercise had been unnecessary; a friend working for the Red Cross had been in all evening in his heated apartment room at the extremity of the other wing. A spare bed with duvet should have been mine. Now, armed with his key, I reascended to catch up on the hot-water indulgence.

# 5

# *Danger on the Edge of Town*

Flynn, Sean Leslie, son of the Hollywood star Errol, moved into 47 Bui Thi Xuan the same afternoon that we met, on our way out of the daily press conference. He had only been in country a week or so. It was the spring of 1966. His old man had never put a foot in true combat boots, merely played the role. Sean really wanted to find out what it was all about, grab the experience by the balls and come out alive with some decent images. He was anxious to shuck his dad's decadent image, to discover himself and create his own persona, no longer shadowed by his parentage.

Both father and son were devastatingly handsome, both ladies' men, both raffish. Except for the looks, the tall, well-built bodies, the moustaches, which in Sean's case came and went, the two were opposites on the emotional spectrum. Sean had been more influenced through his education and upbringing by Lili, his French mother. He was his own man and was not entirely happy to have been cast into the same type of role, on screen, as his father. It was embarrassing to imagine him in obscure B features with such titles as *The Son of Captain Blood* or *Le Fils de Robin*, but he had done it with a quick giggle, a stoned laugh, a flash of white teeth and compassionate eyes. He preferred being on the other side of the camera; the trips turning to lengthy stays in the Nam were the lotus opening of his new chosen path. Like most things he turned his energies to, his photography was eye-opening and ever improving, the tool to the adventure of self-discovery.

Flynn was three years older than I and we were both Geminis. We could have been brothers, and felt as though we were. We would sit for hours in the same room, hardly speaking yet in total communication, a vibration as intimate as between lovers. Photography, dope and adventures were the leyline hobbies; the tracks each chose for the hi-fi were the exact ones the other would have selected: Vivaldi or Jefferson Airplane, Dvořák or the Doors. We hung out a lot together. Going out in the field was always safer with a fellow *bao chi*, especially one not in direct competition. We had no need to compete, only to complement.

His easy-going, unflappable attitude blended in with the rest of the *bao chi* crew at what most of the town knew as Frankie's House, after one houseboy. There were about half a dozen of us, depending on who was in town or out in the field. Occasionally honorary members from the television fraternity would camp over. Somehow we had become the act to be lodged with in town. Our parties, it must be said, were truly the toast of the season. A better-quality event was never hosted than the one thrown to celebrate 'the opening of the first house of legalised prostitution in Pleiku'. Saigon's literati and glitterati clamoured to attend. Flynn lent glamour and street cred to our house. With others he was polite, almost aloof, no time for fools or wastrels. Both a rogue and a gentleman, he would gradually come to embrace a Buddhic attitude to a life which had not provided much serenity. Another soul lost to the Orient, its magnet had polarised him towards the East. The image continues to glow with the passage of time; his aura still seems to haunt those places back in Indochina that had been familiar and even now are revisited.

Fast forward in the film of memory to the planting of a bo tree on the south bank of the Ben Hai River, which runs along the 17th parallel, the one that once served as a border between North and South Vietnam. The tree is in memory of Flynn, missing in action. Should you superimpose a ying-yang pattern over the map of Indochina, you would find that the fulcrum of the shape would fall square on that bridge dot on the blue trace marking the stream that meanders out of the Annamitic Cordillera into the tropic beaches of the South China Sea. It is the old demilitarised zone, the DMZ.

The zone was in theory supposed to be unoccupied and free of hostilities. In reality, both the northern and southern parts of the zone were almost a continual scene of contention. Patrols, operations, reconnaissances and raids were normal procedures. Harassment and interdiction (H & I) were carried out continuously by artillery and every kind of heavy weaponry.

Quang Binh province was, is and will always be one of the poorest provinces in Vietnam. The soil is too poor to yield more than the bare necessities; typhoons annually strip the countryside of the trees grappling in the shallow soils. The higher, rolling scarps tend to be capped with a coarse laterite covered in scrub vegetation and offering tremendous tunnelling and trench and bunker building in its durable bowels. Only occasional villages nestle in folds of the undulating sandy hills carved by lazy rivers which afford the water for sparse paddying. The locals have taken on the stunted look of the landscape. Neither Dong Hoi to the north nor Dong Ha to the south of the zone has any buildings taller than two storeys; well, they both had nice Catholic steepled neo-gothic churches, but the war took care of Dong Ha; Dong Hoi's is still there, reduced to a blackened hulk in the middle of a new housing development, memorial to one of the grimmest points of the US air war campaign against the North's infrastructure.

The Z had its own reputation, the word dragged out to a slow 'zeeee' loaded with all the fear that being in range of the North's rather effective long-range 130-mm through

180-mm artillery could induce. From 1968 onwards, the North Vietnamese army had all the firebases, camps and outposts in the southern part of the zone continuously in its firecones. Any moving around in the Z was done in the dark or at speed during daylight hours.

Before there was a massive American in-country presence, the demilitarised zone was just that, a backwater, an outfield of the cricket game that the separate Vietnamese regimes played out. But as more American units poured ashore, the South Vietnamese were pushed into conducting aggressive operations into otherwise undisputed territory. Territory that Americans in the Pentagon East, on the outskirts of Saigon, were keen to tinge in their colour on their computer-originated maps. The marine expeditionary force spread north from its original beachhead in Da Nang, installing advance-base facilities up through I – pronounced eye – Corps at Phu Bai outside Hue, Quang Tri and Dong Ha. Primitive airstrips which once serviced periodic short-takeoff-and-landing craft resupplying special-forces teams and ARVN forward bases were now upgraded to receive multi-engined transports capable of airlifting armour and artillery with all their attendant logistic support.

Escalation also made conditions of travel on the major highways a bit more of a dodgy business. For the last year and a half I was in country 1965–66, you could easily drive from Da Nang to Hue in two and a half or three hours over the Hai Van pass, then through a series of first mainly Catholic, then flourishing Buddhist villages south of Hue. Hue to Quang Tri, the stretch known to the French as *la rue sans joie* was not quite so secure: cratered, mined or subject to VC toll and checkpoints. On a motorbike the chances of being stopped seemed somehow less as we believed Charlie was going to be only surprised to see a bunch of long-haired loonies out tooling along on customised Jap street bikes. We liked to imagine that they would just stop us, exchange a spliff or two over a cup of tea and let us tool on our way again. It never proved so or otherwise. Jeeping up Route One apparently didn't seem any more fraught with danger. Maybe it was just that Mr Charles knew more about our movements than we did. The bit of road north of Dong Ha was rarely ridden for, unless there was a POW exchange or ICC (the International Control Commission) was throwing a junket, there was no reason to go to the frontier of the country. It was a neutral, controlled, non-violent zone, unlike the Cambodian border across which the VC/NVA could seek sanctuary. Naturally this attracted missions in hot pursuit.

At the frontier bridge on the Ben Hai, each side vied to outdo the other with the height of their giant flagpoles and the volume of their loudspeakers. The last government post was at Gio Linh, six klicks south of the river, a sleepy base with US advisers loath to change the status quo. From there to the bridge, the echoes of the duetting loudspeakers grew ever louder, the 30-metre flagpoles drawing ever closer across the last two and a half kilometres of Route Nationale 1. Suddenly you were upon the actual official border post, complete with red-and-white-poled barrier. The bridge ran 100 metres to the north, decked with thick splintered timbers, the divide in the middle two lots of barbed wire, pull-aside barricades, behind which two scowling NVA could usually be spotted. It was more like the Yugoslav frontier in the early sixties than the middle of a war zone.

Nobody really appreciated photographers turning up on bikes to disturb their placid days. Still, it was about the only place to see a real live enemy soldier without getting blown away, just one of those spots on the map of the globe, an Everest or pole, a Taj, that just had to have its I dotted and its T crossed. At that time it was a gas to get back after dark to the marine-run press centre on the Song Hong River in Da Nang and in response to 'Wot ya bin doin'?' reply, 'Oh, just up to the border and back on the bike.' Their jaws dropped gobsmacked jarheads, incredulous to civilian exploits.

By the end of 1966, there were enough marines up north to have pushed a presence up to Dong Ha, and even a regular air service. Flynn and I hopped an oil-smeared USMC C-47 for the short flight from Da Nang, having heard about the sizeable Vietnamese operation from buddies attached to the ARVN airborne as advisers. Both of us had been out with these crack, or at least better than average by ARVN standards, troops on a number of operations, always getting back with a good photographic take and a better story to tell. The advisers were really into their role with nothing but admiration for their counterparts' tenacity and made a point of letting us in on any upcoming action; of all the advisory groups, they and those assigned to the ARVN marines were the tops, actually press-friendly. It could have been because they only got to see the better part of our corps rather than the desk hackers and bar-stool warriors that had started to predominate.

Naturally the operation did not kick off right away, obliging us to seek a rack for the night in an already overtaxed forward zone. It was to be poncho liners on top, gritty canvas GI cots beneath, in a barrack without mozzie nets at the side of the flight line. The shadowy birds that were to carry us into the zone in the morning flavoured the hot January night with a tang of hot hydraulic fluid, Avgas and Cosmolene. A different aroma came from the hut full of sweaty men, most still semi-clad in case of incoming NVA mortar, rockets or artillery. Dong Ha was front line.

There was a smell of fear about the place, an impermanence to its frontier-town status. The first hooches were up, but with canvas roofs; the sandbags still had a green sheen to them, not split and oozing dirt; there was dust, red and gritty, everywhere, blown into every nook and cranny of your clothing and gear. It had you reaching for a water bottle every ten minutes before passing a quick toothbrush across the top of the cameras. Every chopper added its whirlwind of savage sandpaper, every touch billowed another faceful of grit and spit.

We had noodles and iced Ba Moui Ba beer with the advisers downtown before turning in early for a fitful, sweaty night. You never really drop off in places like that; something is always nagging: a mosquito, a bit of grit, a trickle of sweat, an itchy spot; but mostly you have one ear half-cocked for incoming fire. You are ready to roll out to the bunker thoughtfully assigned to you on check-in. The outgoing artillery fire is much louder than any faint announcement of fatal incoming. Outgoing leaving its tubes becomes a reassuring disruption you grudgingly sublimate to a dealable level, only the first round of a new mission's salvo breaking into your somnolence.

It seems that you are only just dropping off to a dream when it is time to stagger awake. A greasy skim appears to have coated your entire skin, your mouth is dry leather and a cursory hand finds dirty stubble. Gravel is dislodged from the corner of each eye by indelicate probing. Oh for a hot shower! No way. A gargle of brackish water tasting of purification pills, a can of warm Coke when lucky, possibly an overbrewed canteen cup of GI coffee. People stretching, hawking, spitting, pissing, grunting and bitching; they have made it through another night intact, only to find the same old shit still around them. Murmuring forms dimly made out performing age-old awakening rituals, unconscious of each other's ablutions, cracking open another day of surviving. Pulling on your boots, you make ritual order out of the routine of the cross-lacing, making sure the trouser bottom is well tucked in, leech-proof, bug-entry preventive. How long will the boots stay dry today? Why is it that each morning, both boots always seem board-stiff, unwilling to bend to the coming day? Another bitching morning. Another day in the field.

The military world was awake before the sun rose. The HH-34 choppers with their bulbous noses rapidly took on form, the blades spread against the brightening sky, still tied down. Crew members merged with their birds, the rotors slumped loose, innards were probed, the engine cowlings flapped up, then down. The pace quickened to the day as discernible warmth came with the slanting rays. There was a splutter of auxiliary engines, coughing, stuttering, then the main radials started to catch down the flight line, blades started to turn, revs built up and the rotors whirred. Lines of troopers shuffled wearily forwards, bowed under with equipment, the US advisers fussing about getting each pool of men sorted for its specific bird. The Viets' smaller stature made it possible to cram a complete squad of twelve troops into each antiquated marine 34.

The operation had kicked off two days earlier, but had been under political wraps because the airborne had been put into the demilitarised zone; it was the first time either ARVN or US ground troops had staged such a blatant full-scale incursion. The problem was that too many people were in the know, there were too many plane movements, too many realignments of forces to go unnoticed. Flynn and I were hoping to hop a chopper on a resupply or medevac run out to the bruised and bloodied battalion now pulled out of the village where they had bivouacked the previous night, only to be targeted by the North Vietnamese artillery firing those 180-mm long-range Russian howitzers, their heaviest piece of kit. The paratroopers had got creamed: 240 men had been lifted out dead or wounded; the unit was demoralised, at half strength, awaiting reinforcements or extraction. The whole incursion had gone inexplicably wrong, but command was happy to have forced the NVA to play their hand, agreeing that the sacrifice of a few more Vietnamese was the price they had to pay. The advisers were furious that their men had been the lambs in the bait, part of the advance probes to test the feasibility of putting US ground troops into firebases that close to North Vietnam. The North did not approve and would continue to react to provocations.

Dong Ha strip was a newly expanded facility; the raw work in the middle of the dry season created a continual dust storm kicked up by the streams of jeeps, trucks and tracked vehicles while the continual chopper movements blew the lateritic stuff in horizontal palls, causing you to bend double, back to the sandpapering blast, grappling with neck towel to cover chest-slung cameras. The ready shack paired us up with a couple of ANGLICO marine reinforcements about to be lifted out to the surviving airborne. Both packed large radios capable of orchestrating incoming naval artillery from Seventh Fleet cruisers and destroyers 15 kilometres away safely offshore. ANGLICO was the marine equivalent of special forces, trained in para, scuba and special warfare, who were used to recon beaches before landings or put behind enemy lines to coordinate incoming firepower. These two were a reassuring duo to get assigned with on a ride that promised to end in a hot landing zone. They were amused and somewhat chuffed that they were going to end up splashed across the world's media by the son of Errol Flynn.

'I mean, no shit, man, are you for real? I mean, you came here, of your own free will? I mean, I mean, are you crazy, or are you what? I mean, I would be outta here, man! Ya, well, we kinda dig it, too. Too much!'

They were not greenhorns; they had been trying to pinpoint the NVA Long Toms for some time and hoped we would get hit again so they could unleash the navy's new toys.

'I mean, like, Charlie will become a believer when he sees the effect of this shit, man. I mean, would you wanna be on the receiving end of the kinda heat we can de-liver?'

Neither Flynn nor I pointed out that the NVA had survived worse and come back with a vengeance, and had been coming for nearly a thousand years of revolutionary war; nor that they probably expected to have the wrath of the US navy fall on them and had dug in accordingly. We heaved ourselves aboard the 34. The sill on that obsolete old Sikorski

HH-34 is a good metre up, requiring a certain amount of agility to get self and equipment harness, backpack and cameras aboard in one movement, an upward-flopping, top-heavy fish motion. There wasn't time to enjoy the flight, to savour the air-conditioned effect of being aloft, nor even to catch our bearings, for we flew at contour height, barely lifting off the runway, dipping to the west with our wheels only just above the bamboo and occasional tree lines.

There are two theories about flying choppers in a hostile environment: either stay above most small-arms fire at over 1,500 feet or play sports cars at zero elevation so Charlie hardly has the time to see, much less sight and shoot at the treetop bird. When artillery is being lobbed around the skies, it is definitely safer to stay down low. The pilot homed in on the purple smoke flaring out, fast, at the last possible moment, hoping not to attract any more heavy stuff from across the border.

Bedraggled survivors dragged one of their comrades' poncho-wrapped corpses towards the bird as we clambered out; three more awaited their dispirited hands. The advisers were not exactly overjoyed to get saddled with a couple of journalists, but we could stay on the proviso that should we be subject to a ground attack we would have to pick up and use a weapon. We had been put down in a south-facing draw in some low hills terraced with poor, dried-up paddies offering a certain amount of protection against any incoming, and at least we could not be directly spotted from the north. However, we knew that the NVA had watchers hiding, logging movements and reporting within a few hundred metres of where we stood. It was spooky and the hardened paratroopers were on edge too, wanting to get moving. The helicopter having revealed the position we were at, it only had to be a matter of minutes before we could expect probing incoming fire. We tagged onto the command group with the senior advisers, the commanding officer, medics and radio operator. Possibly this was unsafe, since the cluster of senior people, highlighted by a preponderance of radio antennas, could usually be expected to be the focus of any attack. Knock out command and the medical and you could end up with disorganisation and loss of morale. The poor buggers packing the extra 25 kilos of radio gear habitually drew the first firecones: Mr Charles knew that those sets called the wrath of death upon their liberated hearts and minds.

The unit swung out on a southeasterly heading, ostensibly to sweep back through the village where they had laagered up and been shelled the night before, though taking in a couple of other hamlets that had not been checked out before.

It is hard to say which is the worse to traverse: the ankle-wrenching, ploughed, dried-out, stubble-spiked fallow paddy or the gumbo to the knee or deeper of a flooded paddy where the crop is in one of its water-sucking growth periods. Either season, either way, periodically you have to clamber, haul yourself up and over the dykes that divide the fields and form the irrigation system. They can vary from knee-high to, on steep territory, a stepladder job. They were loathsome hurdles to surmount, though ideal cover when under fire. During the growing season we tried precariously to walk along the boot-wide top, invariably slick, greasy and uneven, so that when we got to the sluices between fields we had to leap to the next wet sod. In any given line of men, a plop, followed by cursing, signalled the unfortunate who had missed his footing and fallen into the gloop. The enemy had a nasty habit of booby-trapping the dyke tops in areas they controlled, adding an extra chamber in the Russian roulette of survival.

The sun was still almost straight overhead, it was a good 38°C in the shade, except there was no shade. The pace quickened at the promise of shade and water in the complex of *villes* that were the day's objectives. The strung-out troop closed up dangerously before re-entering the village they had been in hours before. The approach was strewn with evidence of their decimation. Bits of equipment were littered about: punctured helmets, torn clothing, bandage wrappings, bloodied gauze, caked puddles of rusted human drainage. No spent ammo casings or pried-open cartridge cans. This battle had been one-sided, the enemy unseen, heralded by distant, muffled explosions as the rounds left their tubes kilometres away. The rest of it had been an unimaginable cacophony of noise, preceded by a distinct whistle and whoosh just before impact.

The village was well established, though poor. Most of what once had been houses had been roofed in rich thatch, and the rest, including the headman's, were tiled; the walls were mud and wood, the animal pens and rice silos of woven bamboo. The buildings now stood mainly roofless, gaping holes in walls amid the scorch-marked craters and hurriedly scraped foxholes. The inhabitants had made themselves scarce with their few valuable possessions; anything left behind was now either smashed or looted. About the only intact items left were the shelters built into each of these homes.

Most Americans conceived of every Vietnamese as somehow the enemy because every rural family dug, or constructed, a bunker under the floor or adjacent to their homes. This was a wise precaution since they were just as likely to suffer from friendly fire as to be caught in the middle of a battlefield. Virtually the whole country not directly controlled by the Saigon government forces had been designated a free-fire zone. The bunkers and shelters often ended up as specific targets for retribution, with the inevitable carnage of innocent civilians.

A dog and chickens were already back, incongruously sniffing, scratching and pecking about amid the desolation, and, as we slumped to a rest break, a couple of troops flapped off in hot pursuit of a feathered survivor for the evening pot. The dog had barely enough meat on its bones to flavour a soup and was left to its scavenging around the matted rust puddles.

The forward observers had given us a scare while we were filtering into the *ville*; a couple of their 'registration rounds' – that is what artillery called it, so that subsequent salvos could be correctly adjusted – had fallen perilously close, causing everyone to dive for cover. Luckily, no one was hit by the Willy Peter – white phosphorous marker shells. A rice-straw rick was left burning, the smoke a nice column for a North Vietnamese spotter to home in on.

Flynn and I found ourselves together again at the friendly incoming near a house that had taken a hit on its corner, partially uncovering the family's shelter. We both giggled nervously: it was a nervous situation. Then a bunch of small-arms fire broke out to our right on the northern edge of the *ville*, off beyond some tall bamboo. There was return fire, and a firefight started to tat-tat away; odd tracers whizzed by overhead. We all went flat again, Sean and I now agreeing the bunker was to be ours at the next exigency.

The FAC – forward air controller – a young army captain, got on his radio to try and sort out the situation. The artillery lad got his net up and adjusted to help. We were in luck; a prowl of air-force Phantoms were on station five minutes out. They locked on our coordinates, we popped smoke and over the crackle of radios the roar of the attack run could be heard. It was too close, everyone hit the deck again as 500-lb bombs tumbled loose. So close, the concussion waves thumped over our flat backs, showering down dirt and vegetation as we lifted with the force from beneath.

The other F-4 was circling, awaiting its turn. The FAC and the radio operator were busy screaming into handsets, trying to call in adjustments relative to our marker smoke. After the explosions it went deathly quiet, save for the pattering of descending rubbish. The firefight had stopped. Then a few rounds smacked out, just letting you know there were survivors. The second Phantom was called in.

Flynn and I dove for the bunker entrance – an aperture 18 inches square. Into a fetid blackness pungent with *nuoc nam* fish sauce we squeezed, dropping to the softness of damp straw. We felt around the space we almost entirely occupied before being thrown together against one side by another explosion. Dirt fell onto our entwined selves; the breath had been squeezed out of us. Though it was pitch dark, I swear I could see Sean's wide eyes, centimetres from mine. Our breaths touched. This had to be the end: a second explosion rocked the tomb, more dirt descended, we held on tight. Our world was a small one of deafness and dust, near suffocation, a rush of claustrophobia, the sweat of fear, the reek of amonol and cordite, the closer one of spilt fish sauce and body heat.

It went still outside. We breathed out again, uncramping the chest, climbed towards the diffused square of light of the opening and emerged into the flare-bright sun. A pall of smoke was settling, a few heads were up looking around; fortunately there appeared to be few screaming. Figures scurried, doubled over, to a group around the battalion command group. The radio squawked, runners were despatched to check the perimeter, and a semblance of order was being established as the first of the newly adjusted artillery support fires took up the airwaves after the fast movers had done their thing. This time they whistled satisfyingly overhead to dump out of sight on what everybody prayed was enemy and not the friendlies who had pushed out their perimeter after the air strike. They started volleying over in threes, working back and forth, then another fell short. Two soldiers on the move got cut by shrapnel. Back in the hole, or stay up for the photos? The next incoming was theirs, not ours, not heralded by a sound, just the awful somewhere-too-close megablast and scything red-hot metal chunks and heavy earthen clods. Quiet again, emerging again from the stinking bunker.

I think it was at some time on that outing that my nerve

gave, and I decided that this would be my last sortie. The elastic had finally snapped. A yellow card had been shown; the red one was actually in my hand. Send self off the field. War had me whipped, exhausted with its insanities. The images across the subconscious screen were ghoulish negative stuff, the breaking point reached, the shutter opened to maximum aperture and pointed straight at the sun. Flynn had grasped this from me huddling in that bunker, had reciprocated that all-knowing fear and stroked mine back into place so that we could both get on with surviving that day, which was ever elongating.

It was Flynn who had to get me up and moving. I believe I could have camped in that bunker for an awfully long time awaiting whatever fate. A shaken unit, its morale further cracked by the last experience, the advisers furious, everyone edgy, was ordered to swing south, beat a retreat and hook up with an armoured ARVN outfit sweeping up to our relief. A bird-dog spotter plane periodically buzzed over, keeping an eye on our movements, ready to coordinate any requested friendly fire support. This was reassuring; our pace quickened as the shadows lengthened. The tropical night would soon be upon the dispirited column, now intent only on linking up with the relative safety of the armoured unit. We were bunched up, with only minimal flank cover as we pulled out of the fateful village across a band of paddies before climbing what seemed to be a very steep ridge made none the easier by clawing dense underbrush.

As the uphill hack began, the last of the light bled away, sensed, not seen, in the double head-height scrub relieved by thinner patches of stumps and grass growing back to cover the war scars. Going cross-country this way did have the advantage that there were probably no booby traps. We followed no specific path or trail, the point man took the least path of resistance to his machete and locked on a compass bearing. Stumbling we pressed forwards in silence (almost unheard of in an American outfit), just occasional whispers of encouragement in the blackness, twigs gently crackling up and down the column as it staggered towards safety. It was so dark that the forms of the men a mere two or three paces in front or behind me blended into the night, not even the distinctive smooth outlines of the helmets were discernible.

Suddenly we entered an area where we all became boats in a stream, our feet kicking up a glow from the phosphorescence in the jungle's litter. Twigs glowed around us; there were glow-worms and fireflies left, right and centre, electrically weird and ghostly, show-stopping. A ripple of childish joy mirthed down the column, with everybody picking up a piece of the forest litter and attaching it to the pack or helmet of the man in front. Our luminous centipede crawled off again at a more positive pace, making light of the occasional probing North Vietnamese round lobbed towards our line of retreat. Charlie was letting us off the hook and the ARVN GIs could dig that. Everyone wanted to get home to see their families for Tet, a few weeks away. It felt as though victory flowed from the spirits of the lands of the ancestor via the fluorescence and then caught and lifted ours.

It was past midnight when we drew into the perimeter of second-division infantry with their attendant armoured personnel carriers. Sporadic incoming fire was dropping randomly, suggesting that the safest place to sleep would be under one of the armoured vehicles, despite the danger of being crushed, should it decide to manoeuvre. Claustrophobic, too, with barely room to twitch from side to side, any movement of the troops inside amplified alarmingly. In the end we decided to chain-smoke cupped cigarettes with the ANGLICO marine radio lad, Flynn sitting up on his air mattress, poncho liner draped over his head and shoulders, and passing out his flask, once his father's, the Courvoisier burning a coarse, welcome track through mouths that had leathered.

The first wraiths of light revealed foxholes occupied by haggard figures in tattered clothing; the wounded had been laid out on stretchers on the ground. Canteen cups were held over improvised stoves, the solid-fuel pellets made of plastic explosive. We slurped instant noodle soup and coffee from the scalding-hot aluminium; one enterprising squad passed out chunks of congealed rice they had saved in their communal cookpot, and stale baguettes were distributed from the armoured personnel carriers. Hunger grows horns in the relief rush.

We rode the first chopper that got in after sunrise, then got lucky in a lift back to Da Nang. I went on back down to Saigon, leaving Sean in UPI's room at the marine press centre.

Vietnam was an addiction hard to kick, and 1968 found both of us back together in Saigon. It was a very full year; full-tilt boogie, the hatching of the rock-'n'-roll plot to subvert the old order. *Sgt Pepper*, the Doors, the Jefferson Airplane, Hendrix – the power of the music reverberated in our flat on Tu Do Street so the beat could be heard a floor below at street level. Passers-by in the busy boulevard, which ran from the cathedral to the waterfront, could be seen staring up to discern the source of the noise. Sometimes we threw smoke grenades out of the windows. They landed on a solid awning over the sidewalk which projected to kerb level. Our porch was the repository of the airmailed garbage from the cribs the working girls had upstairs. The flat was decorated with hippy tack and military souvenirs: searchlights and parachutes vied for wall space with Day-Glo San Francisco artwork and revolutionary Che Guevara posters. The atmosphere was right.

The heavy staffers on the networks and magazines got a week of all-paid R & R every nine weeks. We in-country wallahs took our flights internally. While others unwound from their post-trauma stress with a gin and tonic or a six-pack, we lay back with an opium pipe. (The opium-pipemaker, the only such service available by phone, arrival guaranteed by Peugeot moped.) The timeless float and the dream-laden sleep erased something of the terrifying inhumanity we had witnessed, and camouflaged some of the emotions too profound to explore right then, lest our reaction would have been to pack up and split on the next plane.

Instead, we went cruising on lightweight Japanese bikes. The later years of the sixties saw the emergence on the market of scaled-down street bikes of between 50 and 90 cc. They had motocross handlebars, hi-lift exhausts, knobbly tyres: the whole senior scrambler circuit in powerful miniature form. Initially, the product was imported as a gentleman's roadster; all chrome appurtenances, signal lights, mirrors – the flashiest kit for a new, gullible market – but soon the manufacturers (Bridgestone, Yamaha, Suzuki and Honda) provided a leaner, more raked model for the developing world. Our first rigs were heavily customised, but at the black-market rate we could afford to change makes regularly. We were obliged to anyway; the theft rate rose to where I lost six locked and chained machines over an eight-week span. Flynn lost two. One day we managed to catch one of the operators in flagrante. Each day he would sneak into the passage downstairs that ran up to the stairs at the back of the Bluebird Bar, our neighbour. He would drip some acid onto the chain before pulling back its protective sleeve to conceal the damage. It took a patient week before he could walk the machine. The gang worked out of the Vietnamese naval base a few blocks away; from there they shipped the bikes out on supply ships and landing craft to other ends of the country.

When Flynn burst in frog-marching the culprit, I was flat on the floor with Monsieur Long, our pipemaker, in attendance. Flynn and his buddy, another famous son, John Steinbeck IV, searched the guy's pockets and found a roll of piastres in commensurate with his official salary ranking of petty officer in the Vietnamese navy – so read his laminated

ID card. More interestingly, he also had a palm-sized slab of black opium – for sale to GIs, he claimed under interrogation. Steinbeck, looking severe in wire-rimmed glasses, and Flynn playing the soft Mr Nice Guy, were attempting to break the by now trembling thief. Having been slapped around, he was Polaroid-snapped against the white-tiled kitchen wall, holding the ID card, the opium stuck in his teeth. Long pronounced the O inferior, but we kept it anyway, along with the roll of piastres and the identity papers. We all went back to the horizontal on the raffia carpet to mellow out with a sense of justice having been meted out.

Riding bikes in the Nam had more than a little of *Easy Rider* about it: open roads, though potholed and bumpy, with little traffic since Charlie had stopped, taxed and agitpropped the buses and tanks. Perfect weather made Ray-Bans and bush hats obligatory; in the monsoons it was best just to pull over and have a coffee or a *pho*, cool out until the soaking deluge had poured and roared through its hourly afternoon slot. Those were cherished, quiet pauses that I enjoyed with Flynn; passing a joint, the road running temptingly either way, the mind loose, the adrenaline just hot enough, the camaraderie of being in such an existential situation, right at the cutting edge. Everything was communicated in the undercurrent of the unsaid.

On a sandbar in the Mekong delta between My Tho and Ben Tre was the seat of the Dao philosophy. Should all religions have been rivers, the island would have been the sea into which they all flowed. Led by the Dao Dua, a former chemical engineer turned pilgrim prophet, who lived up a pole, subsisting on nothing but coconut, was the Neo-Catholic Buddhist Church of Dao, the latter the Vietnamese version of Taoism. This church was all-embracing, subscribing to folklore, philosophy, doctrine and tenets Eastern and Western, endorsing only peace as a way of life for Indochina.

Steinbeck had discovered the Isle of Phoung (or Phoenix) while researching a book on oriental philosophic practices and had become an instant convert. I think we all did. The contrast between the gongs and chanting for peace on the macrobiotic mid-Mekong retreat and the insanity on the river's banks a kilometre away could have convinced the hardest sceptical hawk. We were torn by our work, grooving out on the battlefield, then protesting on the island at weekend retreats.

The balance tilted towards love, the sorties to the field becoming more perverse trips endured for the heavy images we hoped to create. Sean now had a 16-mm camera and was determined to cross over to making the moving image: he believed he could shoot and edit the ultimate documentary, provided he was able to shoot from all sides, including Charlie's. He was becoming increasingly dedicated to this aim, handing in to his regular clients at CBS a fraction of his footage and airmailing the residue off to his long-time amie Cookie in Paris. The stuff getting to New York was regularly airing in great chunks on Walter Cronkite's evening news. The black and white he snapped with his around-the-neck Leicas earned pocket money from UPI and the AP, both agencies keen to use his byline and his images. A long way from the debutante snaps from his first gig as a 'Playboy goes to War' for *Paris-Match* in that spring of 1966.

Apart from his name and the pennant of the yacht, the *Zacca*, where a lot of Errol's money had been squandered, the only possessions he had from his father were two Purdy shotguns. Hunting skills were part of the upbringing Errol had ensured, and these were now honed on the battlefield. Sean fell prey more than most to the press corps, now swollen to more than 600, to the temptation to carry a weapon. More worryingly for his karma, he seemed at times really to enjoy using them. The wardrobe in his room at the Tu Do Street flat was a regular arsenal: an AK, an M-16 carbine, a couple of pistols, grenades (smoke and frag), C4 plastic explosive and a complete inventory sampler of all parties' ammunition. The lockers in the CBS and UPI crew rooms at the Danang press centre where Sean and a photographer friend, Dana Stone, kept upcountry digs, contained stocks of C-4 plastique, enough explosive to flatten the compound. The lads had taken to collecting it competitively. Another contest they had running was to see who could score the most parachute flares. These metre-wide chutes dangled the illumination pumped out of mortar and artillery tubes to light up areas around perimeters at night. They drifted all over the place and made great ceiling artefacts, light drapes, scarves, clothing and stuff sacks. We went after them like kids chasing rocket sticks on Guy Fawkes Night, though it was rather more dangerous.

Some time in that year, or in early 1969, Flynn and I made a pact. Should the unthinkable, the unmentionable, the inevitable happen – going either MIA, KIA or seriously WIA – we would notify each other's next of kin, where possible before officialdom got their act together. It felt very spooky just to say this, any mention of death attracting the bad vibes. That end was left always unsaid.

When the mine that terminated my second in-country tour was detonated, Sean was up in Laos with Carl Robinson, the AP Vietnam photo editor. They had been biking up to Luang Prabang, grooving in the most laid-back country in Indochina, at that time still only just being touched by the war. In fact, the US embassy had sent a telegram to him saying that I had been admitted to hospital as DOA and might die. He was on the next plane back to Saigon out of Vientiane.

Although it was but a dim vision, for I was partially blinded and hit in the frontal lobes of my brain by shrapnel, he appeared magically, a presence in his Indian wedding shirt, exuding the familiar smell of Gallet soap and his musky, slightly smoked tang. He came bearing a small wooden Lao Buddha and a lot of energy towards a recovery that still hung in the balance – I was to have a total of nine hours of neuro- and abdominal surgery. That was the last time we were together, for as soon as I was stabilised I was to process out to Japan and then to Walter Reed Medical Center in Washington, DC.

Later I heard that seeing me laid out like deblooded meat crudely sewn together had spooked Sean to get out while he was still ahead. The two minor nicks he had received from flying debris scarcely counted as purple hearts, but enough people close to him were starting to remind him of the transitory nature of life on the planet and the frailty of flesh and bone confronted by hot sharp metal. Indonesia became his home-from-home, his favoured retreat a beach house on Bali, at that time still unspoilt by tourism, in a complex that he imagined buying with other Nam heads to serve as a permanent base. Odd aerogrammes arrived with drawings of penis sheaths, weird descriptions of prehistoric men in Papua New Guinea, of purple acid sunsets on beaches, as I progressed through a series of hospitals and convalescences in the United States.

I was waiting to go into the Good Samaritan hospital in downtown Los Angeles for a plastic plate to be installed in the large gap in my skull when I got the news, albeit third-hand. A friend of a friend heard it on the radio, and phoned me up, though before he called he had checked with another friend at AP downtown. I knew the man downtown, another lad with a tranche of Vietnam service, and got a confirmation of the information, as yet only rumoured. Then I dialled Iowa to get in touch with Lili.

She had finally remarried. Sean successfully out of the nest, to a gentleman admirer who had worshipped from afar and then wooed and won her hand. Allen Loomis had made it in business having turned his Midwest ice-cream business with Carnations nationwide connection into a food of hall-of-fame entry. He had invented Eskimo pies, a chocolate-coated layer cake of individual ice-cream bars and crumbly wholewheat digestive biscuit, packaged in foil and dispensed from the freezer unit of any shop or gas station. Al and Lili spent part of their time at his place in Fort Dodge and the rest at her house, where Sean had been brought up in Palm Beach. Back in the days of the silent movies she was a superstar, and before Uncle Sam got round to slapping taxes on the wealthy she had wisely invested in property. The semi-Thai style wooden two-storey house on Woodbridge Road was where she had chosen to call home. It abuts the Trump estate.

It was Al who initially picked up the telephone and although I had never met him, I could vibe that he knew why I was calling. Sean, together with Dana Stone, had been captured by unknown units on Route One near the village of Chi Phou in eastern Cambodia, just short of the Vietnamese border post at Moc Bai. News folk going MIA was not unusual at this juncture of the expanding Indochinese conflict in April 1970. We were to find out that two hours before Dana and Sean got taken, two other journalists – one Japanese and Claude Arpin, a French freelance photographer – had disappeared at virtually the same spot on the highway which links Phnom Penh to Saigon. I managed to beat Time-Life, for whom Sean was then on assignment, and the State Department to notify his next of kin. The promise had been kept.

Initially, nobody had a clue where Chi Phou was. We located it in Svay Rieng province, which comprised the jut of Cambodian territory that extends into South Vietnam west of Saigon, commonly called 'The Parrot's Beak'. The Vietcong and North Vietnamese troops sought sanctuary there in supposedly neutral Cambodia. The Parrot's Beak is bordered for two thirds of its southerly quadrant by the Plains de Joncs (the Plain of Reeds); on its northern it was abutted by the so-called Iron Triangle. Here a slightly rising plateau of orange, gritty, lateritic soil provided the home to the hardened core of first Vietminh, then Vietcong National Liberation Front guerrilla fighters. They dug over 200 kilometres of tunnels in the Triangle, many feet beneath the major American divisional base at Cu Chi, established in late 1965 by the Tropic Lightning 25th Division. The Americans never quite managed to suppress local enemy action or pacify their tactical area of responsibility. Mr Charles kept on popping up right in the middle of the base golf course and behind the motor pool.

The flat land with its clumps of bamboo and fruit orchards was either a swamp or hard as concrete. It was always hot, a third of the time sticky. The population devoted much of their energies to the traditional task of cross-border supply and demand – smuggling. Historically, then and now.

It was the height of the dry season, 6 April 1970. The new Lon Nol administration had staged a campaign against the ousted nonaligned government of Prince Norodom Sihanouk, Loyal Sihanoukists had been obliged to take to the hills, joining the outlawed Khmer Rouge, a newly emergent group functioning with the backing of the North Vietnamese. Together they formed the official collective resistance. Lon Nol was an inadequate right-wing general, better known for his corruption; he had phantom companies of troops on full pay, other units fighting at their best for pay pilfered by their commanders.

Sihanouk had cast a blind eye to the North Vietnamese sanctuaries on his neutral turf. Tacitly Chinese and E-bloc weaponry and material flowed from the port of Kampong Som, renamed Sihanoukville, to NVA front-line units. Undisclosed B-52 bombings had been going on since 1968 across the K-zone, the rear area for NVA troops cross-border in the southern third of Vietnam. Here the populace had become inured to the frequent coming and going of to varying degrees rapacious forces. The communists tended to be better behaved, but still exacted a heavy toll on the peasants' meagre resources. After the rains these plains became verdant with paddy rice baking to desert fierceness in the autumn, heralding five months of a dun-coloured, parched landscape. That made it good tank country for that season. Lon Nol's regulars rode to the front on a motley fleet which included buses and Coca-Cola trucks, their manoeuvres announced way in advance to the press. The latest gambit by Phnom Penh to demonstrate its prowess in secure road-holding provided the small Cambodian-based corps an opportunity to head east of the Neak Long Mekong ferry to a look-see. Six journalists would go missing on this particular junket. Dana had been in Phnom Penh shooting for CBS, while Flynn had a commission from *Time* magazine.

From afar I believed Flynn had gone to see the conflict from the other side for the purpose of making his film. They would be released in a matter of a few days or weeks; they had, after all, been taken by Vietnamese, not Khmer revolutionaries. Newsmen and women captured by the VC or North Vietnamese had usually emerged unscathed, with guaranteed *Life* or *Paris-Match* magazine pieces plus the cover. Not a few had managed to arrange being captured by being on a certain bus or driving on a given road at a specified time. The PR worked well for both parties. Making contact with Charlie was not that difficult, especially at the Dao Peace Island, and we regularly met NVA/VC liaison officers in the opium den in Da Nang. They kept a beady eye on the media, probably better aware of its power than their counterparts on the other side.

Days, weeks, months went by without a word of information, not even a rumour. Concerned journalists' committees under the godfather Walter Cronkite were set up, for by mid-1971 nineteen of our colleagues were listed missing, known captured, and/or presumed dead. Time-Life sent in its best Vietnamese-speaking correspondent, an ex-military intelligence officer, Zalin 'Zip' Grant, to look for all nineteen. He returned with nothing but vague rumours, nothing to go on. Louise, Dana's wife, better known to us as Smiser (her maiden name) moved to Phnom Penh to pursue the matter, pumping every source, lead or rumour; CBS most honourably continued to pay her Dana's stringer retainer, and the rest of the media brotherhood stood behind her. Even the photographer Richard Avedon, on a swing through for *Harper's* and *Vogue*, made a piercing portrait of the now emaciated Louise.

On 8 Marth 1975, the Khmer Rouge entered Phnom Penh and immediately set about emptying it of its populace on the pretext that US bombers were going to flatten it. The tyranny of Pol Pot's regime had come to town.

A few weeks later, tank number 854, a North Vietnamese army T-54, rolled through the wrought-iron gates of Saigon's presidential palace. Liberation and unification came on the same day: 30 April 1975. Saigon thereafter was to be known as Ho Chi Minh Ville.

Pol Pot's reign of terror, genocide through Stalinist agrarian policies, probably wiped out one and a half million Khmers over the next four years, and not a single Westerner or foreigner would emerge from the interrogation centres or killing fields alive. Both minorities were singled out for persecution by dreaded Anka, the supreme central committee council.

POWs from both sides in Vietnam had been exchanged in 1973 during Operation Homecoming. Thousands of so-called war criminals, South Vietnamese army officers and government officials languished in gulag prisons termed re-education camps. Hundreds of thousands who had worked for the old regime, and who had done time in the gulags for their sins, turned to the boats for escape, reaching perilously every quadrant of Southeast Asia. The few foreigners left in the south were gradually obliged to leave. Hippies, deserters, traders and outcasts were not needed in the new society of the Unified People's Democratic Republic of Vietnam. There were no more POWs and no more MIAs, or so we were led to believe.

In 1979, former Marine Corp corporal, Robert Garwood, emerged from the woodwork in Hanoi. Taken prisoner by the Vietcong in 1968, he now stood accused by the US authorities of surviving by aiding the enemy during his captivity. A turncoat or, as he put it, just a dumb middle-American white-trash kid hip on kar kraft and little else, suddenly called upon to hack living in a POW camp in the jungle. Taken to the North, he had worked in state motor pools and had a common-law wife. Reluctantly, the Viets let him go; almost reluctantly, the American judicial system and the Marine Corps accepted him back. He was treated with as much leniency as the system could tolerate, and described his survival in a gripping book, *Conversations with the Enemy*. He was last heard of working in a gas station in suburban Washington, DC. According to him, there were no Westerners left in Vietnam. A handful of French ex-patriates had been allowed to linger on both in Saigon and the north, probably no more than a dozen. A classic case was the ex-legionnaire, now a *cyclo-pousse* driver, who used to ply for traffic outside the Thang Nhat Hotel.

Then America was still contending that Vietnam ought to account for 2,200-odd missing US personnel. In reality, there are twenty or so priority cases left to resolve. More than 4,600 photographs released late in 1992 of US POWs in captivity have done much to assuage the US hang-up on this sad affair, but it was still preventing any more steps down the road to normalisation, the lifting of the US-imposed trade embargo that most other nations including Japan, the ASEAN bloc, most of Europe and Australia have all circumvented.

It may be a better policy to remember that the Vietnamese themselves are still trying to resolve what happened to approximately a quarter of a million of their own.

We, as somewhat arrogant Westerners, aliens from the Occident, tend to forget that the oriental values of life and death, ancestor worship, Confucian and Taoist beliefs revere the spirit more than we do. When remains are not returned to ancestral graveyards, the spirit is considered to be wandering, outcast, unhappy, bringing real disharmony to the family. Irreverence towards these matters will only attract a back balance in karma. We clumsy intruders are unmindful of these curious, fragile equilibriums, and this ignorance causes much of our downfall when dealing with society and the local culture.

Someone once said of Southeast Asia, 'The Viets plant the rice; the Khmer watch it growing; the Lao listen to it coming up; and the Thai harvest the profit.' It could be added that the Singaporeans and overseas Chinese bank and invest it. Little has changed, though now there is a direct UN involvement in Cambodia, laying an economic carpet into the heart of Indochina. The major hotels in Hanoi and Ho Chi Minh now accept non-US-backed credit cards.

To believe that someone missing is still alive is a mixture of pain and hope familiar to all families and friends of kidnap victims, hostages, prisoners-of-war; people whose kin go off to remote or dangerous work sites, or on hazardous expeditions, feel the same anxiety. The fate of their loved ones is always in jeopardy, not knowing has always been unsettling. I experienced many of those fraught emotions over the uncertainty of Flynn's fate. I would have dreams in which we were conversing in living colour, or nightmares of battle-lit death. They were not frequent, only disturbingly unforgettable. But it was not until 1989 that I had any news.

Laurent David was a French student doing his dissertation on press coverage of the Indochina conflict 1965–75. He had chosen to study Flynn as his example of a freelance photographer. He had written to me a couple of years previously trying to obtain further information or sources and had included a couple of clippings from the French press at the time of their capture that I had not seen before. His studies then took him on a research trip to the United

States, and when I next heard from him, the boy had been busy. Through the Freedom of Information Act, he had obtained recently declassified Intelligence, Defense and State Department archives and, in particular, some CIA papers from the early 1970s. Black ink censored a large amount of the text, probably the information giving procedures, agent names, locales of meetings, details that could compromise people possibly still alive. However, there were a large number of references to our lads being held in captivity by the Khmer Rouge or resident factions in Kompong Cham province 120 kilometres north-northwest of Phnom Penh, a series of hamlets and villages. The coordinates WV featured heavily, as did the name of one Ta Sabun, a local Khmer Rouge headman. It gave the approximate date of their deaths as over a year after their capture, a couple of hundred kilometres west of the point on Route One where Vietnamese forces had originally sprung the ambush. The date on the files was nearly ten years old, but this was the first time they had come to light.

Although I had just returned from one trip to Southeast Asia, I immediately started trying to put together another. Cambodia reputedly was becoming a cheaper place to function, though public transportation upcountry was unsafe. forcing the rental of vehicle and/or boat. The commensurate amount of fuel would make up the larger part of the bill. Off the beaten track security was definitely bad, but bodyguards and escorts were for hire from the paramilitary police. A few of the old hotels were open for business. The press were not unwelcome, and there was now a foreign-press desk in the refurbished foreign ministry.

The background of the new prime minister, Hun Sen, was a complete cycle of Cambodian political history, although he was only forty years old. Khmer Rouge, escape to Vietnam, retrained, then reintroduced by the Vietnamese. He was a decorated combat veteran, missing an eye from wounds in the field. His rise to supremo had been consistent and rapid. Most parties, both internal and external, had respect for him and his fledgling government's attempt to stave off Khmer Rouge resurgence or Vietnamese reoccupation. Aid was beginning to come in, an infrastructure was emerging from the potholes and craters of a society that had been living without public transport, a postal system or money.

There were still no direct flights to or from Bangkok, the Thai border was still something to infiltrate rather than cross. There was, however, I discovered, an express bus service daily in each direction that left from the Rex Garage in downtown Saigon or next to Phnom Penh's Olympic Stadium.

# 6

# *Getting There Then*

First the bad news, then the good. Cambodian red can no longer be bought down the road from the Paris Hotel, on the street running to the central market in Phnom Penh. You have to go into the afternoon market, a bazaarlike maze, twelve blocks away. However, the top price for the primo flowers will not go above 600 riels a key, around one pound sterling. Sticks are another matter.

First you have to get a Cambodian visa. This is not so easy, since the war-torn Khmers cannot afford diplomatic representation even in Bangkok, slap next door. Naturally, they have an embassy in Hanoi. Vietnam still holds sway over the decisions made by its fraternal clients, since the intervention in 1979 to end the madness into which the Khmer Rouge had plunged the devastated land. The Cambodian delegation is housed in an elegant French colonial mansion downtown; the consular section operates from the basement. It is difficult to catch someone actually at work. The hours posted on the ever-open door are only vaguely adhered to. You can safely leave documents for processing on one of the desks and return a day later hoping to pick them up completed. Likely as not you will have to return again, having scribbled a resumé of your life, which will undoubtedly be committed to a dusty pile in Phnom Penh. I composed a page of poetic licence and sundry historical facts in longhand, and dropped it into the embassy early one morning, on the way out of town.

It was not until I returned eight days later, expecting the necessary paperwork to have been completed, that I realised that in the chilly early-morning scramble, the wrong sheet had been sealed away and the embassy had been given a page of a letter to my wife. A message at the foreign press centre asked us to present ourselves before the Cambodian first political secretary. 'No sweat,' said Tien. 'Formality.' The dapper diplomat preferred Salem Lights to 555s, we exchanged the normal pleasantries, and then I launched into the tale of the confusion of letters, believing that the visa permission hinged on it. I babbled on, using the gambit, the confession. 'I love plastic, smoke dope and am honest.'

His Excellence paused in his perusal of his gift book, cleared his throat discreetly and pulled his horn-rims halfway down his nose in a quizzical manner. 'We sell it in our markets.' The letter could be retrieved in Phnom Penh and, please look, the entry point has been carefully annotated for the land crossing at Ba Vet.

It was latish morning by the time I got to the colonnaded arcade facing the cyclone-fenced market perimeter. An elephant came lumbering through the bemused traffic and crowds, the howdah on its back chock-full of kids on a city joy ride. Along the arcade, the shops all had new occupants, well-dressed Khmers and Chinese presiding over glass cases full of jewellery – their front for money changing. Business was booming. The official rate of exchange was 340 riels to the dollar, but the largest denomination was a red 50-riel note. Changing a twenty bill automatically qualified you for a free raffia purse to haul your bricks of currency.

There is a logical progression to an Indochinese market: the outer rings of stalls sell the most perishable foods. This market had a ring of grinning women squatting behind boxes of Washington State apples, New Zealand pears and Australian grapes – this in a country with no official representation in the West! Behind them crouched the women with catfish plumply wriggling about on large trays. Periodically, one would be pulled to the side and neatly beheaded with a machete, leaving its brethren sliding about in the gore. Turning right took me to roots and tubers, banana stems edging back into fruit. I was looking for herbs and spices.

It was hot under the canvas and poncho drapes which threw a modicum of shade in the alleys between the stalls. No breeze dissipated the pungent smell of everything strange mingled. I ran up against sheet metal, the section given over to hammering utensils out of old oil cans. From the flattened shapes, little forms were snipped and soldered into suitcases, sieves, funnels and classic Third World toys – Cambodian interpretations of planes, trains, boats and buses. They were being edged out by ubiquitous Thai and Taiwanese plastic objects. Smuggled cosmetics and toiletries crowded into bands of colour, masked by a front of detergent boxes, soaps, shampoos and mosquito coils. My trail had gone cold. I kept shifting from stall to aisle, scanning the goods, trying to spot cigarettes, tobacco or skins among the heaped goodies. My Khmer totalled two words: *Ákun*, thank you, and *sabai*, hello, good day. In Viet, *can sa* is the word for the herb. In Lao, *sa* always got you a smoke and *tuk* meant consume. '*Tuk can sa*,' I started to mumble, pointing to a lit cigarette. Everyone caught the idea of a smoke, pointing in the opposite direction to that from which I had come. This took me past a hard core of antique and gold dealers cashing in family heirlooms for tatty red bricks. Business here was brisker than in the arcades outside and a group of bonzes, Buddhist monks, were having a profitable alms pass through these traders.

It felt strange to see the gliding saffron robes, knowing that almost the entire community of all the temples and wats in the country had been systematically exterminated during the

Kampong Cham ferry, security.

Cheung Ek Phnom Penh killing fields.

On Mekong, recon trip.

Begging from up express, Hai Van Pass.

Boat across Red River,
Ho Kien.

Train south.

Lang Cai, Bo Doi (GI), near Cao Bang, Chinese border.

Special Forces, Dac Cong, Son Tay.

Tim Page, Thinh Hoa Pagoda, Da Nang.

Fifty kilo bale of dope in the market.

Ho'Ville bus at Neak Long Ferry, across the Mekong.

Hal Moore and General Giap, Ha Noi.

The beer box containing the missing F4 camera.

Clockwise:

Exhuming the grave at Bei Met.

Lighting huong at memorial site on 17th parallel Ben Hai River.

Witnesses to capture of Flynn and Stone with M.I.A. book, Chi Phou.

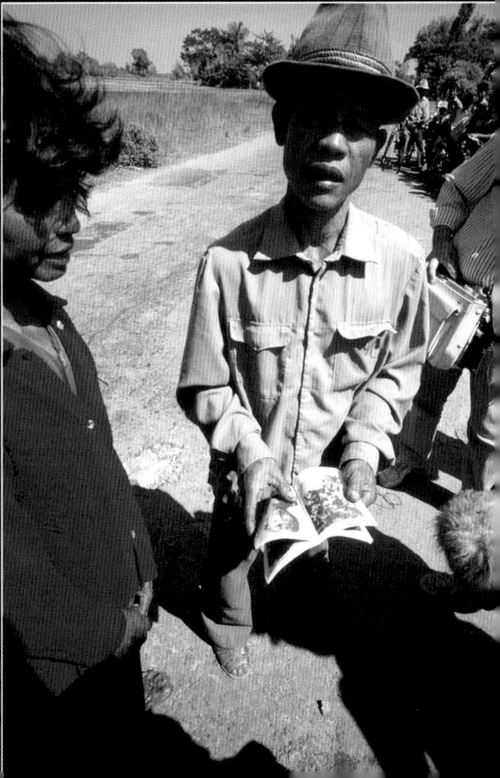

Marble Mountain Buddha Cave, Da Nang.

End of line, north of Lang Son.

Pol Pot four-year reign of terror. Most of the buildings had been trashed when not levelled, though a few were spared to be used as granaries. Now Buddhism was once again the official state religion. The wats were being rebuilt; all along the country roads peasants solicited for meritorious gifts to restore their local one, and the bus, truck and car drivers would slow and toss out crumpled balls of soiled riels. Newly ordained bonzes could be seen on *bindabat* every morning, moving along Monorom Boulevard hitting up the nouveau riche shopkeepers, who were eager to atone for the newly imported air-conditioned Toyotas and BMWs parked outside. Their generosity seemed less stimulated by the continual procession of crippled and mutilated folk. In today's Cambodia you keep one pocket full of selected balls of money to dispense to this pathetic army who plague you no sooner than you have slowed down to look around or take a streetside café seat. The beggars had their own section in the market out on the northern edge of the central hall, next to the recycled metal and the kiosks dispensing Buddhist decorations. I almost stumbled on the unfortunates, packed as closely as though they were still in hospital gowns from surgery, with their stumps, still tied up in dirty dressings, trailing in the sludge next to a main thoroughfare.

I was adrift again, my arms and short vest full of items originally not on my list, but irresistible at the price: a pack of four *kramas*, the traditional Khmer scarf, loincloth, head wrap or sarong; a machete forged from an old car spring: two monk's bags and a couple of Buddhist flags. Besides these, I had loaded up on cigarettes in my endeavour to elicit directions from the vendors.

The variety of recycled bits and bobs stretched across the last thirty years of violent history. Any vehicle imported into the country was here represented in an exploded form. Under Pol Pot, all civilian transport had been scrapped, the vehicles reserved for the favoured few of the Anka, the party's central inner clique. Everything had been turned to junk and now, as the country gradually picked up, the populace sorted through the residue looking for a motor bearing, nut or bolt which could make their day. Great ingenuity was employed to keep things ticking.

I found myself back out in another fruit and veg section devoted to the small seller, the peasant who came to town for the day to dispose of the family's excess produce. The opposite side had been the crops and state-farm stalls. The ground was a patchwork quilt of ladies and their offspring, squatting over baskets and spread sacks displaying the makings of the spicy Cambodian cuisine. Squatting down conspiratorially beside two beaming, betel-mouthed mums flogging herbs and chillies with a few strange roots underneath, I popped out my stash can, flipped off the top and showed them the *can sa*. The patchwork quilt rippled with giggles and titters. Strange white devil after the loco weed. Shrugs and Cambodian babble, old crones pointing in opposing directions. With much loss of face I put them on the spot by taking their portraits.

Staggering in overheated sneakers, soaking *krama* around the neck, I went back into the industrial part. Now on nodding terms with the line and net sellers, I was about to give up. It must have been the third time I passed them in the maze.

One last shot at directions from an ancient whose stock was packs of smuggled Viet and US cigarettes with one pack of Dunhill Menthols in a green and gold flip-top pack (an ace trade item). As I straightened up and was cramming the purchase in my hip pocket, I noticed a dark, bandy-legged man hovering just behind me. He was babbling in quasi-French, '*Avee voulez, musure! Cherchez ou' moi aid.*' On closer inspection, he was clad in nothing save a pair of French colonial baggy drill shorts and antiquated cut-down Bata jungle boots, toes showing. Round his neck was a gold chain with an ivory Buddha. His eyes were bird-beady with the telltale spiderwebs of a true head.

Standing, he resembled an upright frog, bowed legs, arms aflap. He was also extremely grubby, veneered with a sheen of sweat on a hardened body. His *krama* was tied cummerbund-style around his waist to keep the oversize shorts up. He was Rumpelstiltskin crossed with the good fairy. The crone selling me the St Moritz appeared familiar with the shuffling old soldier, giving him a tatty bill to go away. He stayed, plucking at my sleeve, now mouthing. 'Gunja, gunja,' and making smoking sucking sounds. He had obviously overheard my enquiries. The crone and I wiped eyes, the implication that the dude was cool, one of them, go for it. He was already on the move, skipping down the aisle, dodging round stalls in a cross-market beeline. As he passed stalls selling fruit or sweets, he picked up what he wanted with a giggle, bantering with the shopkeepers. The point of the baggy shorts was now revealed – they were a squirrel pouch – and his cheeks bulged with an apple.

On a diagonal heading we passed quickly through familiar alleys. Just past recycled electrics, near the corner where I could just make out the beggars through the foliage of dangling goods, was the vendor I had been searching for. The stand's cover was bottletops, boxes and sacks full of caps ready for crimping beer, soya or oil in the endless bottle bank of the Third World. She also did a sideline in bright gold or silver washers, powder paint in jars and shopping baskets. Propped around the perimeter were gunny sacks, recycled sandbags neatly rolled back at the top to reveal different grades of cleaned weed. Propped in bundles in front of the lot were the sticks; some somewhat soggy with oil, some autumnally crisp, bound with bamboo stripping. Bundles of smaller sticks cluttered the outer edges of the counter.

Having delivered me safely, Rumpelstiltskin was anxious to be off. I delved in my alms pocket and peeled him a couple of wads. Thinking I was being cheap, I then thrust a just-opened pack of Lights on him. He was gone, with an '*Akun. Au voir, musure.*'

Negotiations progressed simply with an implicit trust. I would hold up a sample, Madame scribbling out sums on the back of a cigarette carton. Her three healthy offspring were clambering over her, all the time their waif eyes glued on the foreign apparition before them. It seemed that one bought a kilo for openers. A scale was produced and loaded, with much giggling. The heap was a roll a foot long, ten inches thick, totally unmanageable, the size of a bundled sleeping bag. I took a quarter. While I was at it, I added a hundred grams of two of the loose clean. The formidable pile was wrapped in newspaper and tied off with rubber bands. I stuffed the parcel into one of my new Buddhist walkabout bags. By now, all other commercial activity in the vicinity had ceased to function as the smallholders clustered round, helping me to count out the bills, arguing the total price down a few tatty notes. I was out of pocket by nearly 85p for an amount of grass whose street value an ambitious excise man would probably make into telephone numbers.

Some months later I was back again, this time with the added advantage of a Khmer speaker. A young Bostonian married to a Cambodian student and doing her photographic dissertation in country, Lea glided through Khmer society with a facility not often witnessed in foreigners. Top to bottom they accepted her for her command of classic Khmer and the ribald bantering of the streets. Shopping with her would be a doddle.

Our guidance systems were not entirely stable, necessitating a couple of false sorties into the market's labyrinths. Homing in, we found the locale not by the actual stash, but by the activity in the vicinity. The new crop was just in from Kampong Thom, 100 kilometres to the northwest. Rumpelstiltskin was now fully employed in helping a lady from an adjacent stall and a man in rolled-up trousers and straw boater hoisting bales into slings to be weighed on a primitive hand-held balance. The contents had been tightly wrapped in burlap, the ends covered with recycled rice sacks, all bound together with plastic strapping. One by one, they struggled to get the ropes around the bales and onto the hook, sliding the weighted bar for a reading. Each lot tipped the scales at 50 kilos. Then the load was unceremoniously dumped into the sea of waste and rubbish that had collected from the day's sweepings.

Rumpelstiltskin swung around, uptight until latching on to my grin, and his face relaxed in recognition.

Packaging leaves and twigs is difficult. Large tufts poked out at the corners, blatantly advertising the contents in their new-mown green splendour. Destined for the daily cuisine of ordinary Cambodian kitchens, this herb was the natural start to all soups and the curry pot. Squatting for a low, wide shot of the balancing act, I peripherally caught Rumpelstiltskin detaching himself from the process. He grabbed a tuft and hopped in my direction, an ear-to-ear grin on his face. He stuffed the tuft into my shirt pocket, wedging it down behind the Salems and lighter, then stepped back and, pointing to his stained mouth, ordered, '*Kin, kin*.' In Lao that's 'consume' or 'eat' and couldn't be far wrong here.

Dipping into the pocket forage, I stuffed the dry mix into my mouth and started masticating. I must have looked like a buffalo with a jaw full of water hyacinths. It was tough getting enough juice to digest the wad, but soon my brain appeared to have a seepage, and the heat of the day was all smoothed out. I let Lea do the negotiations with our lady of the bottletops and washers at the adjacent stall. The tune to 'The Camptown Races' invaded my brain and I could almost hear the singing, 'Pick a bale of hash, pick a bale a dale. Lordie, Lordie. Hey, hey, wrecked again. Ho'ville, here I come.' The beat picked up, and carried on.

It was late March by the time we got up to Kampong Cham, 120 kilometres north of the capital. The ride in an old

Toyota took six hours and involved a ferry crossing. Half the distance was well covered by government patrols, every 500 metres or so there would be clumps of raggy mix-and-match men with decrepit, mainly Chinese weaponry, sitting at the side of the road in the shade of a bush or tree. Often they would try to flag down vehicles to exhort tax or just to bum a cigarette. The rest of the way we would hurtle along, dodging as best we could the deeper repair jobs to the war damage.

KC was never much of a town; back in 1968, at its peak, the population never topped 35,000. It forms a small haphazard blob along the Mekong, with no building higher than two colonial stuccoed storeys. Like most French Indochinese provincial centres, its major attraction is the Art Deco thirties central market. There was no hotel open in town; visitors were obliged to put up at the official government guesthouse, where half a dozen of the rooms were permanently occupied by a French Médicins sans Frontières unit and an ophthalmic team from Australia. A Maryknoll father was the only other resident, and the only American I met upcountry who freely admitted that his role to serve up Christianity was a little superfluous.

The guesthouse stands at the river end of a long dual carriageway servicing all the provincial ministry buildings. At one end is a large traffic circle, off which lies the old French governor's mansion, now province committee HQ. At the other end a rusty pink ferroconcrete liberation memorial built in an Angkorian triumphal arc with Buddhistic crenellations perches on a roundabout that becomes the focal turnaround for the youth of Kampong Cham's evening *paseo*, or King's Road cruise, here preferably performed on heavily chromed Pheasant-brand bicycles imported from Thailand. (Back then, the flood of Hondas had not yet surged upcountry.) Downstairs at the guesthouse was a deserted, cavernous restaurant, a room full of bleak brown-painted wooden classroom tables and chairs, the walls lined with crates of beer bottles, mostly empties waiting for an investor to come and rebuild the local brewery. Although we had arrived in time for lunch, the kitchen would offer only instant Vietnamese dried noodles – everything except hot water was off.

Downtown, a block away behind the shrapnel- and bullet-pocked local cinema, there was not much of a selection of feeding stations. A bakery, two soup shops and two cafés fronted onto the market. Away from the river, on the town's only other major intersection and roundabout, is the only place in town to eat. At breakfast, lunch and dinner you can always find the foreign volunteers pulled up at a long metal table consuming from the limited menu which they have supplemented with omelette, steak and fries. There is a lot of swimming oil, but let your Khmer companion do the ordering and be pleasantly surprised. The Café de la Place is relatively clean, that is to say that people only occasionally fall sick, a blessing in a country where it is advisable to take prophylactic Lomotils before you eat.

We had a late-afternoon appointment with the local military commander to discuss the feasibility of getting to the village most referred to in the declassified documents, Toul Ta Kao. On paper it looked to be no more than 15 kilometres due east on the other side of the Mekong, just north of the Chup rubber plantation. There even appeared to be a reasonably large tributary stream heading in the right direction and as far as Suong on Route Seven there was a major highway. North of the rubber town, service roads gridded through Cambodia's largest working plantation. The French had successfully tamed large tracts of forest from the Mekong all the way to the Vietnamese border and beyond with rubber plantations, using indentured labour. The serried rows of trees endowed this part of Indochina with a civilised feeling associated with a drive through Malaya or southern Sri Lanka. Somehow the Chup enterprise had continued to function throughout the troubles in the sixties, the all-out war of the early seventies and, more surprisingly, had continued to export a trickle of latex during Pol Pot's time, when the rest of the country had ground to a standstill. This eastern zone had seen the font and been the front of the revolution; harboured the largest North Vietnamese sanctuaries, endured the heavies B-52 bombings, the most cross-border incursions and the last Khmer Rouge purges of its own ranks. Hun Sen's home town is Kampong Cham. The output from the Chup can still be used as a yardstick of national progress.

Chen, my guide, had to go back to province and sort out the next day's upriver logistics. Approval had been granted, posts ahead notified, they now only had to agree on how much to rip me off. A quick riffle through my wallet revealed a mere $140 to get me back to Phnom Penh and then on to Saigon in a week's time. He returned and announced that diesel for the trip would be $80, the boat hire $20. The colonel commander would accompany us himself. I suspected that he had little better to do and here was a freebie trip. I was still a little miffed at why we would require 600 litres of fuel just to go across the main stream and then up a small creek a few kilometres.

The next morning, before sunrise, we were in front of the guesthouse by the Arc de Triomphe. Five paramilitary types with an assortment of AK-47s and rocket-propelled grenade launchers were already present. We took off for the waterfront, two of the young privates holding hands. The mood was one of a group of kids off on a picnic, not of an expedition deep into the dreaded Khmer Rouge's back yard to try to exhume friends killed two decades ago.

Arriving at the riverbank, I could understand the need for the diesel. My craft was a 10-metre twin-deck river launch with a large Perkins engine midships. Its bridge, a hutch the size of a dovecote, was perched forward on the top deck, oil-tanker style; the new Cambodian flag of red and blue with a gold Angkor Wat silhouette emblazoned across it drooped from a stubby mast whose purpose was to support a navigation light that once had seen duty on some Japanese automobile. The crew were out of sight below boards, banging and hammering; a new prop shaft was being fitted, for which I would be dunned the rest of my wallet. I had not exactly countenanced buying a unit of the Cambodian navy a new drive train. The colonel turned up on cue as the crew fired up to test their repairs; my escort arranged itself across the roof, the colonel procured a chair and we were off for a seven-hour chug upstream.

Our destination was now revealed; we were heading for Kroch Chhmar, a small riverside community on the south bank just round the first big eastering bend north of Kampong Cham. We would be about 20 kilometres north of the village where Sean and Dana were last sighted; the map traced a fine line which I hoped would be a good truck road in this dry season. Why Kroch Chhmar, its name the same as the Khmer for lime or lemon, was never really explained. Maybe it was for the food, for we arrived in the lunch hour, only to disturb the local district officer who stumbled out of his residence-cum-HQ fumbling with his flies. Five minutes later a lady shuffled out, eyes cast down, and went downstairs to start fixing the delegation's meal.

My hopes had soared when we first arrived, for in the godown out behind the compound was a Gaz jeep and an old Chinese Ho Chi Minh Trail truck. The hopes evaporated as the food was served. It would take a platoon of troops for security and much benzine, in fact a lot of riels and dollars would have to be doshed out to proceed farther. The officer offered to investigate for us on his next downcountry swing, and in the same fraternal speech presented us with a bill for lunch for twelve. I peeled off an Andrew Jackson to cover the expenses. We were free to tour the town and the rebuilt wat next door.

Pol Pot had absolutely no taste for religion or philosophy, save his own, so he ordered most of the wats, temples, churches and mosques to be razed. The rather beautiful turn-of-the-century Phnom Penh cathedral was taken apart brick by brick and most of the wats were desecrated, the stupas and tombs ripped open and Buddha images destroyed. Upcountry the amount of destruction had depended on the zeal of the local commander. Often a quirk of the spirits would save a wat from destruction, though it would be utilised as a gunnery or ammo dump. The tall, steep-pitched long-eaved wat Sisowat was now reconsecrated, a group of bonzes resident in a separate building, and local people had restored images of the Buddha in the shrine room. The cool interior had benignly served as a rice depot for eight years, the chipped and scarred floor tiles the only reminder of the hard days. The ceiling paintings were bright and fresh, showing naive depictions of different scenes from the Buddha's life. I lit three sticks of incense, bowed and retreated to sit at the back of the room. It was a wat with a strong spiritual feeling. Children, young bonzes and bodyguards slipped in and equally quietly slipped out, leaving the space a meditation haven.

A tingle lit my hair and ran down my back. I sensed a presence, still but energised, a communication. I believe Flynn had been in this building. A fragment of his spiritual energy was looping inexplicably across time. Rather than leave feeling bummed out, peeved at the local authority for not getting things more organised at short notice, I left the wat light of step, glowing from the encounter, even managing to walk a dodgy springy plank between bank and jetty unhesitatingly. Landing had been a right palaver akin to moving a circus animal.

There was an anticlimactic air to the downstream ride. The shadows lengthened, the temperature still hovered at 27°C or so, the crew and escorts took it in turns to step up to the square fantail to dip and splash buckets of bright-brown Mekong over themselves. Each was modestly breechclouted with his chequered *krama*, wrapped normally around the head and neck. It is the single most important item of Khmer clothing.

The sky turned orange, purple, red; an acid sunset, purely magical. And somewhere on the journey back down the Mekong I had one of those pure thoughts, a thought well lit, an inspiration.

The site of their burial would become a memorial dedicated to all the media personnel killed or missing in the various modern Indochinese wars. I would get to Toul Ta Kao, the mystery would be resolved and a stupa get erected. I must have babbled this to Chen, who babbled it to the supremo and the bodyguard squad. Everyone joined in, costing buffalo carts and bricks and masons and, and . . . The thought sailed on like a spinnaker billowing out with purpose.

# 7

# *The Search*

It was known that no foreigner managed to survive the notorious Toul Sleng interrogation centre in southeast Phnom Penh. Toul Sleng, once a lycée, had been converted during Pol Pot's reign of terror into a prison where all prisoners were obliged to write confessions before being trucked farther out of town to Cheung Ek, the killing field. The guards and interrogators photographed everyone upon their arrival and often upon departure. The macabre portraits now line ex-classrooms that formed one wing of the complex. Thousands and thousands of deadpan eyes, all knowing their fate; death after the most inhumane tortures dreamed up to exact pointless confessions. The purpose of these was to bolster the blanket of security Anka was trying to shroud itself in to conceal its own carnivorous paranoia, its own apocalyptic future.

One wall displayed the photos of the only foreigners known to have been digested by the system. Three Europeans, a couple of Australians (yachtsmen who had inadvertently strayed into Kampuchean waters), a few locally born Indians and an overseas Chinese. Nobody who was taken alive before the Khmer Rouge had come to town. Anka was very meticulous with its bookkeeping; it is unlikely that they would have forgotten or misplaced evidence of our colleagues. Ghosts still haunt the bleak Toul Sleng compound, now a museum to the years of Khmer Rouge control. An apt reminder now that the United Nations has legitimised them sufficiently to enable their participation in the elections in May 1993.

Since the spring recon trip, I had returned to Vietnam for a month partly on assignment, partly sounding out the Vietnamese on the idea of a memorial to all the missing media personnel, sited, as an old friend had suggested, in the old demilitarised zone on the 17th Parallel. The Ben Hai River had been the dividing line set in 1954 at the Geneva Convention on the demarcation of North and South Vietnam. The original bridge there was blown away in 1963 by a typhoon, common during the autumn in central Annam; its successor had been declared a chunk of national heritage.

The concept had been mooted at diverse official levels in Hanoi, but further consultation with other departments – press, tourism, art, culture, archeology and sport – would be necessary before final approval could be expected. In the socialist bureaucracy no one was prepared to go it alone.

The head of the official state news agency admitted that the Vietnamese were hoping to resolve the question of some of their own media MIA and were searching for a suitable memorial to them. The Cambodians, sunnier minds in a brighter, more southerly clime, were prepared to cooperate in whatever way possible. Cambodia was coming in from the cold. Hanoi confused our search with the overall MIA issue, finding it easier to stonewall. (They also threw me a slight curve ball. It was suggested that I might like to help start a faculty of media studies at one of the universities. Hue was mentioned, politically in the middle and once the imperial capital of the Viets. It is the traditional Oxbridge of Indochina. Balanced between the hard-core frenzy of money market and corruption down south and the stolid socialistic realism up north, Hue has always produced the great scholars, generals and statesmen from both Tonkin and Cochin, or, as they call them, Bac Viet and Chien Viet.)

* * *

As far back as 1989 I had heard mention of Ham. His name cropped up in the conversations the staff of the foreign press centre had among themselves. The guides would either be vexed and annoyed or giggling infectiously, whenever I caught the word Ham dotted down the pinging tones of Vietnamese. When really stoned I can make out a good 30 per cent of what is being said; on a straight, my language skills fall right off, a foreign tongue becoming a backdrop to travel. Even to someone reasonably proficient, the pronunciation differs so much between north and south that it can be incomprehensible. The variations are as wide as between southern English and that of the Glaswegian Gorbals. To speak with the accent of the opposite end can lead to heavy loss of face; often northerners end up stonewalled as soon as they open their mouths. Even before colonial times, there was never a great love lost between Tonkinese and Cochinese. Northerners look on their southern cousins as soft, effeminate, lazy, too laid-back: the southerners gaze north to see cold, hard people with little sophistication and no fun. Neither is entirely true, of course. The most noticeable differences are that the south, over 1,800 kilometres from Hanoi and the Red River delta, is constantly 15°C warmer. The diet down south includes more fruit, and the variety of vegetables and fish is maintained year-round. Up north, in the winter, the markets have little colour, selling mostly drab piles of root crops and the one fruit that is making it to the shelves. As the infra-structure improves, more and more produce from the sunny south is found north of the 17th parallel. Conversely, it is now possible to get a decent bowl of *pho*, the tasty broad noodles, in the south.

Young Thang, a guide educated in Canberra, Australia, had once ridden north in the back of my jeep, back in 1985. That was after the 'ten years of liberation' celebrations when the US television networks had been allowed back for the first time to satellite their shows live out of Saigon. It was Neil Davis, then NBC bureau chief in Bangkok, who had this window. Thang had been one of his lads and a good buddy to my man Tien. Tien had told Thang to come by my room to cop some *can sa* for the hip new cadre of the guide corps. Many of this new elite were children of party hierarchy who were becoming disillusioned about the system and whose minds drifted more towards the sex, drugs and rock and roll their parents' generation had been denied. So Thang had come knocking on my room at the Palace Hotel, delegated by his fellow minders to score a collective stash of dope from the newspaper-wrapped bundle Neil had had passed into his jeep in downtown Phnom Penh. An admirer from the years before 1975 must have spotted him. The bouquet had been passed to me for distribution, a duty hardly befitting NBC's man of the moment.

And Thang, had somehow now, got landed with Ham.

Ham makes films, takes stills, both black and white and colour, records sound and knocks off a bit of video, all at the same time. He also tends to get involved in projects that have nothing to do with the media. For example, he would be endeavouring to help establish an Australian brewery in an out-of-the-way place like Song Be or Kampong Cham. His room would still be full of the bits of kit necessary to discharge his press functions just in case there was a time window. None of the gear matched, the systems all different, no lenses interchangeable, all of it obsolete, second-hand and in a deplorable state, having been transported in luggage appropriate only to a hippie or cardboard-city dweller. Peeling leatherette, splitting corduroy, ripped plastic and painted ammunition boxes characterise his baggage.

He is dressed to match: baggy blue shorts, RAF desert issue at a guess, T-shirt, socks and sneakers. Above this outfit rises a craggy face with bottle-thick glasses under unkempt wavy hair. Periodically, a scraggly beard appears and is pulled and tugged continually. He has a lost look, limbs slightly akimbo, hairy legs firmly planted, eccentric and defiant. His affectation is to smoke a bong, the bamboo water pipe indigenous to Indochina. A piece of bamboo about a foot long serves as the main stem, the bottom filled with water to act as a filter. A smaller piece is inserted, sealed with road tar, a few centimetres up the stem at a 30-degree angle, and on top of this a small knot of bamboo, smoothed down like two acorn cups back to back, serves as the bowl. Tonkinese tamp into the bowl a plug of coarse black tobacco, the Cochinese a pinch of blond, the Khmer whatever and the Lao a sprinkle of weed. The bong attracts suspicion and giggles. Many ranking Viet military and civilian officials still indulge themselves with a blow or two out of wartime nostalgia.

His calling cards announce Evan Ham as Normella Films, named after his parents, Norman and Ella, from the depths of Toowong, Queensland. No one in the business and none of the Viets I know has ever heard or seen a completed Ham product, though I admit I have not come across *Australian Aviation* or *Beer* magazine – publications listed on his business card. Ham's quirky character has, however, endeared him to the Khmers and the Vietnamese; they have adopted him at certain levels as a harmless, wacky foreigner worth indulging and encouraging for the contacts he has back home, Down Under. He has, as someone put it, 'both feet squarely under the desk of Indochina's bureaucracy'. Ham was therefore assigned to get the paperwork in Cambodia sorted out. We would meet up in Bangkok, picking up the necessary visas and papers at the Vietnamese embassy next to the hotel.

Ham and John Sheppard, the director and producer, would go via Ho'ville to Phnom Penh to do the research before the crew came out to film. Shep had directed over a hundred *World in Actions*, in one of which I had featured in 1968. The project now was to make a documentary for British television. They were counting on us to solve the mystery of our two fellow MIAs. I would head for Hanoi with the other researcher-cum-producer, Brian, another ex-Asia hand from the 1970s, now parked on the sidelines of Granada Television, Manchester.

We would learn what we could from Hanoi's files, should they decide to let us see them, and try to trace Vietnamese veterans of the campaigns fought in the region where our lads went missing or were later seen moving across. We also hoped to comb the army film archives for possible footage shot in their liberated rear-echelon areas, the K-zone, at the beginning of the seventies. Noncooperation in Hanoi quickly became a source of utter frustration. They knew and we knew that there was more material available, but that it was not politically expedient for them to make it public. We were obliged to build an information biscuit by collecting sundry crumbs; we had unit names and numbers, commanders' movement details, a fairly comprehensive picture of their operational structure. We had even found a teashop where veterans of the Cambodian front regularly meet. The next step was clear.

Suddenly we found ourselves out of visa, bound for Phnom Penh via Saigon's Ton San Nhut airport. The system had been upset by my sidekick's attitude and by our getting close to opening another, in their minds, delicate can of worms, that of the military MIAs. Normalisation could not be run faster than the system wanted it to. It was easier for them to freeze like disturbed, terrified, small, furry beasts than to find a way around the problem. They habitually say no twice before assenting to any joint endeavour.

Shep and Ham were not in town when we got in. They had not checked into the Royale. Passing round the back of the once elegant four-storey colonial edifice to the bungalows, I began to understand why. The bungalow on offer did not have functioning electrics, and the water was full of mosquitoes and rat droppings. The place stank of creeping damp and mould. The nongovernmental aid agencies all had offices or apartments in the main body of the hotel, which had been refurbished, whereas the crescents of chalets, grouped around overgrown semicircular gardens of flowering shrubs, were only now being brought back on line. The pool, once the watering place of Phnom Penh lunchtime society, had a surface life awaiting a biological investigation.

It had been from back here under the shade trees that Flynn and Stone had set off on their last bike ride. The dust jacket of Perry Deane Young's book about their lives and times, *Two of the Missing*, shows them astride Honda 90s, ready to roll east to Svay Rieng. The photo had gone out on the UPI wire a couple of days after their disappearance. Terry Khoo, the Singaporean cameraman for ABC who snapped them, was himself later to disappear.

Shep and Ham got back from the upcountry research and reconnaissance. Ham – now rechristened Hand Luggage, for he was still steadfastly refusing to check in his assorted flight bags, briefcases and silver make-up boxes, keeping them close to his body – had caused Shep palpitations at Don Maung airport, rushing off to locate an ammo can lost on his way to Bangkok just as they were checking in for the Ho Chi Minh flight. Later, when I had a chance to examine it, it turned out to contain three airline ticket stubs, a comb, one sock, an old toothbrush, one roll of very slow black and white, and one empty film canister.

The story had unravelled faster than anyone could have dared to believe or possibly hope for, once they hooked up with Dara and Chanda. Dara had just got out of government service, where he had been boatman and bodyguard to Hun Sen, the prime minster. I had met him briefly back in the spring when he was working for an American photographer on assignment for *Time*. Dara came complete with white Datsun station wagon, Dutch export plates covered with Singaporean ones and finally a Khmer one at the rear. Between the seats he sausaged his folding-stock AK-47, oiled and immaculate. Dara is above average height for a Khmer, built like a boxer, balanced like a cat and can read a situation with the eye of a pathfinder or scout. He is easy of smiles and laughter, though pissed off he would be very dangerous. Definitely someone to have on your side. His spoken English was then minimal but he could understand almost everything, having, I suspect, learned to overhear top-level conversations, file and then report to whatever inquisitive party subfunded his service. In a poverty-stricken country, Dara, with his tenth-hand imported car, was next to nobility. Nonetheless he was honest and loyal and not a party member, merely a skilled survivor in a land where everyone has the most harrowing tales.

As the Germans have tried to put their past firmly into history, so have the Khmer, their attitude enhanced by their fundamental philosophy: forget, forgive and get on with the now. Everyone knows who the bad guys were, who are the people still to ostracise, still with debts to pay; but so much of the populace was uprooted, displaced and still has not returned to their native districts that it is possible for those of dubious history to relocate to fresh fields where their politics is more acceptable. Surviving the years 1975–79 required everyone to collaborate to some degree. Almost everyone in the power structure of government has Khmer Rouge somewhere in their curricula vitae. Nobody really wants to get into deep raps about those times, they are too busy getting on with living. The birth rate is phenomenal, it would seem that every second motor scooter carries a family of five, all the offspring still in the portable stage.

Madame Chin Chanda would be our main interpreter, translator, guide, arranger and spiritual mother for the entire time we were incountry. Then she was still working for the Ministry of Foreign Affairs, as one of their senior interpreters. She had a bustling, no-nonsense schoolteacher manner, and a mane of curly black hair, her slightly portly figure always traditionally clothed in silk sarong and modest-sleeved top. Chanda was well endowed with gold jewellery and expensive threaded sarongs. She was also a devout

Buddhist. Rarely flustered, she was always ready with a placating Band Aid when the excrement and revolving blades met midcourse. Her husband fortuitously owned a clapped-out car, rentable at somewhat extortionate rates, which we used as a backup to Dara's Datsun. He had a secondary job at a ministry as an accountant, though this paid a mere pittance. The legacy of communism is that everyone is obliged to have at least two jobs, which they moonlight in shifts. We paid the ministry per diem for Chanda's services and then made a personal contribution at job's end, making her income in total ten times that of the prime minister, who was on the equivalent of a few dollars a month.

The upcountry recon mission had basically uncovered the lads' last days. Their story would never, of course, be fully known; too many people had disappeared in the interior, too many memories dulled by time and the trauma of survival. They could not give me every detail, needing me to appear fresh on the trail when the film crew got in to record the search. A scenario was already being scripted, though the final sequence of filming was to be decided by the research still to be undertaken in the eastern provinces around the point of capture.

Most auspiciously, Shep and Ham had been in Kampong Cham at the same time as Hun Sen, who was back in his home town planting a sacred bo tree, one of thirteen saplings he had been given during a recent visit to India. The bo tree or pee pul, a member of the banyan family, is the tree under which the Buddha achieved enlightenment more than 2,500 years ago at Bodh Gaya in the northeast Indian province of Bihar. In the East it is known as the *bodhi* tree. India is the principal aid donor, sending archaeologists and technicians to restore and preserve the temple complex at Angkor Wat, and was also one of the first states to recognise the new Vietnamese-backed government in 1979. Hun Sen, then in his early thirties, served in it as foreign minister under Heng

Samrin, gaining the finesse and language skills the Viets had been grooming him for. He was still their ally, but had become ever more Buddhist and patriotic Khmer.

Hun Sen was familiar with the eccentric Ham, and Shep, with his height of nearly two metres, was only impressive. The nod must have gone down to the local people, for full cooperation and access were accorded. Once they had crossed over the Mekong, the trail had warmed up north of Suong, the rubber-plantation town. The twenty potholed kilometres of Route Seven were theoretically secure, 'prone only to banditry', though every bridge or culvert had a government militia unit bivouacked in the immediate vicinity, likely as not extorting tolls from the lucrative route to the Vietnamese border at Tay Ninh. The declassified CIA documents had not been far off; the places they had reported the captives held at were only two and a half kilometres different from the new coordinates. The closer Shep and Ham got to the X on the map, 10 kilometres north of Suong in the Sangke Kaong district, the more volunteers with information stepped forth. Word of mouth spread up the track.

Tuol Ta Kao, my original destination, is three kilometres to the northwest of where a bounty hunter had finally gone digging in what was once a banana plantation at the back of a small hamlet now called Bei Met. Kong Nhar, a frail old man, still farming at past sixty years, was not native to the area, having come back here with other commune members after the fall of Pol Pot. During the bleak years, many of these eastern zone villages, heartland of the original Khmer Rouge movement, had to be purged, so the inhabitants were moved west to a gulag on the other side of the river to work in the nonsensical irrigation projects. These schemes were designed by non-engineers and had canals trying to run uphill; medics in the camps were often aged twelve to fourteen, licensed to perform unanaesthetised amputations. A society upside down and brutalised finally returned to its native villages, taking along survivors of families evacuated from towns and other liquidated zones. Kong Nhar probably had listened to stories of the old days of the Vietnam War. In 1983, after hearing of a reward up to $10,000 being offered for information leading to the recovery or the bones of MIA Americans, he started digging. That tease had been broadcast by the Khmer service of Voice of America radio based in Bangkok. Voice of America is a spooked-up American version of the BBC World Service. Kong Nhar and his fellow villagers had exhumed two bone fragments, three teeth and a large filling.

There was no way he would be able to get to an American consul, much less embassy, from the middle of Kampong Cham province. The United States did not recognise the existence of the state of Cambodia. (Officially, at the UN, the country was represented by the Khmer Rouge, although in practice this never really occurred.) Phnom Penh would come and take the bone fragments away, giving no reward – not a riel – but the wily villagers and Kong Nhar had kept back the three teeth and the filling.

When we went back to dig again, hoping to unearth some more evidence, there was a somewhat chilled air at first, the villagers fearing trouble from so many foreigners and Phnom Penh folk suddenly arriving in their sleepy backwater. Once it was made known that there would be a small recompense (5,000 riels) per interview or house usage, the attitude loosened up. A liberal number of snapshots taken on the recon and imported cigarettes also helped.

The commune of Sangke Kaong/Toul Ta Kao had originally been a Muslim one; most of the leading cadre were ethnic Chams, Cambodia's indigenous Islamic adherents. During the holocaust, they had been slaughtered like Gypsies under Hitler. Singled out for extermination, the mosques were razed or desecrated before the Buddhist wats. Back in 1971, one of the young front cadres, El Am Noas, had been assigned to guard and watch over Flynn and Stone.

When we met she was one of the respected leading

lights of the community, a handsome lady in her early forties with a substantial house in the southern part of the village. Then, she must have had a teenage crush on the tall, though thinned-out, Flynn, judging by the look that came over her face, a softness to her eyes as she spoke of him. Leafing through a book of photos of the MIA journalists, she immediately recognised Sean and Dara, both pictured with and without glasses, and moustaches. She told us of the time they had travelled together fleeing the invading South Vietnamese forces, being subjected to bombing raids and talking of home, chatting on the trail. Flynn was remembered not just by his character, but by a distinctive gold chain and round amulet. She recalled his ability to speak French and Spanish and that his parents were big in cinema, Hollywood maybe.

Of the two captives, Flynn had been the less despondent, and had picked up some Khmer during their months of captivity. But then, he did not have Smiser Stone waiting for him in Phnom Penh. Dana was madly in love with Louise, and she with him; he even wore a plait of her long hair around his neck. Dana liked to get back in from the field each night, back to the security of Smiser's arms. Before he was married, he used to disappear up in the hills, walking point with recon patrols for weeks on end. Domesticity had taken the edge off.

Sean had just finished a lengthy stint in Indonesia, mainly in Bali, soaking up the gentle spirit of the East. He had initially gone to Indonesia on an assignment to cover Nixon's first visit – the first by a US president to that country. For half the time he had been staying in Jakarta at Joe Galloway's ample villa, compliments of UPI, for whom Joe was now bureau chief. Joe had been one of the people living in Frankie's House, 47 Bui Thi Xuan, in Saigon in 1966 when Sean had first arrived there. The rest of the time Sean spent mainly down in Bali in a beachfront complex with Mike Boyum, one of the first American expat surfers, who had discovered the perfect place with its purple sunsets.

Flynn had intended to get his kit out of Saigon, and out of his Paris flat, make a last trip to see Lili in Palm Beach and move permanently to a place he would buy with Mike in Bali. This was after an impossible love affair with the seventeen-year-old Princess Laksmi, which had ended in disaster, Flynn in jail for days and a villain's Mercedes Benz minus any external glassware.

The last Christmas in Jakarta in 1969, he had turned up in a cyclo with a sapling flame tree for Joe's yard. It was planted in front of the porch and Sean announced that the man he had bought it from said it would flower in a year's time. Before he left to start the process of the move to Bali, he had pointed to the tree and said he would be back for the first blossoms. Two years later Joe wrote to me saying the tree was over seven and a half metres and still had not flowered; he believed there was a good chance that Sean was alive as long as the flame tree did not flower. Much later, in November 1972, he wrote again, 'I must report to you that this week Sean's tree began putting out the first flowers since it was planted exactly three years ago . . .'

What had lured Sean to Cambodia was the headline in the *Stars and Stripes*, the forces' paper, 'NVA advance on Phnom Penh'. *Time* promised gigs and Dana was already down there stringing for CBS as a cameraman. A last trip to the front, perhaps the chance to see the action from the other side for the definitive home movie he had been preoccupied with for the last couple of years. The movie he had declared would not be complete until the enemy's point of view had been shot.

Full-scale incursions began in the spring of 1970, when 70,000 US and Vietnamese troops were committed to cross-border operations to discover COSVN headquarters, theoretically somewhere just inside Cambodia between Mimot and Snoul. The operation, the largest combined allied task force used since 1967, did not achieve its aims of finding or destroying the elusive HQ. It did, however, succeed in uncovering vast caches of military supplies, which had been brought down the Ho Chi Minh Trail or trucked up with Cambodian government connivance from the south-coast port of Kampong Som, renamed Sihanoukville. The neutrality that Sihanouk had desperately tried to keep balanced had fallen apart with his ouster by the Lon Nol group; fortunately at that time he was on vacation in France. He went into exile in China, where the coalition opposition FANK front was formed, the first time that Sihanouk was obliged to sleep with the now emerging Khmer Rouge. The KR had been brutally repressed by Snooky in the early 1960s, but their power base was now being enhanced by the North Vietnamese, who needed to stabilise their cross-border areas and havens, having been so badly clobbered during 1968. Old nationalistic animosities had to be swallowed by both communist factions to present a united front, for it must be remembered that French colonisation had succeeded in endorsing the gradual southerly spread of Vietnamese domination, enabling French power to create Tonikin, Annam and Cochin as three separate principalities, all owing fealty to their European masters. Cambodia and Laos came as afterthoughts, buffer states between large chunks of British empire and the expansionist, neutral Thais. Saigon had once been a Cambodian fishing village.

The American raid into the Fishhook and the ARVN one into the Parrot's Beak began an invasion of Cambodia that escalated until forces were being pushed across the border almost continually. South Vietnamese strength in Cambodia was to be maintained in division strength until the onset of liberation four years later. Retaliation by the Khmers resulted in thousands of Viets being incarcerated and slaughtered, the Mekong carrying hundreds of bloated bodies. Traditionally, the Vietnamese had provided the bulk of Cambodia's artisans, fisherfolk and, more recently under the French, mechanics, shopkeepers and administrators. A whole infrastructure was being bloodily torn out.

An all-Vietnamese raid to the Chup plantation with a stop line on the Mekong at Kampong Cham was ostensibly to neutralise the base camp of the 5th and 9th NVA divisions and their K front; effecitvely it just obliged the enemy to move farther west into Cambodia, destablising whatever efforts were being made in Phnom Penh. This widening of the war throughout Indochina drew many newsmen to Phnom Penh, even though much of the action was actually closer to Saigon. The Lon Nolists were foolhardily running press trips up to their side of the Parrot's Beak to show how much control they could now exert. The media tended to get film and photos of retreating ill-led troops while catching more and more glimpses of NVA, VC and Khmer Rouge mixed units. It was now becoming a regular event that individuals as well as small groups of media personnel travelling together for safety were being taken prisoner and after days, sometimes weeks, released with a front-page story. The communists and resistance recognised the value of their side receiving coverage that had previously not been accessible to the Western media.

As the war spread, the unwritten rules changed and the attitude towards the media veered dangerously. Twelve went missing in a ten-day period, none to be seen alive again, though initially everyone at the Royale Hotel believed they would come back as before, Louise going so far as to refuse dinner invitations in case Dana would suddenly show. In actuality, they were being marched and trucked in stages across three eastern provinces; we can only hypothesise where exactly they were since they were then still in the hands of the Vietnamese, who have not been very forthcoming.

I can't help wondering what my buddies, traipsing along with their captors, thought about the massive allied onslaught that they could witness unfolding around them as they were moved to the rear. They were now on the receiving end of the awesome fire power unleashed on the sanctuaries. B-52 bombers were flying round-the-clock support missions for the offensive.

The secret bombing of Cambodia by the high-flying bombers had been going on for over two years, camouflaged under the code name Menu, the first missions aptly called Breakfast; by now the 7th Air Force was down to Dinner, which must have been a six-course spread, plus *digestif.* Flynn and Stone were tracking across the perimeter of the fire power. It appears from evidence we dug up that their hosts had no need to bind or handcuff them – the chances of escape were minimal and they probably imagined they were to be released shortly, anyway. Did they hear of the American rape of the rubber town of Snoul, seven kilometres from the border? This incident evoked the US campus demonstrations that culminated at Kent State, Ohio, when national guardsmen opened fire with rifles, killing four students. Did the new mood of protest and disillusionment seep down the propaganda chain in those pre-CNN days? Did Charlie listen to Armed Forces Radio or Voice of America? I still don't know.

We will probably never know the exact date that the Vietnamese decided to relinquish control of the lads to the Khmer resistance. In line with party directives from Hanoi, Caucasians and foreigners captured by Vietcong or Northern Army regulars were to be handed over to the local liberation forces, as part of the process or legitimising their new allies. There are unconfirmed reports that both Sean and Dana were in NVA field hospitals at different times: Sean with malaria, Dana with shrapnel wounds caught in transit. Those MASH units would have been in the vicinity of Chup, north of the Mekong.

An unreliable sighting had them in a POW camp as far north as Kratie, way upstream, in a compound adjacent to a newly liberated government regimental base on the edge of that town. Supposedly up to ten Caucasians were being held in relative comfort in a barracks building with separate washing facilities and an exercise court. Later we were to inspect this base, of which only a laterite runway remained, overgrown with grass and weeds, though the white centre-line dash markers were still traceable. At what was once the HQ building and entrance, two concrete building bases could just be discerned. Nothing else, and few people in the neighbourhood.

There would have been some kind of official miniceremony when they were transferred to Khmer Rouge jurisdiction. One theory has this taking place south of Kampong Cham on an island, but it was most likely much later, in the autumn of 1970. They were assigned to a stilted house a hundred metres up the street from the local security centre in Toul Ta Kao. For the first five months they were lodged with Lek Lang, who also remembers the gold chain and medallion. When they arrived, in the bean-picking season, they had a small bag between them. There was one camera left inside and 20,000 riels. It is unknown what happened to their other equipment, whether it was stolen, sold or just went missing in transit. To find any film they may have shot would be a coup. They had only one set of clothes apiece, black pyjamas. Sean wore Ho Chi Minh sandals made from rubber tyres, the thongs cut from inner tubes; Dana no longer had footwear, nor his spectacles. They were miserable, gaunt, thin and lightly bearded.

For the first month they were in the hamlet, the local populace was not allowed near them. When the quarantine was lifted, a number of village girls came to stare. This evidently upset Dana, who shouted, 'Why are you looking at me like that? I'm not a monkey in a cage!' Lek Lang's children would be despatched to the local market in Trapeang Sey by bicycle to purchase little treats like milk biscuits or coffee. She also did the cooking for the lads: charcoal-broiled river fish, pork stir-fry, and ganja for desert.

In fact, nearly everyone they met on their travels with the Khmer Rouge cites giving or selling them ganja sticks.

Without prompting, villagers who had been in contact remembered Flynn for the head he was. Dana was fonder of the local palm wine. Once they had settled in at the hamlet, they were free to wander down to the noodle-soup stand and the small general shop. The villagers, though bemused by their presence, had shown typically Cambodian hospitality, supplementing their meagre rations with gifts of fruit and smoke. When out and about among the locals they were outwardly smiling, apparently happy, integrated in the community to a certain degree, no longer treated as aliens. The extra security problem their existence created was resolved by expanding two or three houses of the compound where they were lodged. That would have made it about half a dozen stilted, rice-thatched and tiled dwellings scattered around a clearing on the side track between the Chup rubber plantation and the river crossings at Rokor Khnr and Phum Chhlong. With a 30-metre year-round well, the yard had, and still has, papaya, lemon and mango trees, bananas and coconut palms. Flowering bushes and herbs fill borders, pigs root in their basement pens next to where the buffalo are tethered. Everything is swept and tidy. The rice is stored on platforms out of reach of domestic animals and rodents in separate stilted huts. Behind the protective screen break of bamboo lie the paddy fields, banana groves, the semi-cleared land with fruit trees. When we visited they were trying a more profitable crop of coffee to replace the bananas, which had run their useful cycle. Transport is still by buffalo cart, most families usually owning a bicycle between them. Now the popular Thai-made Honda is spreading upcountry and during the dry season a rudimentary truck or bus service is operating. Locals, then as now, rarely venture too far away; Phnom Penh, though still another world, is now much more of a known entity, its vision now disseminated by increasingly numerous television sets, dependent on small portable generators.

The 1971 January–February ARVN attempt to neutralise

the NVA base camp in the Chup rubber plantation was probably doomed to failure from the start. The South Vietnamese were now almost self-reliant militarily, and less than a couple of US divisions of men were left in country. A lot of air support, fixed-wing, transport and fighter-bomber, and the helicopter units, had been pulled out. The retreat out of Indochina was at full flood. Training cadres, technical and teaching personnel were left, many military personnel in civilian guise. ARVN units were still resting from the drubbing they had received during the incursion into the southern Laotian panhandle. Attempting to cut the Ho Chi Minh Trail and its crossroads at Tchepone, 12,000 of the best newly equipped troops had been thrown across the border, ineptly, into the jaws of a well-prepared NVA trap. Anti-aircraft fire on home territory was radar-controlled, simply plucking over 100 American-crewed choppers out of the midair. Half a million artillery rounds would be fired by some of the last batteries left in country; the logistics had been American-coordinated. Sixty per cent of the expedition never got home again, morale plummeted and generals were fired and shuffled around. The effort towards Chup would be the last ARVN thrust. Unfortunately, slap in the middle of the area where our friends were lodged was the old rubber-plantation airstrip. It would become the forward operations base for the ARVN thrust. Long-range 175-mm artillery would range and armour would roam from this position. The evacuees would return to their home village to find it nearly obliterated.

ARVN intelligence and operation planning had never been at all watertight, the whole Southern regime had been infiltrated right up to the president's latrine. The whole of Cambodia knew through the grapevine what was coming. It is not easy to camouflage what is happening when it involves armoured vehicles and their logistic train, and the overflights alone would have given the show away. The plans could have been published in the *Saigon Daily News* for disinformation.

So the liberation forces had ample time to pull back out of the immediate impact zone.

Towards the end of January, preparations to leave were made. Madame El Am Noas, then with the militia, was assigned as the lads' security. She first met them on the road outside Toul Ta Kao, later giving them some tomatoes, which they ate messily. During the ensuing siesta, they had awoken her and pointed up through the rubber trees to where a passing plane was hit by anti-aircraft fire, crashing nearby. Later that day they all got lost in the forest, ending up in the village of Kapop instead of getting to the staging post at Ramving. Much later that night, they had arrived at their destination on the banks of the Mekong at Rokor Khnor.

Flynn and Stone were lodged immediately in the monastery. The wat in Rokor Khnor dates from Angkorian time: the foundation stones of the wooden temple, itself 250 years old, go back a millennium, while next door a modern steep-eaved red-tiled wat was, when we visited, just completing its restoration back to a functioning teaching monastery with a complement of *bikkhus*. Its easy access from the river made it a target for Pol Potists desecrating buildings during the later years as the eastern-zone Khmer Rouge cadres were purged for their gradual coalition with the Vietnamese.

The captives' arrival in Rokor Khnor had initially terrified the populace, who, as El Am Noas tells it, shouted,

> 'Let's run! The Americans are here!' They were later told that these Americans did not come to kill them, they were journalists. The villagers then asked, 'Was it true that Americans knew how to eat sweet potatoes?' I said I did not know, I would have to ask them first. When I asked them, they said, Yes, they knew how to eat sweet potatoes. So we brought them some sweet potatoes. After one or two bites they stopped eating. Later I was asked to go away, not to talk to them. So I went to stay in a house at the back.

She had gotten to be real buddies with the pair during her escort duties, but especially with Flynn, bantering with him on the trail.

> I slapped the tall one! You, American, are you going to give me the gold chain? He said no. He said it was his souvenir. He said if I were his wife he would give it to me. 'As you are not my wife, I won't give it to you,' he said. I said, 'You are much too big, I wouldn't have you as a husband!' We then measured ourselves. I only reached his shoulder. Then I joked with him, saying, 'I won't marry you!' He then laughed and said, 'If you don't marry me, I won't give you the gold chain!'
>
> [Another time] I said to the tall one, 'You don't help me carry the gun. Is it because you don't like me?' Then he took it. After we had walked for about 100 metres, he gave the gun back to me. It was at night. He said, 'Lady, please take the gun back.' I said, 'Please help me carry it.' He said no and threw the gun on the ground. When I saw it I laughed and said, 'You don't pity me. I am a woman; I'm very exhausted. You are so strong. You can carry three guns if you want to.' He said he was also very tired. I took the gun and we continued to walk together. They wore hats. When we stopped to have a rest, they took their hats off and sat on them, just like this man here. They looked hopeless. He, the tall one, told me he would not be able to do what I was doing. He said, 'You are engaged in a revolutionary struggle, yet some drive cars and you walk with heavy guns. Throw it away.' I said, 'No, I'm afraid of Anka. I will not throw it away.' Then we kept walking. I asked the tall one whether he had been to the Mekong River. He said yes. I asked him why. He said he was a journalist. I asked him how he got there. He said he got there in a helicopter. Then he pointed at the direction where the Mekong River was.

The ARVN–Lon Nol operation had petered out rapidly. It never really got into top gear, for the commander, General Don Cao Tri (young, inspired and well respected by his officers and men), was killed in a helicopter crash. With him in the chopper had been senior members of his staff and a veteran French correspondent, *Newsweek* bureau chief François Sully. François's legend had started back in the postwar colonial days; he had seen Dien Bien Phu, Diem and the arrival of the Americans; only to perish in an accident due to mechanical failure (most helicopter losses were so incurred). ARVN maintenance schedules, part of the Vietnamese programme drive, had not achieved the necessary levels. The method of conducting warfare, American-taught, was highly reliant on armoured vehicles and air mobility, effective only when constantly looked after.

Although our lads were away up on the Mekong in a secure zone, they were still receiving the periodic attentions of the VNAF (Vietnamese Air Force) and the Cambodian Luftwaffe. Many of the houses in the villages along the Mekong banks had to be rebuilt after this period: the air force's criteria for success were as ever measured in structures destroyed and guesstimated enemy body count from air strikes. The original dwellings where Dana and Sean stayed are long destroyed and replaced.

The villages of Rokor Khnor, Peus, Kroch Chhmar and Chkor Amlou were all visited, their spiritual scent adhering to the fabric of the wats they lodged in. The feeling is real but indescribable. The villagers who fed them, got them ganja, tried to find big enough new footwear, those upon whom they were billeted all had fond, eccentric memories relived in front of the TV camera.

The captives' departure from the various places always seemed to occur at night, to avoid the patterned aerial reconnaissance while maintaining Anka's mysterious, threatening aura.

They would have been up in the neck of the woods at

the height of the dry season. It is a hot and dusty 35–40°C, so the whole day is punctuated by the need to refuel; the access to water is a necessity and the Khmer are habitually drawn to wash in ponds or rivers at the first opportunity. The Mekong recedes, creating long, cultivable islands with sizeable communities. The sandy banks become cliffs and mud flats. Birds and people descend to happily fish.

A Cambodian expression says, 'Where there is water, there is fish; where there are women, there is money.' In the shallows it is easy catching, though a long way to transport watering cans for the vegetable plots which creep closer to the water's edge, terraced on the steep stretches. Sweet corn, pumpkins, cabbage, sweet potatoes, even sugar cane zoom up in the enriched river loam. There are fewer mosquitoes and the temperature at night never gets too cool. A hammock suffices for the normal rest period as well as the siesta, which becomes a necessity the longer you are here. Under every stilted house are hooks to sling your hammock as well as king-sized split bamboo beds for communal gathering, daydreaming and dozing. It is also the easy time of year to travel the numerous small rivers fordable; the ground not too soft, not too hard, an abundance of food, fruit and coconuts for free.

In a time of war there would still have been food, but less of it and less variety. Each village tends to overdose on whatever crop is ripened, a diet of manioc and sweet corn or yams and little else can be boring and undernourishing. Sean and Dana were reportedly consistently very thin, underfed, Dana more haunted-looking, a bit helpless without his thick spectacles. More and more, I suspect, they were blending in with their surroundings, hardly remarked upon. A curiosity, yes – but not threatening, weakened as they were with thin diet and malaria, hardly inclined to try to escape in a countryside where foreigners stick out a mile. I wonder whether they were actually making any pictures with their remaining camera – had the Khmer Rouge or the VC swung around and let them document their captivity? Had their captors decreed that an artistic impression be made an exception? We do know that their passports had been kept by their subsequent detaining bodies, but the documents have never surfaced.

The ARVN mini-invasion retreated back towards the border, the southern republic's army now seriously off balance with the losses from Lam Son 719, the incursion into Laos which had totally soured. From now on it would be an armed force on the defensive. The territory the government could claim under its control was now at its most extensive, but largely through the activities of counter-terror teams, the CORDS teams, the successors to the Phoenix programme doing evil in Vietcong turf. The figures were a corrupt, hollow victory, for the terrified population could only face ripoff or death. Civilian casualties rocketed at this time.

Our lads began the hike back to their adopted home town north of the now abandoned Ta Pao forward operating base. Before and during their retreat, the invading forces had stripped bare the countryside, plundered anything of value in the houses and workshops, pilfered bicycles, sewing machines. All rice stocks as well as the seed rice had been shipped out east. What could not be moved was levelled, burned, dumped and spoiled. The population was on starvation rations, and our lads, as punishment for what the local commander saw as justice for most recent American crimes, were put on half rations, denied fish or meat, subsisting on rice, fish sauce and some fruit.

Ta Sabun cropped up in the declassified CIA documents, his name spelled in various ways but obviously the same person. We find Ta Sa Bon, Tea Sabun, Ja Sam Bon and old Saboan. In the terrain that the lads travelled and lodged in, his name was familiar. He had been Anka's main man, the local commander. Initially he must have taken to the poor foreigners, for on his periodic visits to the local security centre, he would bring them cigarettes and fruit.

A revolutionary, he claims, from 1947, though intelligence traces him to being a Khmer Rouge cadre in 1968 who had graduated to district chief by 1970. Tabaung Khmun district was known as Region 21. He had been briefly promoted to member of the party's central committee, rebelled against Pol Pot and, unlike his boss, Uk Saren, who met his fate in the Toul Sleng interrogation centre, followed by execution at Cheung Ek, had gone on to be a minister of social action in the Heng Samrin government after the Vietnamese liberation of 1979. Uk Saren's confessions are neatly preserved in the library at Toul Sleng, macabre lies to disarm the interrogators, though the torture continued ever after confession had commenced. The only release had been death or execution. Ta Sabun either made the decision to terminate someone in his control or transmitted the order from his commander to do so.

Long Sokha Bouny, a plump 34-year-old lady now working for an aid organisation in Phnom Penh as liaison to the government, had survived through being educated, one of a few in the communist camp, made up mostly of disoriented and deluded peasants. She had been a happy lycée student in Suong until the Lon Nol coup had disrupted education nationwide and student demonstrations were savagely repressed. She had taken off for the liberated zone 20 kilometres away. A few older fellow students went along, too. They were allowed to talk to the foreigners in their newly acquired English and French, and she recognised that Sean also spoke Spanish. She went on, 'The tall fellow used to chat with us. He was very fond of me. Sometimes he would ask me to buy this or that for him. He told me that his family was in the movie business. That he was very happy in his country. He said that if he survived, he would not forget our care and kindness.'

Although she was bedecked in naff gold jewellery, overdressed, chubby, with heavily lipsticked face, it was still possible to see in her the giggling teenager, not unattractive, flirting with Flynn, or going off to compare notes with her older buddies assigned to the front's training unit, where their high-school education qualified them for training as medics. She recounted her brief exposures to the prisoners with a soft smile, a fondness for Flynn apparent in her visage; poor Dana leaving hardly any impression or only that of a sad man, barely participating in conversations, blinking continually. On finishing the interview, for which she had originally asked $500, she settled for $200 because, she said, 'I can't remember the short one. He didn't stick in my mind. I only remember the tall one.'

Madame Bouny had put herself on the line for her two bills, pointing a heavy finger at Ta Sabun, He did not want to go on record about his own past, denying what he had already admitted to a few weeks earlier when asked questions. When bluntly asked on film about missing Americans, this shifty, retired government functionary glared balefully into the camera, his eyes trying to avoid the lens's focus. He could not avoid the probe of Mike Blakely's interrogative Aarton camera. His evasions were tantamount to guilt: too many people we had talked to had his name as the main man and he admitted his promotions through military postings to Tabaung Khmun district chairman. Maybe some day he will reveal all. In today's Cambodia the future is uncertain; any official with even the slimmest governmental connections, especially with a history stretching to the 1960s, is naturally guarded, considering that UNTAC, the UN transitional government body, was then talking about conducting war-crimes trials. Many outside Cambodia would like to see Pol Pot and his lieutenants brought to justice and executed. The Khmer themselves are doing their utmost to forget the past and forgive those living in their midst who they know were once evil. There is basic return to Buddhist principles of karmic law, which they believe will balance and redress the past horrors.

Back in the village of Bei Met, the ARVN safely back

across its borders, life for the lads did not improve. They had been model prisoners, causing minimal inconvenience to their hosts. Now, at Dana's suggestion, they started to remonstrate for their repatriation, their release. The question had arisen before and been sidelined. Now they became more insistent, writing to the district, province and front chiefs, pleading for a review of their situation. By now, everyone knew them to be journalists and only sympathetic to the cause and Cambodia. They went on a hunger strike. That was Dana's idea. They moved no more than 50 metres to the well, listlessly staying in the house or their hammocks, keeping to themselves, despondent, weakened. Neither of them even smoked.

Bin Nhiv, who owned the house where they lodged, tried to persuade them to eat something; he thought it was weird that they were refusing, and proffered both cigarettes and ganja. Madame Bouny filed another repatriation request, and probably Ta Sabun turned up again with the orders. Bin Nihv was not around at that time, so he was surprised when he returned to find the lads no longer about. His wife said they had been led away, arms tied behind their backs, after ten days of the hunger strike. He had simply thought, 'It's finished', and, being terrified of Anka, had not dared ask further in the village. The tall one, who had walked with his arm around Bin Nhiv and called him 'elder brother', had passed into realms better left uninvestigated.

That last walk was not so far; and it must have been familiar. Probably they knew, or sensed, what was coming. An awful doomed resignation, a cloud that had been pushed away on previous occasions, would this time not disappear. This was to be the end. The spookiest, the most frightening, anticipating moments of any life. The last guaranteed time left as a breathing witness to the planet. The fear of seeing no more. The sheer terror of the unknown. No more aspirations, no more hopes. Dana trying to grasp that there would be no more seeing Smise; Sean's ebullience finally punctured. We can only pray that the hunger strike had made them so spaced out that the last walk, the last moments together, were being seen rosily in a cloud of near ecstasy that abstinence can induce.

Sitting in the now rebuilt house, talking with Bin Nhiv, I knew that I too had to make that walk from the cool interior with its slatted bamboo floor out along the hard, dusty path, now winding between coffee bushes planted the previous year, to a point triangulated by two mango trees. The time warp created by that walk in the late-morning heat transposed two decades. I feared what I was going to feel, whether or not we would unearth more traces of their fate. For I already knew the story and knew roughly what to expect. Yet we never know how our emotions, our spiritual tunings, our vibrations to the supernatural, will actually manifest themselves. We are prepared, yet can never be totally prepared, for the weird will focus in the here and now, the conscious. The very thought made me sweat with palpable expectation.

Our Khmer lads, our bodyguard of militia, could easily have been the security detail doubling then as the execution squad. They wore the bits and pieces of military uniform – communist mustard-green tunic, *kramas*, sundry headgear – and East-bloc melange of weaponry and webbing that have been Cambodian fighter fashion for over thirty years. Our lot packed a light machine gun, the RPD, a rocket-propelled grenade launcher with one round, an anti-personal one, looking like a toffee apple stuck in its spout; four or five lads had AK-47s, the magazines worn in traditional flat harness, tabard-style on the chest. A few additional heavies from the local army post in Suong, whom we had picked up in the drop-side blue Zil truck, had fanned out before we trooped the last walk.

Everyone was a little nervous, mostly because we were once again going to be disturbing spirits, but also because this was the fourth visit that parts of our team had made to the neighbourhood. The local banditry, the die-hard Rouges, would now have been fully alerted to what was going on. So far no foreigners, no aid teams had been attacked or held up, not even those doing business with the Chup rubber. But in Cambodia you still get the feeling you could be the first. Kong Nhar, the old man who had initially 'robbed' the grove, walked slightly ahead, dubiously in control. Even Shep was hanging back, uncertain what new fate would appear. It took the old man some time to decide where exactly to once again start digging, for, as he explained, 'People digged the place once more later. It's now a mess. There is nothing left. They have already digged this place twice.'

He had started his probing with a stick and dug all over for a period of months until he had unearthed a bone.

Some hoes were passed up, big, stout-handled tools, with blades six inches across, eight deep, weighty enough to drive into paddy slush or hard dirt. Shovel, mattock and spade in one, a handy, balanced three-kilo instrument of construction. Or destruction: for in order to save ammunition, a blow to the nape of the neck from a swung hoe was the favoured method of extinguishing life in the Khmer Rouge's killing fields. Sometimes, you hear, the executioners felt twisted and did not deliver the coup cleanly, aiming to injure and pain. Laughing and sadistic. I pray not.

We met no one who had been witness to the act; but then a lot of eastern-zone cadre and fighters had been killed in the last purges after Anka, ensconced in Phnom Penh, finally got word of the zone's preparations for full-scale insurrection.

I felt that the dig should be preceded by paying homage to the disturbed spirits that I sensed must be still here. A candle and three sticks of incense were lit with difficulty. The slight breeze gutted the small flicker we induced with a Bic lighter; the incense took forever to smoulder. Madame Chanda had thoughtfully brought along a tiny fresh wild-flower nosegay, a bright-red hibiscus dominating the spray. She laid it next to the candle, which had given up the unequal struggle to stay alight.

Even before the first hoe blow to the hard ground, I knew that we were not ordained to find more remains, nothing as concrete, as tangible, as a skull. The digging ended after an hour, the trench line beginning to remind me of an aerial photo of Flanders during 1914–18. We asked them to go deeper, but it soon became obvious that anything more than a shallow grave would have required explosives or something mechanical.

It was easy to walk away from the dig. The snapshot an easy frame to remember. A hopeless moment. Hard to believe that we had just realised what had been a twenty-year dream – or had it been resolved? It felt so, but it was hard to step back emotionally. The rest of the day, talking to rubber officials in Suong, and the last bump back to Kampong Cham passed ethereally.

Some time not so long after the murder, Bin Nhiv's wife had become pregnant. Bin Nhiv told us, 'She had a dream that the tall one gave her the gold chain. They both came back to see her and the tall one gave her his gold chain. My wife said she did not want to accept it. She said that as they had already died, she did not want his gold chain. The tall one said, "Take half of it", and gave her half the gold chain.' Later, she lost the piece, but both he and she agreed it was because she was pregnant. Had they really had the chain, or part of it?

> Later in the pregnancy, about the sixth month, she had another dream that the small one came to ask whether he could come stay with her. She said, 'How could you stay? I haven't given birth to my first baby yet.' The baby who was born did not speak any Khmer until he reached the age of six. When he was a baby he did not know how to speak. He only made noises like 'Im, oah, ih, ouh'. He

couldn't speak Khmer. My father was worried and asked people whether the child was going to be mute. When he was six years old he began to speak. I was told that when he wanted to play with other kids at a banana grove, they said no. They were afraid of the American ghosts. So he went there alone and said, 'Ih, ouh, in, ouh,' and made gestures.

Here he imitated someone with arms tied, kneeling for execution and having his necklace cut off. He continued, 'An old lady saw this. She understood and she cried. That's why I feel pity for him. Eventually he began to pick up Khmer but could reveal no more. He could tell no one anything else.'

Bin Nhiv says the boy forgot. Though this was after he had been heavily dosed with boiled eggs. It is a Khmer belief that the consumption of eggs will evoke forgetfulness and Bin Nhiv was frightened that should the boy speak English Anka would arrest them.

Both of the sons are still alive, the younger, eighteen years old, hovering in the background during the interview. The wife and the older egg eating boy had gone downcountry shopping. The boy was certainly tall for a Khmer, the other allegedly quite short. I couldn't believe that these poor farmers were lying, there was no way they could have invented any of the story. Sheppard and Ham were only the second lot of white men they had ever encountered. The tale was nothing but plausible. They had all been only too happy to reminisce with us. They had too many of their own near and dear still unresolved missing, so our quest was totally understandable.

At our interpreter's suggestion, each person was given a bundle of riels equivalent to $5 at the end of the interviews. No one saw another getting the same. Convincingly, those versions of the same story all differ in small detail, many details blurring and erasing with the passage of time. The discrepancies are reassuring in their naivety. Maybe it is just that we need to believe in resolutions so badly, maybe the Cambodians have it easier, their faith allowing them to believe in reincarnation.

The next bit of the journey, the spiritual-path fantasy, came as a surprise. You know that spring skies will lift the heart, but it is impossible to predict when their rays will start once more to infiltrate the becalmed mind.

Hand-luggage Ham had casually mentioned, before he left to organise the next stop in Hanoi, that the Cambodians were probably going to come up with a token of their thanks. To seal the solidarity of the memorial that we were trying to create in the DMZ, they believed that it required an auspicious act to consecrate it. Who gave the fraternal nod to the concept I still know not, and there must have been some sort of liaison between parties, ministries, governments; some knowledge of the minor peculiar event. Relations with Vietnam were at the time neither hot nor cold; smuggling to Vietnam from virtually wide-open Cambodia was almost unchecked. Customs duty was imposed only when someone was overtly flagrant and the right officials had been left ungreased. The border was porous, not just to consumer goods destined for markets right up to Hanoi and beyond, even through to China, but to a systematic semi-clandestine pilferage of the timber of Cambodia's jungled eastern mountains. Huge log convoys highball down the newly hardtopped Routes 13 and 14. Along these roads ammo and supplies had been carried up to the cross-border offensive; now the same trucks, belching fumes, haul lumber out along the old invasion routes. The Viets are running logs as fast as possible until the UNTAC border controls finally slam down. The trucks still roll business bigger than officialdom.

On a daily level it is easy to watch; take the Phnom Penh-Ho Chi Minh two-dollar express bus ride. You start off with a roof rack full of, say, 35 Honda scooters; they all leave the bus a couple of kilometres short of the border and reappear on the other side. The back end of the former Osaka municipal bus fleet has been stacked with Thai cement sacks. A good half, say sixty, of the passengers get off before the frontier at Moc Bai and climb back on out of sight, just down the road from the Viet customs post, the Han Quan. There is now emerging a flow of stuff out of Vietnam where the dong is stabilising, the exchange rate staying close to 10,500 to the dollar, fluctuations within a couple of hundred either way. Good-quality silk and cotton clothing is fast becoming a major export earner; what had once ended up in the E-bloc countries as exchange for weaponry is now enabling market stalls to be filled. Vietnam is also serving as a pipeline for smuggled goods to China. As relations warm, the northern border opens, and Chinese products arrive in Phnom Penh overland rather than as they had before. A lot falls off the back of the lorry.

We backed our Phnom Penh tourism Hiace van up to the red and white pole on the Cambodian side; my old main man, Tien, had got the Saigon Tourist (Du Lich) backed up on the other; and we proceeded to shift nigh on thirty pieces of luggage. This included the minimum of fifteen silver boxes that every film/TV crew seems to have with them. The last item passed across the backed-up vans, the astonished customs police and immigration having virtually waived formalities, was the basket containing the tree. It had been beribboned and decorated with a saffron-orange cellophane frill, the sort of Woolworth's adornment you would expect to find around a birthday cake. The white silk *krama*, the one bought especially for the morning's ceremony, had been draped over the handle hoop to keep some of the scorching mid-morning dry-season sun from inflicting more burn on the sapling bo tree. It had only five delicate pale-green leaves to start with, a very fragile plant to be out of the nursery solo, in a glazed brown pot. Well rooted, it was already a good year on from its original grafting and setting.

This baby had been originally taken from the bo growing on top of the Phnom, the hill that is the focal point of the Penh. The mound is surmounted by a 500-year-old wat with the slopes clad in flowering shrubs and majestic forest trees.

The sacred status of the bo tree is universal in the East. In northern India and Nepal, whole deforested slopes will have but one or two trees left standing, lone banyans or bos. The seed of the *bodhi* must first passs through a crow before it is ripe for germination. (In Sri Lanka, a devout Buddhist land, it is against the law to keep a crow, for the blighters are easy to train to steal anything shiny and it is illegal to kill them, pests though they are.) It is a benevolent, shady tree, much given to harbouring friendly spirits. Habitually bo trees are decorated by passing folk, offerings placed at their bases. They are often the only trees to grace the central space of a temple's grounds. In theory, when a limb of the tree breaks off, it is supposed to be separately cremated to placate the latent spiritry.

The Cambodians had decided among themselves that as part of the resolution of our MIA case and as a fraternal gesture towards their not so neighbourly neighbours the Vietnamese, the tree would be a perfect symbol. It was designated the centrepiece of the nascent memorial. The bo could at least start to attract a few benign spirits to hallow the spot which had been notionally proposed on the Ben Hai River, along the 17th parallel. The tree would grace a garden wherein, we hoped to build a stupa or similar shrine to the approximately 300 media personnel of all nations killed or missing between 1945 and 1975 in Indochina. Their names could be inscribed around its base chronologically, much like the names engraved on the Vietnam Wall in Washington, DC.

The idea for the location had come from Don Wise, a gentleman of the press who had devoted most of his life to the Orient since World War II when he was a POW on the Burma railway. Later he had roved for the *Daily Mirror* before becoming a senior editor at the *Far East Economic Review* in Hong Kong. Donald had been spiritual father to three generations of reporters on the Indochina scene.

The whole number with the tree was taken with total seriousness by the Cambodians; two days before the ceremony, back in Phnom Penh, Dara, our driver and bodyguard, and Chea, another interpreter, had insisted my fortune be told before Chanda would take me off to be introduced to the senior abbot at the temple who would supervise the presentation of the bo. We drove out almost to the edge of the Viet town, to a temple near the southern bus depot. Against a backdrop of shanties and other low buildings, the temple was barely discernible save the walls, which were freshly stuccoed; the gate was properly hung and painted, the ground out front swept and tidy. Incongruously, Dara beeped his horn to tell an ancient custodian, who shuffled out doubled over, to undo the gates and allow us to park inside the neat walled courtyard. From the hieroglyphic motifs on the gates and the heavy wooden doors, I presumed the place was of Chinese origin. A place of ancestral spirits, Confucian and Tao. A shrine benefiting from donations from the trading community, both Viet and Chinese. A shrine whose ambience was said to impart auspicious forecasts in a country where battles are not fought nor matters of state conducted unless the omens are correct; soothsayers run the course of public and private life.

Inside, the pillared entrance hall gave on to a long space leading to the altar table. Red-lacquered pillars ran either side of the meeting space, going up to the tiled roof. Crenellated windows allowed in a slight breeze. It was baking hot outside, somewhat cooler here, barefooted on the tiled and concrete floor. Rice-straw mats had been spread in front of an enormous low mahogany table serving as a podium for the gods, buddhas, urns and vases – the spiritual centre of the establishment.

Divination here would be conducted with wooden sticks somewhat slenderer than chopsticks. I had purchased a packet of incense, which I lit and offered to the presiding three deities with three bows before placing joss sticks in the urns in front of the effigies. It was said that during the Pol Pot years the statues had been taken away by the temple custodians and buried and hidden. The three ancients shuffling around must have had quite horrific tales to tell of their own survival, but then in Cambodia, anyone born before 1975 had to go through their individual hell. These custodians were all skin and bone topped by broad wrinkled smiles, the idea of a foreigner possibly believing in their line enhancing their rising mirth. One asked me to choose a colour – red, yellow or green. I went for the green, whereupon a lacquered vase full of green-topped sticks was handed me. This was to be shaken between the hands in a position of prayer while concentrating on the Buddha on the shrine, so that three sticks would fly out of the pot. Should the lot come out, the go was null and void. It sounds easier than it is, for the pot contains between twenty and thirty sticks and they wait to come out en masse or not at all.

All activity stopped in the temple as I shook the pot. It was like being at a spiritual coconut shy in a fairground. There was a rush to pick up my artfully jettisoned trio. A ripple of approval gushed from Chea, who showed the sticks to one of the ancients. There was almost applause. I had hit number 12, considered to be the definitive number for someone of my birth date and on this particular day. Cambodians also feel that the number twelve is the goods, simply pure good rites and good luck.

This was divined by one of the ancients, who turned out to be the keeper of the texts. On a side table lay a pile of hand-bound books of sutras, which could have been Sri Lankan or Tibetan. These contained the interpretations of the various numerical read-outs of the sticks shaken. The answers were gauged by cross-indexing in the computation of the *I Ching*, giving two sets of hexagrams, and hence the answers were firstly generalised, secondly specific. Chea interpreted, for once hardly hesitating or muddling words, a graveness to his softly spoken translations. We wrote down at the time:

Number 12

Passing to and fro without harm.
The talent of the poor will promote to wealth.
Better-quality clothing.
People who pick this number will fulfil their wishes.

This was the first, generalised message; the details emerged with a little more translatory problems:

Tests will be passed with facility.
Desires will be realised.
The court will decide in your favour.
Six people will overcome their maladies.
Will only maximise 90 per cent of the total income.

Two slips of paper were handed to Chea for translating. The Khmer predictions were neatly written on the back of a slip of paper printed with a Day-Glo buddha in the teaching position. The Chinese one was on a rice-paper slip, bookmark size, printed with five columns of hieroglyphics. The ancient summed all this up merrily, albeit toothlessly, accepting two Marlboros, and wished us '*bon voyage*'. Chea, who had been in Vietnam for schooling, added that they all liked to use the expression *Vao thien*, 'Be mindful', but as a Vietnamese word it was said in an undertone.

The decision to go to the temple had been on the spur of the moment, and the emotion of it had washed over and by before I could snap a frame. To be dunked deep in Cambodian mystique was unsettling but simultaneously calming. I am not overly superstitious; I have had my fortune read perhaps five or six times, once a decade in totally diverse places, East and West. It is hard to recall whether any of the forecasts have actually panned out as predicted. Normally, then, I would not require a reading before a venture, but now the visit had somehow seemed a necessity before the next cross-border step with the Bo. Great care had to be taken threading this spiritual needle.

The venerable patriarch Gohzananda was out behind the wat squatting on the wall of what would have passed for an octagonal garden house in the UK. He was overseeing a handful of *bikkhus* engaged in the unlikely pursuit of carpentry. Normally monks do not work or manufacture, it is against the ethics of retreat; but in Cambodia it's everybody to the oars. Special dispensation has been given for the order to accept money during *bindabat* – the morning food alms gathering – as there is still a need to rebuild the desecrated and destroyed wats. In between small asides to his acolytes, he gradually related the story of his survival. A small slight man with expressive hands and long nimble fingers, he looked twenty years older than he was. Originally from the west of the country, near the second city of Battanbang, he was already a senior monk when Pol Pot liberated the land. Forced into a gulag, he and two fellow *bikkus* had been dumped in a pit to break their morale to force a ridiculous confession. The camp commander had relented, or he had spotted an inextinguishable light in the *sree* ('honourable'), and put him to work as a buffalo boy, the Khmer Rouge believing it would be demeaning for a ranking prelate to have to live with animals. With a sparkling gleam in his eye he went on to describe how happy he was talking to the cows, guarding the calves, cajoling the bulls, providing milk for the few surviving children and for the sick and weak. The horror and terror he sort of whisked aside with an elegant hand. His is a politically loaded dharma.

We climbed up three flights of tiled concrete steps to the top shrine room. The shutters on the tall windows were open only at one end of the chamber, bathing the images in a bright white light, the rest of them were closed, keeping a coolness to the whole. The doors at the east end, overlooking the Ton le Sap River, stood open. They still had not been able to replace their main Buddha statue, so the altar displayed the head salvaged from the images trashed by Anka. The flowers and lotus blossoms were morning fresh. A couple of monks with whisk brooms discreetly withdrew, leaving four of us to chat. The chamber would host the ceremony at first light two days later. That would be on our last sunrise in Cambodia.

Before the crew, cameraman and sound engineer had arrived in Ho Chi Minh to begin the actual shoot, Chea and Brian, our researcher and bagman, had gone up to the point of capture in Svay Rieng province and then to Prey Veng, where the lads had later been spotted, to patch the front end of the story together. They, too, had hit the motherlode of luck. Six and a half klicks east of Chi Phou, within metres of the point of capture, they came upon two middle-aged peasant farmers, the neighbours Ouk Sin and Madame Kao Saphan, who had witnessed the Vietcong North Vietnamese patrol stop and arrest our boys. They had not, however, seen the prior ambushing of the Mercedes from which Claude Arpin and the Japanese correspondent were led away. They were never seen again, no more than a rumour of their fate. Claude's brother René had talked to a clairvoyant who had seen Claude cross-border in Chau Due province, one-armed, married to a local girl and rice farming! No one we found had seen the joint patrol stop the vehicle and shoot its tyres out.

Back in 1970, the small cluster of housing at the junction of two tracks had been occupied by North Vietnamese Vietcong. Ba Vet, just up the street, had not yet been attacked by the Phnom Penh forces. Three Vietcong soldiers had been lounging behind their rice-sack barricade when the Merc turned up between eleven and eleven thirty. The white man, the Japanese and three Khmers had been led away; Flynn and Stone had biked up to snap a couple of long-lens frames from 200 metres away and gone back west. Half an hour later they had reappeared and ridden up to the checkpoint and the dead Mercedes.

They had come from the little market town of Chi Phou, or Cipou, where Western press members had holed up for a cold one, having ditched their Cambodian government escorts in Svay Rieng, 20 kilometres back towards Phnom Penh. Everyone was up in the eastern neck to witness the government's attempts to displace the Vietcong and their FANK clients. Like most Lon Nol PR efforts, it was a shambles; anyway, the area is only a couple of hours' drive from the capital, provided the ferries across the Mekong at Neak Long are running. So the Information Ministry special had long been abandoned. A group of French journalists overheard the lads arguing at a nearby table in the town's café, which commanded a good view of Route One heading east and west, where government troops were streaming by, retreating towards Neak Long. From what the ORTF, the French TV crew, reported, Flynn and Stone were in heated discussion about whether to head back up towards the Vietnamese border and the shot-up Mercedes. The situation was decidedly dicy, security nil. I can see Sean insisting, 'What an opportunity, man! I mean, we can get some great shots from their POV. Chance we've been waiting for, think of the film CBS will run, Dana. Man, c'mon, let's do it. Let's get the fuck out of here and all these boys and competition. Let's show 'em where the picture is really at.' Dana reluctant, thinking of Smise back at the Royale, New York needing film, good stuff already in the can.

The café is no longer standing; the whole market area and the shops were razed during 1975–79, when trade was deemed unnecessary and anything this close to Vietnam considered evil by association. Rebuilt shanties and stalls now jostle for space amid the shrapnel-torn columns and bits of wall left from then. A small flourishing market, full of goods from Thailand, Vietnam and China, caters to the continual flow of traffic between Saigon and Phnom Penh. The Khmer Rouge have not got much support in the area. There is security; Svay Rieng is booming and building.

After about half an hour in the café, to make his point, Flynn had thrown the bike keys out of the window. They had trooped out, cranked up and headed east. The film purportedly shot by the French cameraman of their departure has long disappeared from the archives in Paris. As the two in floppy bush hats aboard red Honda 90s burned up the two-lane blacktop towards their demise, Flynn had called out something to do with Pathet Lao, the communist resistance force in Laos. This could have been a deliberate red herring to the ORTF crew, who were not regular residents.

The VC unit probably thought they had a fat catch; two free bikes and a lot of neat black camera gear. They succumbed to the temptation, though they had explicit orders to handle all journalists correctly; the party knew the value of the press and the persuasive power of propaganda. Of the fifty-eight Western members of the press killed during the US involvement with the war, the 10,000-day war, only six had been hit by bullets. Four of those who had been in an ambush in Cholon during Mini-Tet in 1968, a Mini-Moke-full taking the wrong turn at the height of confused and heavy fighting. Across the border in Cambodia, though the Viets kept to their disciplines, the Khmer tended to go feral.

Ouk Sin and Kao Saphan had secretly watched the VC flag down the lads. They were told to dismount and remove their shoes; hats and shades were also taken. They then faced an agonising couple of hundred metres along tarmac bubbling in the midday heat before taking off down a sandy cart track, where denser bamboo clumps offered cover. The arresting unit led the boys off northwards towards wat Thlok, shadowed by an adventurous Ouk Sin. Here the Vietnamese made him go back home. Somewhere along the four-kilometre track a greedy local headman had liberated Flynn's Rolex. The three VC/NVA platoons operating in the district, recon units from the Tay Ninh front, used the pagoda as a forward operating base, possibly holding their headquarters and communications. The wat, once prominent, with a steep tiled roof, when we saw it was a mere raised base indicating its former size. The surviving buddha statues were cushioned in a temporary bamboo meeting house while the new wat was being built. The landscape is as flat as paddies can be, not a *phnom* in sight, the horizon broken only by tall clumps of giant bamboo and sugar palms. The nearest high spot is Nai Ba Den, Black Window Mountain, 40 kilometres north. It guards, legend has it, Tay Ninh city, home to the Cao Dai sect with its own pope and Holy See.

Another man, Sann Thank, had squatted in the shadows at the edge of the Vietcong compound, witnessing their first interrogation. He claims there were hundreds sitting about looking on. He could only understand the questions asked in Vietnamese; their answers were unintelligible, but a VC soldier next to him translated one as 'At a time like this, they say they are just having a walkabout', or 'they go on a picnic in such a situation'. I can hear Flynn saying, 'We're just scoping out the scene. Seeing, ya know, like what's happening up here. Did ya meet my man Stone here? C'mon, Dana, say hi to the nice VC.' They were not roughed up, only questioned. They were held at this spot overnight, and the next morning they were moved to the west.

The trail is cold until a 77-year-old man, Poch Yim Int, and Ong Douen from Cheach Chour village in Kamchey Mea district in northern Prey Veng province, are unearthed as having billeted the lads for three nights. The local resistance cadre had come and requisitioned half their house for the Vietnamese, their Khmer interpreter and three prisoners. It appears that a Canadian woman was now part of the entourage, though no records show any Canadian missing after capture. The rear part of the house was kept curtained off from Poch Yim Int's family, no one being allowed to communicate with the captives directly. It was a time of much flux and danger, nobody willing to get far out of line. Looking through the concerned journalists' handbook of photos of all those missing, they were 70 per cent certain about Sean and Dana. However, to all the Khmer who looked at the portraits, Westerners tend all to look alike. Height they could remember more distinctly, especially the fact that Sean was tall, whereas Dana was of their build. Again the lads and their captors left at night, heading for Porm farther up on the province line with Kompong Cham. After that we have no more information until they reappear in Khmer Rouge and resistance-front hands.

The ceremony to receive the *bodhi* tree bore the severity of emotion of a Gregorian mass chanted in a cathedral or the clear tones of a flute in the hills. The top shrine room had its louvred doors wide open, the first light of day softly flooding the decorated hall. Rush mats had been arranged around a low silk-covered table upon which stood the perky sapling in its decorative basket. A notable's burial casket and its cremation decor stood to one side. Besides the *sree*, four senior monks were in attendance. There was a short period of chanting of a sutra, a blessing, a pause for translation, then the basket was handed over.

I welled to a fountain of tears as the plug was pulled from the emotional bottleneck. The mystery had been unravelled.

Going east along Highway One for the last time on this trip evoked a sad anticlimax, retracing the lads' last ride once again, now for the third time this trip. Everything was too familiar now, somehow used up, squeezed dry. An empty feeling, as though the ultimate had been achieved, and not knowing what could be done next.

The shop in the Domestic Departures waiting room at

Ton Son Nhut was manned by two bored middle-aged Vietnamese ladies who had been peacefully knitting until what we thought was possibly a mixed-sex mud-wrestling team lunged in. Mike Blakeley, the cameraman got into a fractured conversation with one of their *Gruppenführer*, the ones in shiny polyester tracksuits, blue with white stripes, and plastic trainers. He announced they were Albanians. One does not often meet Albanians anywhere outside Albania. This was before that closet land shrugged off its tyrannical Socialist shackles. Except for the leader, they were all hopelessly overweight, ill dressed with black as the predominant colour in their styling. Both males and females of the group were equally hairy, and judging from the prevailing odour, unwashed. Somehow we had got tangled up in one of their economic expansion holidays. Never have so few bought so much of so little value in so short a time. (Never have so few manhandled so much.)

The cases held locally made products as mundane as soap, hair clips, cheap belts, lacquer boxes and a tatty selection of cotton shirts and underwear. The shop also sold the only refreshments available, priced in hard currency like the items dustily displayed in the cabinets. There was nothing you would want to buy unless you were desperately hungry, when the peanut nougat, lotus tea or prawn crackers could have staved off the pangs. In one corner of the room was a display of ceramic elephants, graduated in size, a classic Viet souvenir, the large ones over a foot tall and weighing nearly twenty pounds. The mud wrestlers snapped these up like candy. Peer pressure, Shep and I supposed, for we had spotted their Toyota van on a souvenir hunt downtown earlier and it was already starting to overflow with the ornamentation. Now those who had missed that hunt could catch up.

The whole group had already exchanged its suitcases for expander trundle bags, the sort with flimsy zips allowing you to make a carry-on shoulder bag into a metre-high receptacle. The Vietnamese-made Robin brand comes in bright red or sky blue, emblazoned with the logo 'Yachting Sub Sports'. Manufactured out on the Binh Hoa highway in a revamped textile plant, the Robin bag can barely stand the stress as an over-the-shoulder item; called into service as a heavy-duty shopping skip it will shed one or more of its insufficiently attached caster wheels as well as losing a strap. Many of the overstuffed Robins now had rope trussings and plastic string bowlines. The same strapping materials had been brought to bear on protecting the Day-Glo flock-velvet 'Last Suppers' (Tijuana-style) and peaceful-paddy-with-buffalos paintings. The Christo school of travel art. They were working themselves into a heavier funk with another 20–30 hand-painted kilos before our eyes. Their travel video could have been entitled *Beyond the Planet of the Apes Goes Shopping, Part III.*

The flight called, we got caught in their crush to get aboard first. They jammed doorways with their armfuls of paintings, ceramics, bamboo model boats and houses. Some were even attempting to get the three-wheeled Robins out on the tarmac as hand baggage. They reduced even Ham, king of the hand luggage, to a pauper among packers. Our mere twenty-five pieces, including all the silver boxes, paled beside their heap, more befitting a heavy-weapons platoon.

Loading the plane took double the normal time; polite Vietnamese stewardesses in blue silk *ao dais* tried to communicate with the mud wrestlers and wrest some of their bulkier items away to stow in the toilets. The Albanians fought back, clinging onto their hard-won souvenirs, squeezing into the three-abreast seating clutching their charges. The Albanians were almost as wide as they were tall so did not fit the seating any which way, their girth increased by the additional clothing they wore, which had been displaced from their suitcases to accommodate the purchases. I hated to think what our takeoff weight had become or what would happen in an emergency-landing scenario.

A heavy pong of body odour pervaded the sealed fuselage, heightened by the inadequacy of the Ilyushin's air conditioning. Several of the Albanians immediately lit up foul-smelling cigarettes and had to be corrected by the now desperate stewardesses. It was a long hour and a half to Da Nang.

Russian aircraft were never conceived with comfort in mind. Passengers are almost an afterthought in planes designed to fulfil dual roles. In time of war they can be used to convey military cargo or be converted to a bomber; either way, they sport nacelles fore and aft, equipped to accept the mounting of anti-aircraft guns combined with a bombardier's compartment. The normal fixtures and fittings of passenger travel – life jackets, air vents, overhead luggage racks – are nonexistent. By the time that these craft reach Vietnam third or fourth hand via Luftflug (East German, now defunct airline) or Aeroflot, even seat belts are a luxury. On five occasions – no, not on the same plane – I have been assigned a seat with only half a belt, and three times, a seat that would not stay in the upright position. Still, passengers, victims of overbooking, are obliged to sit on the floor back by the toilets holding on to the loosely stacked overflow baggage. It was only in 1991 that check-in at an internal Hang Khong Viet-Nam Airlines counter stopped requiring the passenger to put himself with the baggage on the scales.

'Hang On Airways', as its users know it, has one of the worst safety records. Their Tupolevs and Ilyushins fall out of the sky with a monotonous regularity of at least a couple a year. One of the risks was running out of fuel. At Hanoi's Noi Bai airport, mechanics could be seen probing fuel tanks with bamboo poles to ascertain whether it would be safe to remove a few hundred more litres for resale on the black market. This problem has dissipated with the increased pumping from Vietnam's offshore oil fields and the booming market economy. Unsecured excess baggage and freight can also cause an aircraft to go into a terminal spin, should a banking turn be too sharply executed. Maintenance is, at best, rudimentary, and spare parts originating in former E-block countries are becoming increasingly difficult to obtain, so essentials like filters and hydraulics are often recycled. In the great proletarian society, it was assumed that things did not fall out of the sky; the people's machines and industrial prowess were infallible. And old habits die hard.

Security is also a rather lax affair, though one would imagine the hijack would be a favourite way out of the country that put boat people on the map. In the spring of 1993, a Hang On flight into Ho'ville was hijacked by an ex-AVRN officer. He demanded that the plane circle Saigon while he and an accomplice shovelled anti-government tracts out of the cockpit windows before he donned a parachute and jumped. He was captured without difficulty, the leaflets all 'disappeared', and the poor one-time army major is now doing twenty hard years.

Luckily, on our arrival at Da Nang International Airport, the same low-slung ferroconcrete terminal that had functioned as the 12th aerial port in the war, our silver boxes turned up before the disintegrating effects of the mud wrestlers. We parted company, they into a waiting, decidedly dilapidated, Russian minibus, we into a brand-new air-conditioned Toyota Hiace belonging to the town's tourist department. However, we would recollide back at the departure lounge for the onward hop to Hanoi.

The Albanians were last sighted two and a half days later, all of us getting out at International Departures, Noi Bai; we filmed our last shot with the Thai Boeing as a backdrop, and returned momentarily to the terminal to see a somewhat downcast mud-wrestling platoon awaiting boarding of a Balkan Airways long-haul to Sofia. They had been relieved of most of their outsize cases, reduced to bulging shoulder bags and the odd vase, and the tax-free goodies in the Hong-Kong-sponsored shop were out of reach of their spent-out hands. Still, they may now be among Albania's newly elected elite, guiding the impoverished ex-Stalinist land to an economic miracle.

By the time we finally arrived at the Huong Giang, the Perfume River Hotel, on the south bank in Hue, it was dark and damp; we had driven the last stretch from the Hai Van Pass north of Da Nang in rain showers. Three damp, somewhat glum local officials were there, knotted in consternation, trying to resolve the next impasse. It looked as though the film with its tight schedule was about to be thwarted at the last scene. Someone, somewhere, up in the proletariat machinations of Hanoi officialdom had failed to give the necessary approvals during our absence in Cambodia. Road blocks were appearing on our leg line.

Getting the project off the ground involved negotiations with all governmental bodies, from the top of the people's pile in Hanoi, through the departments associated with culture and ideology, and down to the local people's committee in the district where the memorial garden was to be inaugurated at Gio Linh. All of them, party members or not, knew by now of the purpose of the mission. Both Tien and Mum had been despatched south from the foreign-press centre, at our expense, to coordinate the six of us and the twenty silver boxes. Neither of the lads was unaccustomed to surmounting the obstacles that occur with monotony in a dogmatic bureaucracy-laden environment. Yet now the local officials were acting as though this was the first they had heard of the creative project. It was a farce clearly scripted from above, none of the players quite believing they were having to do it. Eventually the delegation took their leave, promising nothing. We had laid out the complete concept for them, Shep pragmatically explaining the shooting schedule, myself raving on about the spirituality. There were no guarantees but we could hope.

We swung by the people's committee in the morning to pick up our local delegation. The cast had swollen; we found the senior bonze from the pedagogie, the main Buddhist seminary in Vietnam, deep in conversation with the dean of the Arts, Letters and Languages Faculty at the university. The foreign minister and information chief were on hand but were too busy to take a day off to go north, so their local representatives from Quang Tri district would join us at Dong Ha. The monk turned out to have taken part in the Buddhist demonstrations of the mid-1960s; he could have been in one of the images I had shot in Hue in 1965 for *Look* or *UPI*.

We left in convoy for the 90-kilometre run up Route One. The road from Hue to the DMZ has seen more conflict since World War II than any other. In the early 1950s, the French staged a series of raids and operations using seaborne landings, armoured ground forces and parachute drops to keep control of central Annam. Their machine was badly mauled in the process, leaving a hard core of liberation forces in the area for the Americans to try to pacify. This task had fallen initially to the marines, later to the airborne and the army; none ever entirely succeeded. To the west lies the Annamitic Cordillera, the mountain range that always harboured guerrillas; to the east is the South China Sea; in between is a fertile belt of rice paddies giving to an infertile sandy fringe up to five kilometres inland. The Street Without Joy runs up this barren stretch where the verdant rice gives way to scrub and pines. Half a dozen rivers flowing out of the massif required the colonial engineers to build substantial bridges to carry the road and railway. These became strategic stop lines during the NVA-initiated offensives of 1972, when the North first threw regiments of armour into the fray. Areas outside government positions were all heavily mined, the allegiance of the populace only assured with a military presence.

Even today, the land has a poisoned feel; large tracts of land, once bases or airstrips, are still littered with half-destroyed blockhouses and bunkers, the surrounding land still hard and sterile, the trench lines and revetments vaguely discernible. Most of the war scrap has gone. Up to the mid-1980s there were still tank carcasses, shell casings and runway platings decorating roadside landscapes. These have just about all been recycled, the scrap steel either exported to Japan, Korea or Taiwan, or sent to the country mills turning out reinforcing rods, plates and girders for reconstruction. However, individuals are still combing the terrain, scraping up small chunks of shrapnel, tank parts or hanks of barbed wire. A canny operator could clean up renting out metal detectors, or having the scrap fashioned into war souvenirs somewhat on the lines of Zippos with faked period engravings that have become the 'in' item on the tourist shopping list. The latter cottage industry appears to have its roots in Hue right next to the bus station, where a suitably naff engraved lighter costs a couple of dollars; down in Ho'ville they're going for five.

Route One, north of Hue, is still eerie in the mist, the dampness dripping from the scruffy pines into the white sand, turning it dingy grey, tinged with rust. Blown-away souls haunt the small copses that are clawing back root space, for the low hills all seem topped by the mournful obelisks that mark the centre of a *liet si*, the liberation forces' war graves. The spirits of thousands of ARVN troops and countless civilians had been left wandering. There is still little joy up this stretch of coast, past the 17th parallel and almost up to the frontiers of Tonkin and the estuaries of the northern delta rivers.

The ancient citadel Quang Tri was once of a provincial capital. By the time of its final liberation in 1975 it looked like Stalingrad after the siege – craters and rubble. It may never be rebuilt. Dong Ha, farther up the highway, was also erased from the map, but is in a more strategic locale and has seen reconstruction. A large bridge spans the Cua Viet River just north of where Route Nine turns left to head into and over the hills to Laos and the Mekong. The US marines turned the town and airstrip into a huge advance base covering their operations all along the DMZ up to Khe Sanh. The river was navigable for landing craft into the town centre, and their hard ramp for unloading is still in place by the new bridge being built. The old span is a rickety, much patched one of odd-length sections quilted together. Alongside that are the pylons of two others. One lot of wreckage earned Congressional Medals of Honour for the two bravely insane US marines advisers who blew it up as North Vietnamese tanks and artillery tried to storm across under a rain of artillery fire. Their efforts were merely delaying: other forces had encircled the town farther up to the west in divisional numbers.

Dong Ha is thriving. It is the last town in the old south still imbued with more than a trace of old-regime guile. A goodly number of the residents served in that regime's military and care not for their northern neighbours whom they fought so bitterly for so long. There are a lot of amputee beggars cruising the bus and truck stops and opposite the post office, adjacent to the old French-built watchtower, a few American fighting vehicles stand rusting. The M-48 driver's hatch still has DAVE stencilled below it.

On the south bank, next to the historic bridge, is the busy market, descending with concrete steps to the river's edge. It is a collection of stalls and shacks located on the bulldozed remains of the town's old marketplace. The only relic to have survived the war's passage and the ravaging of time and typhoons is a perfectly formed, ten-metre high bo tree. It was right at its flowering peak as we passed.

Gio Linh's only claim to fame could be that it was home to the most northern firebase in the southern republic. Before it was finally overrun in the 1972 offensive, batteries of the giant 175-mm Long Tom howitzers had been based here to lob harassment-and-interdiction fire north of the parallel into the North's equivalent gun emplacements at Gio Vinh. The people's committee was moving out of the erstwhile ARVN barracks into a purpose-built two-storey structure designed by someone who failed Lego in Cuba. On the germinating lawn in front, a section of one of the Long Tom's barrels lay forlornly under a line of damp washing. The officials we had picked up in Dong Ha disappeared inside party HQ, re-emerging after a quarter of an hour with the minister of information, culture and sport, doubling today also in the foreign portfolio.

Like most of the party officials and government flacks in this corner of Vietnam, the minister was a war veteran, a former North Vietnamese *bo dồi*, whose combat past was etched into his face. The whole visage was a spiderweb of shrapnel, not a centimetre including the eyelids, was untouched by dirty black filaments. In most US ordnance, steel wire is tightly wound around the casing of the grenade, mortar, artillery round, rocket or bomb, then serrated. On detonation, the explosion throws out small hooked strands of hot wire, designed to maim and incapacitate, rather than kill. Any untreated wounds in the tropical heat tend to turn septic within hours. This man must have walked right into an exploding M-79 round or something like it. At that time, it did not seem good manners to pry out his nightmare.

He was a cheerful soul, our liaison official, his appearance notwithstanding, jauntily wearing a black beret. I got the impression that he probably slept in his beret, jacket too, at this chill time of year. December is the winter here, too, and today was the twelfth; auspiciously, twelves kept coming up on this gig.

It was still grey and drizzling as we climbed up the final ridge above Gio Linh through where the McNamara Line once ran, the 25 kilometres of electric fences, minefields, blockhouses, bunkers, sensors and lights intended to stop infiltration into the South. It was of little use, for Charlie just walked calmly round the inland end of it through jungle and hills that he could claim as his own and where marine battalions would regularly get mauled trying to deny him this passage.

After liberation, the area had been cleared by the troops who had once manned the line. The poor soil is useless as agricultural land, the poisons of war are still leaking out and few people live here. Instead, there are many neat cemeteries with white stone-markers. Most of the graves are empty for their men are missing, disappeared in the hills or on the Ho Chi Minh Trail, or evaporated by the fire power brought to bear as they transited the DMZ. The Z was always spooky, inspiring tales of phantom NVA choppers, swirling mists and strange lights in the sky. The people here are fervently religious, or superstitious. Nearly every house will have a small shrine, like a bird table, outside the front door. Sometimes it has a small Buddha effigy, often simply a small vase or pot with sand which whoever passes or wishes may place lit incense, *huong*, to honour the spirits. A small bowl of rice, fruit and a posy of flowers are also proferred to the spirits daily.

Just as you roll up the last incline before the drop down to the Ben Hai plain, partly hidden by a hedge, some young fruit trees and a fast-growing eucalyptus windbreak, a family have artfully incorporated an old M-41 ARVN tank hall and turret into their kitchen, the barrel drooping northwards. This house must by now have some listed-building status for the property has changed hands four times that I know of, with the tank obviously included in the deeds.

Slipping down the last switchback slope onto the floodplain is still a surprise, the vista across to what was once the source of hostile fire and a foreign land still echoing in the mind's eye. During the war I had driven up this far not only on the Honda motorbike but also twice from Da Nang in one of Kim Chi's jeep specials. He was a tailor in the centre of downtown Da Nang who changed money and had a small sideline in white and yellow jeeps from World War II and, more esoterically, three Willy's Overlands. The latter were stretch-model jeeps with a civilian, rather boxy convertible car body; a real American classic at ten dollars a day. The drive had taken a leisurely four and a half hours with a quick refuel in Hue. No police or army post nor Vietcong or North Vietnamese patrol even bothered to flag down such a vehicle. There was no way a military man or a spook would have travelled in something so conspicuous.

Back then, in the mid-1960s, the frontier should have been a tourist zone. Theoretically anyone could drive up to either side and gawk, as people used to into East Berlin, though the only people officially allowed to pass were the ICC – the International Control Commission. This was the body founded at the Geneva peace talks on Vietnam in 1954, when partition was officially sorted out. The tripartite commission was made up of Poles (basically representative of communism), Canadians (capitalism) and Indians as neutrals. Mostly the officers flew in rickety white DC-4s and -6s between the capitals of Indochina, worrying about the impossibility of their task. The middle of the bridge was the only place in South Vietnam where you could look at the opposition without getting shot at. The bridge was erected after the typhoons of 1963 blew the original French one away, and was intended to be temporary. A new one has been promised in the next five-year programme.

The triangle of land edged by the dyke leading up to today's span, the old road trace and the riverbank is approximately two and a half hectares of seasonally flooded grassy soil into which the sapling *bodhi* was to be planted. Some years the water laps almost to the deck of the bridge, covering the whole proposed memorial site; some years the river hardly spills its banks. The triangle-shaped plot was almost dry when we arrived, our convoy disgorging a gathering of an importance not witnessed hereabouts since liberation. The few locals swarmed out to stare at the hottest act in the commune.

Where to plant the sapling? It was as though I was expecting divine intervention. Feeling a right twerp, decorated basket in one hand, camera in the other, I lurched around in zigzags and circles hoping a magic arrow would pierce the gloom and point out the spot on the partly waterlogged turf. To no avail. Shep was starting to flap, agitating for a decision. When in doubt, head for the high ground. The highest spot on the allocated isoceles was occupied by the square raised brick of the vanquished southern republic's massive flagpole. I hoped this would come down to permit the erection of a stupa around which we could engrave the names of our fallen and missing comrades. It could look magnificent in the white marble that comes from south of Da Nang and the sandstone of the Cham ruins, reminiscent of Ankgor, southwest of Da Nang, at My Son. Much of the statuary of central Vietnam, of Annam, has traditionally been sculpted out of this mellow ochre stone. Classically a stupa is made of nine steps, signifying the steps the Buddha took towards nirvana. The realisation, or ninth, is in Sri Lanka often represented by a crystal, sometimes donated by the Burmese clergy. The Czechs, who lost two *bao chi* in the conflict, took it upon themselves to offer the crystal to attract and simultaneously dispel the energies of the spirits of those missing.

I let the committee man from Dong Ha take me by the basket and lead me to a slightly rising piece of ground barely five metres from the dyked road. We came to a mutual stop and the pack squelched up and spread around, an American football line-up awaiting the next called play. From the shack at the apex of new and old roads two hoes were produced and Tien insisted on taking the first hack at breaking ground for the memorial. Meanwhile I was energetically thumping the phoenix-embossed pot on its bottom, attempting to dislodge the sapling and preserve the simple but symbolically beautiful ceramic. The plant was good and root-bound. The Foreign Ministry minder from Hue took over, grabbed a hoe off Tien and gave a good crack to the pot. The ceramic was shattered, and we interred the pieces around the tree in the metre of dug ground.

The sapling had but two of the original leaves left; the others had withered in the truck and on the plane even with the plant covered in a *krama* and the soil continuously moistened. It appeared relieved to have made it back to terra firma. We scraped the soil over the roots, filling the hole, and stood back. The monk from Hue now had the delicate task of placing his and the Buddha's blessing on the project without offending the state that still tightly controls religion. (For example, getting into the clergy of any religion, creed or sect in today's Vietnam requires a degree in philosophy.) He stayed safe, talking of the tree and the awareness and enlightenment that the Buddha had received under one similar and how he hoped it would bring the same light here.

Our last task was to build some protection for the tender plant; not so much to give it shade, but to stave off attacks by the wandering goat population. Soon after liberation a friendly north African nation of good socialistic persuasion had generously sent goats as part of an aid package, hoping that the Viets would take to the supplementary meat benefits. It is hard to find goat on the roadside slabs next to abbatoirs, or anywhere on a menu. The people just have not taken to eating it the length of the land. Consequently, large tracts of central Vietnam are becoming denuded. Goats are not known for their ability to distinguish between sacred trees and food. Buffalo, on the other hand, can, yet do not, browse off *bodhi* trees. Tien had bought in Dong Ha market a basket or cage that looked as though normally a fighting cock would be cooped under its dome. Made of split, then woven, bamboo strips, it afforded lots of light but would foil any beast trying to get its lips round the tender surviving leaves. The basket was pegged tight down like an igloo with small plaits lashed to the dome.

Our group withdrew from the little green hump, leaving a congregation of surprisingly quiet local villagers, from babes in arms to just ambulatory crones and elders. Traffic had pulled up on the bridge ramp. The silence was of respect. We all hoped the meandering souls would now find peace.

To round off the TV programme, Hand Luggage had supposedly orchestrated and scripted the Hanoi final act with the press and culture folk. We had hoped for a commanding general from the 5th or 9th Division, since theirs was the recon unit that had apprehended our lads. We got instead the national treasure, the poet laureate of the North.

Duat had served on the Cambodian front in the early 1970s as soldier, correspondent and poet. His despatches of glorious deeds in the party's name for the greater cause of national unification and liberation had made him a folk hero. He had turned this, not unlike Oliver Stone, into a career change, pursuing the movie business as writer, actor, director and now, he hoped, producer. He came equipped with a young thing, a beautiful student in her early twenties from the foreign language school, introduced as his assistant, in reality interpreter. Crafty Duat let it be known that he would recite his requiem to fallen comrades on camera. This was negotiated over copious consumption of various liquors. Our national treasure was a lush, a true alky, a marvellous character once wound up on the booze. Sober, he was a drag and boorish; shabby, sad, his vanity punctured. Another tattered vet.

We took him out to the temple in the Lake of the Restored Sword in the middle of downtown Hanoi, one of the seven lakes that give the capital a lot of its charm. The beautiful temple, Ngoc Son (meaning 'Mound of Jade'), is reached by an ancient wooden footbridge. A pavilion with red-lacquered columns faces the water. Legend has it that during the resistance to the Ming domination 1418–28, King Le Thai To was given a magic sword by the Divine Tortoise. After liberating the country from the Chinese invaders, he took a boat to the centre of the lake to return it. The Tortoise is said to have risen up and snatched the sword from his hand,

and it was never seen again. They appear to have created in this pond an Arthurian Excalibur legend crossed with a Loch Ness monster. The lake and its temples are the heart of Hanoi, shade trees and carefully tended gardens forming the backdrop for Duat's reading.

Duat's actor's mien was too stiff for the final cut. The national treasure ended up on the cutting-room floor, a few metres away from the next episode of *Coronation Street* at Granada's Manchester headquarters.

### Remnants of Leaves

A group of infantry waiting to advance
all looked up into the sky:
the black remnants of bamboo leaves falling,
the nearby forest was fiercely burning.
I looking at the sky at that time too
noticed the fall of such black butterfly wings.
The fighter by my side kept sitting down then standing up
anxious for bamboo's explosion.
The older officer sitting on the grass
intently looked at the falling leaves.
The enemies were on the opposite side of the hill.
The mortar shells fired at random in the bamboo forest
are a symptom of something happening.
The sky is full of leaves; black snow falling.
Our troops have densely surrounded the hill.
The enemy is unaware, as they are setting fire to
bamboo forest,
from the silence will arise a fire storm
and in the noisy hill fall down the ashes.
Over the hill, who are they?
The puppet troops in Indochina or Americans?
As the evils had become their doctrine and many things in
black appear.
The infantry man is always anxious.

Ten minutes to wait isn't a long time.
The black remnants falling down above us
have fallen so for thousand years.
Humans are born for endless suffering
as houses burning seen in every village.
As long as there is enemy there are ashes of palm leaves
and the black remnants keep falling.
Our troops have densely surrounded the hill.
There is no shelter for the enemy.
Tomorrow there will be nothing but rain falling
and only butterflies and birds to be seen.
The remnants are slowly falling
but tracing over the sky the lines too fierce.
The order gun then bursts, smoke covers up all forest.
The remnants of leaves flying up and down.

Pham The Duyet
Translated by Tien.

Shep called me from the cutting room up in Manchester. The film had been shot, we had gone, come back, the issue resolved and then there was to be a preview in a couple of weeks. Now, the title of the thing had finally landed on his palate. The Doors' riffs had been echoing through the whole project. We had listened to them way back then, we had listened on the road and he was still hearing the refrains in the edit suite. There had been and there was 'Danger on the Edge of Town'. (Shep and the Doors went back a long way, for he had made a documentary, *The Doors are Open*, back in 1967 during their first UK tour.)

# 8

# *Getting to Know the Generals*

The highlands of Chu Phong mountain and the mist-wreathed Ia Drang valley form part of the backbone of Indochina. It was down through this forested plateau that Unclo Ho had whacked his trail. This monsoon forest was known to swallow battalions alive, as well as the trained recon dudes and covert teams that went monkeying about in country that basically was Charlie's personal yard. The Ia Drang had been a wicked place to learn to fight a new kind of war. One side had almost unlimited aircraft and the other had giant crossbows launching bamboo spears into the heavens.

The terrain offers the defender the advantage. Baked dry, the greens dissolve into buffs and browns not quite autumnal. Termite hills watch over clearings strewn with old fallen trees, possible landing zones. The elephant grass, full of bugs and dust, has sawlike edges that open up your hands and gash any exposed flesh. Good cover but burns beautifully when dry. Small streams, the headwaters of the Ia Drang itself, have carved gullies in the massif's spines. A lot of mahoganies and teaks are big enough to support hidden snipers artfully placed with RPDs, their light machine gun, to dominate any possible landing site or open territory. Like the three downed crews we were attempting to rescue, the giant twin-rotored Chinook carrying the entire heavy-weapons platoon had got mortally stitched settling in to land. Someone figured sixty hits, but who was counting? The surviving Huey crew members were huddled behind logs off the clearing, the pilots with their .38s pointing into the trees, loose cartridges in the flight helmets; another lot had demasted a door gun and were putting out a staccato sweep into the foliage. The NVA lads up in the branches had got the whole expedition pinned down while their comrades contributed blank fire mixed with rocket-propelled grenades.

Joe Galloway had arrived out in the Nam, a junior wire reporter for UPI, hot to have a go, out of shape and naive. He came back from just such a sojourn up in the hills in the autmun of 1965 a changed man. The officer commanding the battalion, Harold Moore, then a lieutenant colonel, had in later years become fast friends with Joe. The battle, one of the most decisive of the entire conflict, haunted both their lives, a common shadow that had passed and left a scarred light. There was even an old boys' association, a unit fraternity, which visited the Wall in Washington, DC, on the anniversary of the battle to remember their fallen comrades, whose 305 names were etched in the black reflective marble.

Now Joe planned to do a twenty-fifth-anniversary article for his magazine *US News and World Report.* He hoped to go back to the scene of the battle with Hal Moore, who had retired in the 1970s in protest against certain administrative policies, having risen to the rank of lieutenant general with three stars. Joe also wanted to engineer a meeting of erstwhile enemies on the old terrain. As an old friend since the glory days of Frankies' House in Saigon, he asked me to help at the Hanoi end.

Bringing together opposing sides after the fight is always fraught with tension. Usually they both want to forgive, but can never forget. The bonding is that of superglue from hell.

Old soldiers have a love of anniversaries of battles, especially when they believe they won, irrespective of the casualties, and this lure was one that the old boys clinging to the waterlogged party system could get their obsolete ideals around.

At this time, the East bloc was crumbling and the south of Vietnam was enjoying a boom of capitalist perfidy. The hard core of the Politburo were not prepared to see the south breaking away again, and to prevent it were even beginning to think about adopting some form of liberalism. But Hanoi has a maze of bureaucracy, designed and proven against revolutionary, excessively radical ideas invading the citadel of power.

These protective walls have also served to prevent the destruction of Vietnamese culture and the family-network way of life. The country, especially the north, has maintained an integrity to community and social structure. People still have others' welfare on their minds. There is harmony, though this is in the process of unravelling, as it has done south of the 17th. Ho'ville has become an old tart of a town. Old colonial structures are being ripped down for new concrete and glass high-rises in the name of business, overseas money flouting laws quicker than they are passed or ratified by any central government up north. Corruption on a scale before unheard-of has ensued, billions of dongs creamed off in investment scandals, dollar millionaires skipping the country, others going to jail. It is hard to achieve anything without a sizeable persuading wad. Yen, francs and dollars make them perk up, but it is always difficult to change pounds or cash sterling traveller's cheques.

Politics anywhere boils down to the evil of money. The war may be long over, but the battle for the buck is still raging. The amount of trade lost to the embargo is in the billions, the opportunity lost by General Motors to power the new Vietnam given on a plate to Toyota and Nissan. Even Ladas get a better showing than Land-Rovers, for nary a soul in the UK embassy speaks the local lingo and the British sales force is barely able to pinpoint Vietnam on a globe.

In contrast with Ho'ville, Hanoi has a grey-brown bleakness in the winter months, similar to the fifties smogs of Britain; a damp, arthritic layer seeps into the ferroconcrete and traditional mellow brick of which the city is built. Fuel is scarce and, when available, consists of lorryloads of lignite dust which are dropped at strategic blocks. The local residents then designate a squad to go out and make patties from the wetted slurry. This polluting substance is the only source of heat available. The electricity supply is at best erratic and subject to unpredictable surges. One bored UN official, who took to monitoring the fluctuations, found that it oscillated from less than 100 volts to above 300 over any given hour.

Keeping warm therefore involves the consumption of many *cafés sua* followed by thimble-size cups of the green, bitterish tea. The locally produced coffee and tea have traditionally always been ace brews, the coffee from the central highlands having a noticeable amphetamine overtone. Hanoi now has more cafés than there are pubs in working-class British boroughs. The onset, albeit grudgingly, of a form of private enterprise has led to the mushrooming of soup kitchens and coffee or snack bars from people's street-fronting parlours onto the broad tree-shaded pavements.

Canned lambada was blasting out of the video box at the corner café I favoured. For a time after Bob Marley died, there was a kind of reggae beat undulating up and down Vietnam with drivers bootlegging cassettes, but apparently not enough was brought in to sustain a market, and except for Cuba there is little direct connection between the Tonkin Gulf and the Caribbean. Anyway, the café, with its little groups of squat-height minichairs and bamboo tables overhung with flowering shrubs, was a good laid-back place to broach gently to the minders the plan to bring an ex-general and old friend back to the scene to tell it from both sides of the field later in the year.

When the time came, we would have to wait it out, just for the visas, for a week, the US magazines budget being sorely tested by the protracted excuses. Joe and the general holed up in a luxury hotel while I carried out long rambling discussions with Dy the press attaché. Dy reported directly to the Foreign Ministry in Hanoi. His English had been honed by a copious collection of videos, the most replayed being *Faulty Towers* and *Spitting Image*. We had first met back during the *gai phong* celebrations, ten years of liberation and unification. Dy, recently returned from studying in Canberra on a scholarship, had been attached to the NBC TV team headed by Neil Davis. It was Neil who had negotiated the opening of the doors to allow satellite transmission in for the first time. Dy had been Neil's right hand and senior among the guides, minders, fixers and interpreters needed to service more than 600 members of the foreign press, a good 30 per cent of whom had sent reportages back from Vietnam in another lifetime. It had become as much our reunion as their celebration; the media had taken over the event from the party.

Half a decade later Dy had ascended to chief councillor and number-one overseas information gleaner in Bangkok. It was good to see his diminutive cheery self again, to sense the warmth of a friendship now matured by time. We could talk securely as buddies, ignoring party dogma.

One day, when unseasonably late rain poured down outside the garden office, Dy started to tell me a story longer than I had ever heard him recount before. It was also the first time he had spoken of the war. He had been one of three brothers. The eldest had gone off to fight in 1972 as a company officer in the campaigns capturing the DMZ and the territory all the way south to Quang Tri. The north had lost thousands of men in this successful advance, stopped only by timely American reintervention with B-52 strikes and flights of missile-firing helicopter gunships to bust the massive tank and armour thrust for the first time southwards. Neither side ever really had a chance to remove their dead from the battlefields and bury them at home. Dy's eldest brother was among those killed, and the soldiers under his command had marked and remembered where they had buried him, notifying the remaining brothers when they finally got home.

When the push of liberation came in 1975, there was a vacuum of euphoria into which our lads leaped. Liberating a Russian-made motorcycle with a sidecar, they zoomed off towards the 17th parallel to retrieve the family remains. There followed an epic journey, Dy's experiences mixed up in the flow of a victorious force towards the reclaimed southern provinces. The classic ceremonies were eventually held at home for the remains. The moral of the story was in the sheer persistence, which led in the end to accomplishment of the task. I dodged back to the grandeur next door and its soft, cool security to recount to Joe the same tale. His patience was not impressed.

Even before we left Thailand, Hal was in culture shock. A fitness freak, he had gone jogging on his arrival without realising the state of Bangkok's pavements, which ill conceal the monsoon drains beneath. Irregular slabs at earthquake angles form an obstacle course, interspersed with kerbs to driveways at anything up to half a metre in step leap. On the straight stretches, creeping tree roots trip the unwary. Soup barrows, vendors, garbage and construction rubble also impede the pedestrian's progress. The general came a cropper down a drain. When I first met up with them he was bandaged, scraped on arm and leg, hobbling and ashen. Joe was almost sweated to a standstill. They both still had that beady-eyed 'want to go get some' look that Americans overseas glow with. We weren't going anywhere for a week which, *enfin*, was good for the general to lick his wounds and for us all to kind of get to accept each other.

★ ★ ★

When the visas came through, it was at the shortest possible notice, and after a typical Hang On flight we arrived at Noi Bai International with no one there to meet us. Sweating profusely, nerves unravelling, we escaped as quickly as possible from Noi Bai's apron swirling with greeters, traders, secret policemen and petty criminals. A taxi took us past paddies dotted with stooped, rag-clad peasants. New billboards sang of joint overseas ventures beyond the reach of those toiling beneath them. The traffic all appeared to be jalopies befitting a *Grapes of Wrath* exodus; they crabbed towards us on threadbare wheels, smoking and puffing, overloaded and unpredictable. Domestic farm animals, poultry and peasants scurried between them. The main road still rippled from the insufficiently filled bomb craters.

The general was agog, pointing and jabbing at items of interest. This was the enemy's home ground, the heartland of the *bo doi*, the North Vietnamese grunts who had died so hard from his men's fire. Most veterans, people that only saw the war as fought down south, imagine there will be Vietnamese in pith helmets carrying AKs behind every bush. Instead they find a country totally at peace, the war merely history, though the whole place has a primitive air of forgotten, obsolete technology. Few Americans coming to the north can believe that it is correct still to keep punishing this stoic peasantry.

For Hal, it was his first real submergence into Vietnam proper, for in his tours of duty it had been rare that he would find himself out in the street or the paddies without an entourage of staff, bodyguards and other fellows in olive drab. The US army had let few of its men get really close to the natives, be they friend or foe; all were clumped into a generalised dinkness and therefore 'them', the opposition. Few Americans had the chance to get to grips with the language, much less the culture. Hal Moore, then a light colonel, had had only an Instamatic glimpse of the people against whom he had been pitted.

Hal still had the posture of a career military man: the erect carriage, pulled-back shoulders, a clear gaze to the horizon, the bright-blue eyes for ever scanning, ascertaining. However, he was going very deaf, and his hi-tech space-industry hearing aid did not work well in the sticky post-monsoon fug of Indochina. The power cells kept getting knocked out.

It was midafternoon by the time we got downtown and the press office was closing, no one of responsibility was around. The army guesthouse staff were unsure since our bookings had been on and off the boil for a week, but we could be squeezed into a suite. Hanoi has probably still a thousand decent hotel rooms per night short; back then, with many foreign enterprises and UN missions moving in, space was gold dust. We were all too knackered to wander farther than the depressing neon-lit restaurant with its isolated prim tables, enormous curved leatherette bar stocked with empty scotch-bottle boxes and canned Vietnamese pineapple jam. The enormous TV sat at one end, the volume turned up to a mindless Singaporean disco beat backing a shopping tourist extravaganza video. The two bored waitresses were keeping an eye on the programme (they must have seen it hundreds of times, it being one of only three tapes to choose from) and another of the two UN Development Programme types seated at different tables picking listlessly at unidentifiable food. The menu was twelve items long, and to those in the know, an Australian-introduced grilled tomato and cheese sandwich was available. The same menu also covered lunch and, with the egg dishes (three), breakfast. It was the only vaguely foreign food then available after nine o'clock. Even during the height of E-bloc colonialism, Hanoi did not have a decent Czech, Hungarian or Balkan restaurant. In the 1990s a number of new joints have opened that serve a passable burger, pizza and omelettes.

Joe got the room, the smaller one with desk and red plastic phone. He was, after all, mission commander and holder of the bankroll. Hal and I drew the honeymoon chamber with Naugahyde buttoned trim and queen-size bed. It will probably be the first and last time I or any member of the press has sacked out with a three-star general. The next night we all got our own beds.

It was Sunday, and there was a good vibe on the streets. The north was preparing for national-day celebrations, a state-sponsored event guaranteeing a small flood of goodies onto the market, parades, block parties and a round of cultural shows. All around Le Petit Lac, the downtown centrepiece, there were vendors, photographers and mini cafés. Crews were out stringing lights from Heath Robinson Romanian-made cherry pickers. Most folk had on their best, and my first impression was of a lot more colour in the clothing, and revisionist messages on the T-shirts. Few people now came up and accosted us in Russian; English has become the lingua franca of practice. Retired *fonctionnaires* in berets still nodded '*Bonjour, M'sieu*', secure with their old colonial memories. The tourist was no longer a rare bird in Hanoi; the American-sneakered, bum-belt-packing traveller hardly merited a second look any more. The remaining eastern European technicians now looked doubly dowdy, their purchasing power eroded overnight, their special privileges curtailed. The Vietnamese were naturally suspicious of these erstwhile communists now snapping up imported consumer goods before their recalls home. A new school of die-hard sceptics could be heard trying to persuade themselves that the collapse of the Berlin Wall, the volte-face of Moscow, would once again go full circle. The lakeside proletariat knew otherwise, expressing it with wads of newly printed 5,000-dong notes.

Tien got to us later that day. He was his usual cocky self and we all breathed a sigh of relief that the system had assigned us someone. He had been learning video editing in Tokyo and acquired a 90-cc bike, so he could guarantee local mobility.

We were looking for generals, we were loaded for generals

and we were American. Our attitude was a little fresh. People became unavailable, saying that the rules stated that the department had to front any interview requests, and then that the department did not have the final say. The liaison office directly under the Foreign Ministry did, but they had to relate to culture, whereas the Defence Ministry had jurisdiction over their generals, retired or otherwise.

Maybe we would care to interview some other ranking folk? Not an original idea, since Joe had requested even before he left the United States a series of backgrounders from leading officials. The trouble was that those being offered were of less interest to Joe and the general than his NVA counterparts. The heavy stars of that period were now being wheeled out less at official functions, their praises sung less and their advice unheeded. Bringing them upstage was not part of the programme of the bureaucracy, the desk-bound jockeys. They were the grey men, the party faithful who had successfully managed the war to its conclusion.

Joe calmed somewhat at the arrival of an air-conned Hiace minibus assigned to us for the duration. The general had already been introduced to the lap round the Petit Lac at sunrise, always the most pleasant time of day in the tropics. The perimeter track around this lake in the early-morning cool must rank as one of the better city walks on offer anywhere. Along the western shore clusters of pensioners practise their tai chi; on the eastern side workers' clubs and union societies hold group exercise classes come rain or shine. At the southern end several al fresco cafés have sprung up. The Buu Dien, the main post office, towers all of six storeys, and was in 1990 the tallest building in town. Inside, occupying the entire rear wall, is a faded Mercator world projection, sundry fraternal places picked out in pea bulbs, the rest of the planet apparently uncontactable. As modernisation and normalisation progress, these quaint residues will most likely be ripped out, to be replaced with corporate logos.

The city was left relatively unscathed by the war, off limits to US air power, that is until 1972 when Nixon decided to try to force the North Vietnamese to their knees at the Paris conference table and unleashed the Christmas bombing and mining of the ports. The principal quadrants of aerial attack were around the Long Binh Red River bridge and out by air-force headquarters in the suburb of Bac Mai. At the latter the strike went horribly wrong, hitting the hospital and killing a French surgeon, which was bad publicity. Downtown, one span of the bridge had been dropped and a residential area nearby was flattened by near misses. Haiphong, the major port downstream on the estuary, was also clobbered by B-52s, the dock workers' housing adjacent to the riverside harbour obliterated, while the channel was sown with the latest high-tech mines, denying any major vessel access. Ironically, tonnage imported increased, surprising the crews of the B-52s, who were now being plucked out of the sky by a barrage of flying telephone poles, SAM-3s, the Soviet-made surface-to-air missiles. Pilots had reported a sky cluttered with streaking rockets and bursting flak from anti-aircraft weaponry. Neither had a lack of fuel prevented the MiG-21s from taking off to tackle the latest threat, though their success ratio was minimal, since US fighter crews had been champing at the bit to get to tangle with a live enemy and put notches on their guns.

One notable success was scored by MiG number 2125 on Christmas Day, piloted by the only Vietnamese to reach outer space as a cosmonaut. His bird now sits atop a concrete plinth in the new air-force museum in Bac Mai. Pham Thaun himself is wasting away from space sickness, relegated to a nonoperational maintenance-overseeing role with a wing at Noi Bai. Most of his outdated MiGs are nonoperational.

Anti-aircraft guns are the first display you see upon entering the war museum. Once the domain of just the army, it has been recurated to take in the whole of the north's military history. It occupies part of the old French cantonment, which included Hanoi's original fortress. Around the back of the first block they have erected a hillock of aircraft scrap topped with a MiG-19 flaunting itself over an array of fins, wings and engines.

Hal had been a bit gruff and flag-waving, muttering anticommie, pro-Uncle Sam stuff about going to a place dedicated to glorifying the defeat of his one-time brothers in arms. But when we got to the first exhibition hall the historian in him took over.

We both froze in incredulity in front of the North Vietnamese solution to the mines seeded in their home waters: a cast-iron boilerplate yellow submarine. Well, peeling grey, rust and yellow. It was so Rube Goldberg it had us reeling about. It was a rivet-seamed six-metre oblong box with stubby wings, a singular caged propeller and narrow conning tower with a viewing slit. It was welded to a tricycle undercarriage enabling it to roll down ramps – a sort of flying start on its underwater missions. How many sorties this particular truck-battery-powered creation and its two-man crew had returned from was not explained, even in the Vietnamese legend. It could have been a dream prototype. However, two years later I was to discover another one, prominently featured in the front yard of a coastguard station on the downstream bank from the Long Binh bridge opposite the city; that one had been painted blue.

We pored over tanks, weapons and cabinets full of assorted memorabilia. It was strange to see photos displayed, shot by colleagues, with the caption details completely different from the actuality of the situation as I remembered it. Upon liberating Saigon they had acquired an excellent photo archive composed of the libraries of the wire services, US government as well as South Vietnamese official and newspaper sources. The attempts to rewrite history, as revealed behind curtains of both bamboo and iron, are pathetic. Simultaneously the population were being exposed to pirated copies of such classic

Vietnam War films as *Apocalypse Now* and *Platoon*. The party was fighting a rear-guard action.

What really chuffed Hal, what really got him stuck in the bunker, was a relief map the size of a basketball court recreating the battle of Dien Bien Phu. The exhibit was not running at full tilt, the power was off for restoration so the various phases of the campaign were left unilluminated, motes of dust settling on the miniature tanks and planes and positions in the shafts of afternoon light. Hal recited a litany of the brilliance of the battle planning and its strategist General Giap. He had brought along on the trip a number of Giap's writings, hoping to get the author to sign them at a hoped-for and requested meeting. The museum put a twinkle back in Hal's eye, simultaneously giving him a sadness that had not been evident before. I think the Vietnamese were now emerging as a people rather than the enemy or the folk he had been obliged to liaise with.

At the end of the first week we were told to be at the foreign-press centre at breakfast-time. Major General Hoang Phuong, chief of the Institute of Military History, who could unlock all their archives pertaining to the battle Hal had taken part in and who had been one of the senior planners at the time, would top the batting order. He was a totally professional military man, someone after Hal's heart, with a mind full of minutiae. During that campaign, which had been the first head-on clash with the newly introduced air mobile units, he had kept detailed diaries and sketch maps. After preliminaries and the normal sparring that always happens between Americans and Vietnamese, Phuong warmed to the pleasure of reminiscence, overjoyed with the set of maps and after-action reports Hal presented him with. I think the meeting was all too short for both parties, they could have gibbered on about this and that movement or position all day.

Officialdom caused Phuong to scamper back off to his archives prematurely, saying, however, that he would open contacts with his battlefield subordinates and buddies who were now full generals. Promises were made which remained unfulfilled for over a year.

The three horses pulling the chariot of war are Leadership, Organisation and Strategy. The ideal general should have a balance of all these assets combined. By many analysts' appraisal, as a strategist, Vo Nguyen Giap was at best a gifted amateur, but he had strong organisational abilities and was a charismatic leader of men, who both gave and demanded loyalty. His early association with underground movements of youth and labour meant he demanded loyalty to the party as well, though he describes himself as not a man of dogma. Most attribute his success to his willingness to sacrifice any number of lives. He once said, 'Every day in the world a hundred thousand people die. A human life is worth nothing!'

The area Giap came from, just north of the 17th parallel, is sandy and poor. By Quang Binh province standards his family were relatively well off when Giap was born in 1912; his father rented out land but also had to work the fields – he had fallen from the mandarin caste. More importantly, Giap's father was literate and familiar with Confucian classics.

At the age of fourteen Giap went off to work as a messenger for the Haiphong Electric Power Company. Two years later he got back to school, a lycée in Hue from where he was expelled, reportedly for subversive organising. Eventually, at the age of twenty-one in 1933, he enrolled in Hanoi University. He graduated in law and history with a degree equivalent to a doctorate, although in the colonies France did not allow this honour to be bestowed. *The Peasant Question*, his first book, brought French attention upon him, so with many other left-wing intellectuals and activists he took refuge in southern China during the late thirties crackdown on revolutionaries.

In May 1941, in Changsi, Giap met Ho Chi Minh for the first time, and when the Vietminh was first founded, he formed the army out of a ragbag of guerrillas fighting the Japanese at Tran Tao in 1944. Later he was to forge this peasant band into a coherent fighting force that would win the Vietminh war, culminating in the battle of Dien Bien Phu in 1954. Asked to purge landowners and incorrect cadre, he had thousands tied together in batches, like cordwood, and thrown into the river to drift towards the sea. This practice was known in a whisper as 'crab fishing'.

Veterans of this campaign provided the nucleus of the 325c division, formed in response to the computerised military planning and sophisticated communications of the US army, which moved by air and hardly ever walked. In his book *Big Victory, Great Taste*, outlining his strategic response, he explains that he had attempted to match the American advantage in mass or movement or, where not possible, to shunt it aside. He was still searching for a winning formula when handed victory in 1975. His dogged logistics genius stood the test of time, providing the means to the end. The doggedness was also his downfall.

Two years later, with Pol Pot in power in neighbouring Cambodia, cross-border raids were becoming more frequent; tension between the two countries was rising, a state of war imminent. Giap proposed a gradual setting-up of an anti–Khmer Rouge guerilla force in Cambodia, similar to the Vietminh or Vietcong. By 1978 the problem had turned septic, and the Politburo, who had earlier vetoed his proven protracted methods, opted for a Soviet-style solution: tank blitzkrieg, airstrikes, the works. Giap opposed it, though he lent his weight eventually to the planning. Pol Pot was overthrown but it turned out not to be the long-term success originally hoped for. For the sin of having been right when all others were wrong in a collective leadership decisionmaking process, Giap was eased out of the Politburo. When I met him in the early 1980s, he was confined to ceremonial functions.

It was the Tet New Year, and I was waiting for Tien to pick me up early in the morning to catch a plane out of Hanoi. At dawn I pushed open the original revolving glass-panelled door of the hotel. The giant wrought-iron gates of the Labour Ministry were opposite, the beige stucco of the building just emerging behind. The first workers were pedalling stolidly off to their state-run day, and a buffalo cart laden with iron pipes slogged along, banned from normal traffic hours because of its slow pace. Squad Number One of the besom-packing street-sweeper ladies scythed down from the direction of the state bank to the right. I lit a little roll-up to prepare for the day in transit south. It was rather mellow just standing surveying the awakening, the pastels of the first light; it felt really good to be.

The light brightened. People now flowed by in a continual stream on motorbikes and cycles; the first Czech-built Karosa bus lumbered towards the bank and the old city. Nervously I read my watch; six o'clock. Tien was half an hour late, and it was pointless ducking round the corner two blocks to the press centre, because no one got there before seven. The seedy bar in the foyer came to life so I got their first shot of *café sua* and tried not to panic but go with the Asian flow.

When the car appeared, a rare beast, a land cruiser, newly imported, Tien came straight to it. 'We see him in fifteen minutes.'

'Who, Tien?'

'You know.'

Ah, Giap. 'What! Look, man, all my gear's packed up.'

'No problem.'

'Hey, you know I'm dressed for travel, not for . . . Where's this thing at, Tien? How long we got?'

What does one wear to meet a general at breakfast? Tennis shirt? Fatigue designer chic? Maybe that's too naff. I dug a short-sleeved bush shirt out of my padlocked grip, got out of my dirty running shoes, the comfortable ones, and put on formal heavy hikers. Flash-pack batteries, leads, different lenses and films had to be gathered into the carry-on work bag.

I smoked the reserve number I had ready for the trip. This was a mistake because suddenly I was really stoned. I didn't dare ask Tien about the flight or the new programme. He intimated that all was just fine.

The state guesthouse was just down the street, but we still took the truck, regally getting the palatial gates swung back after a charade of paper mumbo with a senior fool in a red-banded hat. One side of the guesthouse compound, across a large formal garden with bonsai trees, is the monolithic official state hotel, where guests of the government and their entourages are put up. Opposite stands the governor's old mansion with reception rooms and conference chambers.

We were shown into the main reception room. No one else was there yet. As a place to take a photograph of, it was magnificent: red carpeting, beige walls, gilded columns, velvet drapes swathed around the tall french windows. But to work in for a portrait the room was dim, the verandas screening out a lot of the morning light, the 40-watt wall-bracket fixtures glowing only faintly in their own vicinity. The obligatory tea service was set out at the far end on a glass-topped coffee table with its Tet bouquet in a small porcelain vase. The Thermos of hot water would arrive together with a bowl of fruit once we had all been seated. We were joined by the chief of the press department, Duong Minh, all suited up and goofy grin plastered on.

Duong Minh had been a second secretary in the southern republic's embassy on Victoria Road in Kensington under President Thien. The whole time he was a Hanoi mole, hung in there like a Le Carré novel character for three and a half years. His English was fluent, he loved to rap about

London, and loved Cadbury's chocolate. Sad to say, he is now deceased.

The formalities over, Tien began nudging me, telling me Giap was coming and to think up some questions. A beige four-door Lada swept up the drive ramp. A liveried attendant opened the front door and out sprang Robin; his Batman was in the back with a briefcase. For a man of such standing, he was astonishingly small. It had never crossed my mind that a man who had won so many battles would be so short, only a shade over five foot, though perfectly erect. His smile was cheerful, almost cherubic, beneath a balding head carefully stranded back. At once his eyes locked to mine – a test fire, a blink, an inner nod, a firm hand. It was somehow natural to address him in French; he had been educated in that language and I presumed he preferred that to his last foes' American English. We both mumbled apologies for having no time, though the tenses got a bit confusing.

It was time for me to take the photos. They all wanted a custom pose of the general, Duong Minh and the aide-de-camp. I tidied up the table a bit, tweaked the flowers and backed off down the pile rug running the length of an alley of dead wood, at the head of which we had been having the tea party. It was going to have to be a low stacked-up frame on a longish lens, the 85-mm or the 90-mm. Flash and available light. Damn! I was wrecked, the sync cords were getting tangled, the bounce card fell off the strobe head, the Leica slipped off my shoulder. It was a real mess. A quick glance back towards the sitters revealed quirky smiles, tolerantly amused, willing to look benignly on foreigners as clumsy children.

Regaining composure, I got set up, sussed out the right lens, got the sync cord untangled, popped a test flash and dropped to a squat for the shot. That's when it came unglued and I toppled sideways in a crunch of gear and rolling lenses to end up like a turtle on its back. The whole group twittered like summer sparrows, enjoying the circus – no particular loss of face.

The next ten minutes were more relaxed and the shoot went well. After another round of smiles and firm grasps, both parties sprinted for their respective vehicles, and we made the plane.

When I was finally able to arrange the meeting of generals in 1990, Joe and Hal looked like attorneys off to a trial, loaded down with tape recorders, books and files, maps, all manner of archival stuff. Both were sweating profusely as we entered the same tall-windowed hall I had clowned in before. The light had not improved, though someone had thoughtfully left a set of TV flood lights in one corner. They proved not to function.

Hal had on that all-American look of genuine admiration, the happy gun dog waiting for a command. He was fighting back a lot of emotion. The enemy was now to be befriended – the honourable opponent – the whole warrior code was called into play. But just as we entered, his hi-tech hearing buttons went dead again.

Giap's eyes too lit up when the photos, maps and briefing papers came out; that broke the ice. Hal and Giap pored over common ground, the language difficulty partly overcome with the documentation. Poor Hal strained to catch what Giap said, or Tien translated, bending forward and cupping his ear. The cathartic, historic experience was nearly ruined by $2.49 watch batteries.

Among the archives were some copies of one of Giap's books translated into English. He got so excited that I doubted he had seen this edition, and he was probably hoping for a present after all this talk, but it was not to be, they were only for his autograph. His smile collapsed, but his visitors consoled him with a sheaf of maps and plastic-encased documents.

We were going into the last round of formalities and fraternal messages, getting the blessing for a more intimate future trip, when Hal sprang up like a jack-in-the-box. Pulling his wristwatch off, he thrust it at Giap, who was completely stunned by this move, having quite a nice model on his arm already. Hal's watch looked like solid gold, an upmarket item with a flexi band. He hugged the dapper little man in his parade uniform with five stars on each shoulder board, and sat down again with an exhausted look. Tien caught my ear and whispered, '. . . in the cigar box with twenty-four others!'

It would have been a farce but for the tears in Hal's eyes. Giap looked piercingly long at Hal and gently touched the shoulder of the safari jacket. We were free to go in peace.

Later that night, back at the digs, Hal had dug another Timex out of his ample luggage to cover the white strap mark on his tanned forearm.

Promises, promises, bottles of high-grade cognac and Black Label were despatched, envelopes with entreaties and Pentagon documents slipped across, all via the doughty Tien. It came to naught. The other generals our lads wanted to rap with had gone to ground, no doubt for political reasons. We sat around waiting for the call, and the Americans were getting bored. I had to get them out of town.

Hanoi's resident foreign population, then peaking at 4,000, retreated at weekends to designated resorts within an easy drive. Do Son fitted the bill, a bright fishing town whose beaches were the talk of the diplomatic circuit. It sits on a promontory of land jutting out into the Gulf where the Red River finally meanders to its conclusion. On one side of the spit the waters are a rusty colour, the other clear and clean, except where the typhoons blow everything back up.

Do Son is to the nouveau riche of Tonkin what Brighton was to a Victorian gentleman. New single women in town are scored by the Western studs, the shakily married aid technocrats and the slick movers hunting new recruits for the networks. To the lads it was Coney Island and Cannes.

The main town is full of day trippers, gaudy and gay, down from Haiphong and Hanoi on decaying charabancs, to float in tyre tubes and gobble Vietnamese fast food: dried roast squid, cuttlefish, pineapple chunks, swigged down with beer iced with lumps broken from sawdusted blocks. Young punks perform exaggerated manoeuvres on their chrome-flash scooters past dowdy, pale factory girls queueing to rent swimsuits. Off-duty soldiers and sailors walk hand in hand, unable to compete against the urban cowboys clad in imported jeans abulge with newly minted dong. Over a spine in the promontory, a series of lidos line the seashore, tall coconut palms running to the top of the high-water mark. French villas with stone-pillared verandas dot the hillside. Lunch comes fresh out of the gulf, the best up north.

A mansion built for the last emporer, Bao Dai, as his summer house up north, occupies the whole spur of headland, its own hardtop driveway pulling up in a circular drive, the lawn dotted with ornately clipped shrubbery and topiary. At one side of the drive where it entered the covered portico, free enterprise had created a small café dispensing coconuts, teas and sodas dripping cold from a smuggled Thai cool box. Customers sat at the standard doll-size garden furniture, children ran the orders to the tripper's tables. They had come to pose in the last vestiges of decadence, to saunter through the cavernous blue-shuttered rooms, most unfurnished, though upstairs a few chambers were kept for VIP rentals. The staff said it was difficult to maintain a hotel out here for there had been no water for some time. Power was equally dodgy.

A circular marble-floored dance platform with two viewing parapets stuck out on the seaward end; perfect backdrops for honeymooning couples still in their rented costumes. It could have been a surreal movie set from the thirties in autochrome colour tint, faded pastels. The sea could be heard swishing below; junks batting up the coast rounded the headland into the Red River on the tide. Black on gold silhouettes, long shadows, the first bats flitting. We wished we could have stayed longer.

The press centre got the last laugh, hitting Joe with a monstrously inflated bill for services rendered although these had been frustratingly few. That put Tien's salary on a par with a minor, slightly corrupt, minister. Joe coughed up reluctantly, only to be handed the van rental on the way to the airport. It was as though the Vietnamese had counted his stash and decided how much they decently had to let him keep to get through two nights in Thai transit. It was their pound of flesh, their way of getting back at America at large.

The territory was badly deforested. On the crest of the nearest hill stood a square brick blockhouse or observation tower; guy wires led from its antennaed top into the scrub. Up the gulley to the left were some anti-tank obstacles and a couple of burnt-out vehicles, the whole area studded with stunted shrubs and large grey rocks. These foothills rose to larger jungle-clad peaks in the distance.

We had been bused here, fifty klicks out of the capital, in the press centre's Hiace. Ham and I were the only foreigners, crammed in with ten of the giggling junior staff, all freshly issued with state-of-the-art videos and cameras. There was a picnic-outing atmosphere all the way to Son Tay.

The name Son Tay had gone off like a bell in my head. Special Forces had led a raid on a POW camp here in the early seventies. Airforce Jolly Green Giants had delivered a platoon of crack troops right into the compound, having deliberately crash-landed a Trojan horse. Storming the complex, they had killed twenty-five North Vietnamese and suffered no casualties themselves. The rescue attempt was one of the most daring missions ever carried out, and an unqualified success – apart from the fact that the POWs had been moved some days before.

Most of the kids in the bus were too young to remember

the war, much less this feat of Rambo bravado, but they were fascinated to learn a bit more of the lore. Anyway, part of the reason for our presence was to enable them to practise their language skills.

Son Tay is home town to the Dac Cong as Hereford is to the British SAS, Fort Bragg to the US Special Forces. Ham and I were to be the first Western press allowed inside. Little is known about Vietnam's special units, except that they operate in the densely wooded areas astride the border, where the Ho Chi Minh Trail once wound. In the 1970s and 1980s, there were frequent border incursions into Cambodia, and until late in 1992, the Montagnard resistance movement (FULRO) was still active, staging occasional raids and ambushes against Vietnamese from their base deep in the jungles of Cambodia's Ratnakiri and Mondukiri provinces. The Dac Cong's job was to stop them. The Montagnards are a hill people living along the border with Cambodia and Laos. They surrendered en masse to Uruguyan marines of the UNTAC peacekeeping force after being 'discovered' by an American journalist, Nate Thayer. By then they had been eroded from more than 4,000 fighters and their families to a group of 450, who were evacuated en bloc to resettlement in North Carolina. Their leader was captured and executed summarily by Pol Pot having been lured to Phnom Penh.

Sitting in the grandstand at Son Tay, we watched the special units strutting their stuff. The unarmed-combat demonstration teams included a couple of Spetsnatz, great hairy Russians, who had taken on the aggressor role against a couple of women recruits. Young Lions, teenage fanatics, had gone through their paces, while on an adjacent range an infiltration, demolition and booby-trap course had been delivered. The infiltration demonstration made me realise that during the war no place had been totally secure. We watched a three-man team, naked save for shorts, squeeze under foot-high tanglefoot wire with trip mines and flares laced throughout, then mount double-high coiled razor wire in a matter of a couple of minutes. Admittedly in broad daylight, and not in a hostile environment, but still impressive. With their gun and kit strapped in a fishing-rod pouch along their spines, the first lad had thrown himself against the flesh-shredding teeth of the wire, the second had run up him and draped across the top, the third loped up both their backs and jumped clear. The second one then rolled on out, the last dropped down and, having tied the springy coils together, snuck through underneath. The other two had parted the coils on their side. To get past the low-slung trip devices, they had simply taken small split lengths of bamboo to lift up the offensive wires.

We were side by side on the viewing platforms with a special Lao delegation and a cluster of attachés from fraternal nations fielding trainees in the performance. There were Cubans, Libyans, North Koreans, Russians, Czechs, Chinese, and dark men whose identity or nationality was never revealed. A lot of these guys were sporting rank and medals. The CIA would have loved to get at the majority, and one bomb would have taken out a good 30 per cent of the Vietnamese top brass. Ham and I were not allowed to document these opening stages, though our press-centre juveniles burned up endless footage and tape. The dark men did not want to be recorded by outsiders, and many had donned sunglasses, enhancing their spookiness. Off the record we were told of a wartime raid mounted into Thailand which had penetrated the Sathahip air base and blown up seven B-52s on the ground. The United States had not revealed the details back then.

Once the paramilitary hit squads of people's democracy had left the stage, we were photographically unshackled. So far, the whole exercise had been conducted by a stout, tough-looking guy sporting a gold Rolex and glued-on Ray-bans, his voice fluctuating on and off to the vagaries of the karaoke mike system he was wearing around his neck – the sort of rig Bob Dylan had in the sixties for hands-off harmonica playing. His buttoned up dress uniform caused him to strut more than necessary; the peaked, gold-braided hat toned with the tan dress looked more South American dictator than the world's number-one hard core. Each breast of the jacket held an array of medals the size of an A4 sheet, from lapel almost to belt, with a lot of overlapping gongs. This was General Nguyen Van Cong, double hero of the revolution, chief of covert and intelligence forces, barely mentioned in the gazette lists, and then only as in technical services. To be acclaimed a hero of the revolution is like winning a Victoria Cross to a Commonwealth military man, or the Congressional Medal of Honour to an American. There was no press release of General Cong illuminating his feats. He had the air of a Prussian Sihanouk, a similar squeaky voice, but did not smile a lot. He had conducted the performance by commands given on a gold whistle on a braided lanyard.

Cong now paced in front of us, whistle in hand, his training fields empty as a backdrop, giving a long lecture, partly lost to us by feedback, on the winning and delicate art of camouflage. During the war, enemy bodies were regularly found with a loosely woven rattan place-mat affair on the back of their webbing. The troops were disciplined always to stick foliage of the terrain they were passing through into the rosette. The pith helmets also received new foliage on the move. The whistle blew again and a whole battalion of Dac Cong, clad in buff cotton boxers and tiny peaked forage skullcaps, emerged from their chrysalises of rock, sod and bush. We were invited to move into the pit and make a few snaps. Clambering down the bank from the grandstand, I almost trod on other concealed men dressed as turf and still motionless and flat. All had bird's feet painted on their skin in camouflage-stick paint, the stencil of jailbirds' uniforms. Others had arisen from buffalo wallows and muddy puddles, totally black except for now open eyes and parted pink lips. It was hard to guess anybody's age, much less try to discern a face for future identification. There was nary a grin among them; their eyes just tracked me, the whites swivelling in the darkened faces. Aliens to be watched.

Ham looked as if he was from another planet, a world apart, his spindly hairy legs ending in patterned nylon socks and sneakers. His slightly maniacal smile was partially hidden by thick glasses. He had brought all his gear to record this display. None of the cameras had interchangeable components so he was strung about with a single-lens reflex, a happy-snappy compact, a Hi-8 video, a wind-up cine camera and a separate tape recorder. A spare still camera and assorted bits were carried in an American ammo can painted bright yellow. Cong had met Ham somewhere and taken a shine to him.

The other foreigners took off, leaving us to wend our way to the officers' mess, together with some lucky member of the Writers' Guild. Twenty round tables occupied the outdoor covered section, four the inner sanctum behind still closed doors. The surfaces groaned with food for battalions, symmetrical arrangements of 555s and bottles of liquor in the centre. By the time we arrived, the herd of senior colonels and generals had opened a number, and their toasting had heightened the atmosphere. Minions darted by with more platters, others dispensed a continuum of beer, bottled and canned. This was neither proletarian nor army chow, but a series of dishes befitting an imperial feast. As honoured guests we got chopsticked morsels speared our way before the hosts, represented at our table by two generals and an admiral.

As we sated out, the speeches got shorter, the toasts more frequent. Everyone was getting ploughed under with Ruu Chanh lemon vodka and cognac. Ham had his bong out, a fine head of smoke up, passing from one three-starrer to a two, and back.

General Cong joined our table to promote international understanding and get a hit on the bong. He had removed his shades, and his small piggy eyes were furtive, avoiding lens contact when I popped off some snaps. The top brass were falling over drunk, lady generals included. There were some serious frames to make here, true revelatory moments behind the scenes of power. These normally invisible figures were prepared to pose, a full roll went into the bag. Two female senior colonels got me as I was changing my film, pulled me into a chair and, from what I could gather, were extracting the price of having their photo taken: I would have to down a drink. My protestations that alcohol does not pass my lips were overruled. Three generals joined in; I was pinned back and four shots of raw Ruu Chanh tipped in.

Skunked for the first time in a decade, I remember nothing further. I suppose we left, for I found some group snaps of everyone in my camera bidding the adieus.

# 9

# *Foundations*

Those days I was spending an inordinate amount of time hanging out in the foreign-press centre in Hanoi, bored by the inane activity around the glass-topped tea table and four collapsing Naugahyde-covered banquettes in the office. The room was shared by the bookkeeper and petty-cash dispenser, the assistant chief and Quang, the director. An adjacent room, possibly an old serving pantry, held the secretarial staff; that is, one or more of the interpreters who, when not actually on-line, had to peck out the multi-carboned request forms needed to implement their colleagues' programmes. The typewriter, once liberated from the South, was a sit up and beg American job, looking more like a cash register than a writing machine. There was also an obsolete photocopy machine standing idle for want of toner and paper.

The bureau had one phone line, to Quang's annoyance often used for cross-town chats by the newest intake of kids. This Levis and sneakers gang infiltrating the Essex men of Hanoi was a new generation grown up with more freedom of expression and knowledge of the outside world. They had absorbed Hollywood's concept of their history from videos of *The Killing Fields*, *Apocalypse Now* and *Platoon*, besides shows from the abysmal TV series *China Beach* and *Tour of Duty*. They were hip to the renewed international interest in their country, and highly clued to the need for the correct ways of promoting it.

Unfortunately, it would be years before the new blood seeped to the hydra's head. I was back trying to push the memorial idea further along the ideological track, and getting stumped by lack of communication within and between departments. Delay and frustration had set in with a Tonkinese vengeance. Since that day when we planted the tree on the south bank of the Ben Hai, accompanied by the cream of the province's committees, the goal posts had once again been moved. They had divided Thua Thien province into two, probably to create more jobs in local government when unemployment was running at over 30 per cent, but also to divide up the rampant corruption. Anyway, it would mean having to negotiate with a whole new slew of officials, who were now uptight that they had not been previously consulted about the project. Their objections had been forwarded to the Hanoi Cultural Information, Sport and Tourism crowd, who, faced with a minor dilemma, just said no. I suspect that middle-rankers were blocking the scheme because there was no pocket money in it for them. Had we been a large international charity, dripping dollars, the bureaucrats would have expected a good 40 per cent fund bleed.

The trouble was to try and keep tabs on a project happening in the middle of Vietnam, a country ill served by transportation and with insufficient phone or fax lines. It is impossible to orchestrate a complete local committee assembling simultaneously. We had encountered this problem during the planting ceremony, upsetting a couple of absent Dong Ha officials. Their protests now ricocheted back up the nervous system to control central, the cultural crowd. Someone else had thrown a spanner of confusion into the works by leading members of the ideological department to believe we were building a memorial to all the dead of the Indochina conflict. The religious branch of the cultural lot were taking umbrage at the sectarian aspect of the Buddhist stupa. They did not have any suggestions of their own, although the chief of the Vietnamese News Agency wanted to put up a shrine or plaque to the members of his staff who had perished during the liberation struggles. Remains of six of a nine-man media team blown away on the Ho trail while heading south had only recently been recovered. At an official meeting he had given the impression that he would put his weight behind our mission. Now he was rescinding this aid, saying there was a problem about putting the southerners' names next to those of the true patriots, the northerners.

With Tien, Mum and a bunch of the youngsters, I retreated to one of the pavement cafés to think it over. Madame Hao beavered away on our behalf behind the scenes in the cultural department. Hao is an aristocratic lady, whose father had been a foreign minister in Unclo Ho's first cabinet. She was one of the chief interpreters and translators at the press centre, assigned to the serious English-language papers – the *New York Times*, the *Washington Post*, the *Guardian*. She was also possibly the best literary translator that the north has had, both English to Vietnamese and Vietnamese to English. (Among her credits, *Bright Shining Lie*, the Pulitzer-winner by Neil Sheehan, and the controversial *Ridding Their Devils* by Frank Palmos.) At her house in the old southeast quarter of the city she regularly hosted a salon of painters, poets and literati. Hanoi's writers and artists are generally too poor to get into the big hotels, though desperate to have contact with the foreign and new, and to show their works. You could buy for a few dollars magnificent pieces straight off her living-room walls. The spare upstairs rooms were let to overseas youths on Viet language courses or to the daughters of the well-off who wanted them to have a finishing-school touch, learning manners in four languages. At this time she was chaperone to the *Asahi Shimbun* Bangkok bureau chief's daughter and a girl whom she termed 'my adoptive daughter', a sixteen-year-old whose parents had obviously come adrift of the system.

I needed to see the memorial site, do some measuring, take reconnaissance photos, start planting some flowering bushes, and get things moving. Above all, I wanted to check on the *bodhi* tree's growth, and ascertain that the dollars we had left for protective anti-goat fencing had been used for that purpose. The last report we had had was when Tien talked to a guide in charge of a coach that had stopped by the site. He made vague signs at head height or above to indicate the tree growth. However, there had been a couple of killer typhoons since we planted and the Ben Hai at that point flooded right up to the road dyke, which is usually brackish with tidal water from the gulf.

Hao came up with a suggestion; she would find a vehicle we could all go in – the two virgins, Hao and I, and Thuan, a poet bent on writing an ode to the tree and designing some garden for the foundation. A beaten-up Russian Ruf minibus with driver could be had for a mere $350. Hao arranged for our expedition to go as far as Hoi An, 70 kilometres south of Da Nang, the old port up the Song River where, three centuries ago, Chinese and Japanese trading vessels had plied regularly. Their captains and merchants had constructed a street full of temples and another of warehouses. Faifo, as it was then known, had been part of the inter-Asian trade pattern stretching from the Sakhalin peninsula to the Straits of Malacca and into the Indian Ocean. Junks had come to collect the porcelains, tiles, silk and lacquer, leaving goods that traded all the way across the Annamitic Cordillera to the Mekong in the kingdoms of Laos and Cambodia. Cham roadways stretched from here back through the bombed ruins at My Son, 60 kilometres inland. During the war these ancient tracks had become North Vietnamese infiltration routes, subject to intensive interdiction campaigns conducted on the ground and from the air. The millennium-old complex at My Son in the heart of what the marines had called 'the Arizona' was subjected to a B-52 strike, leaving much of the ancient city in rubble. Delicate *apsaras* (dancers) and buddhas carved from the local ochre sandstone are scarred by shrapnel and many have been looted away.

Once a year, two Polish archaeologists come and make a vain attempt to clear the bush back and do a spot of restoration. The ministry in charge of historical sites and monuments, also located within the Cultural, Ideological, Tourism and Sport Ministry, assigns three workers a year to aid the flagging Polish programme, which is based at the end of a tortuous trail winding through bomb craters four hours from the nearest road head. A lot of unexplored ordnance litters this countryside, causing grief to city migrants encouraged to resettle to plant coffee bushes in the poisoned and devastated terrain.

While we were still in Hanoi awaiting permission to head south with Hao and the two girls, Tien and I tried to find a blue flowering bush, a water pump and a sturdily built *cuong* – a small votive platform or shrine of the type commonly seen in Annam in front of people's houses. These shrines are often cast from concrete but are usually made of wood, though in the northern provinces of the old south, one still sees many created from ammunition cases, the 20-mm cannon variety, the best-selling model. The *cuong* signifies a certain sanctification upon a place or dwelling, attracting the good spirits and appeasing the unappealing ones. Although many Vietnamese now follow some form of organised religion, the old ways, the ancient rituals, are slow to expire. Without due care, the delicate balance of inherited animistic mores will be upset, leading to untold calamities. These superstitions are held even within the heart of the most dogged communist. To deny the existence of the spirits is tantamount to tempting fate.

Erecting a *cuong* next to the bo tree could only be a good thing I believed. Most of the Tonkinese officials with whom I was negotiating concurred, and Madame Hao, whose family originated in the old Annamese capital of Hue, loved the idea.

The section of the city five blocks west of the little lake is devoted to workshops making and selling Buddhist paraphernalia. Incense, altars, candles, flags and *cuongs* were all to be found here. We commissioned one to be built sturdy enough to withstand central Vietnam's weather. Three days later and 60,000 dong poorer, we took delivery.

In the meantime, Tien and I had visited the market for second-hand electrical appliances, a cluster of businesses by the railroad tracks on the southern fringe of town. Dumped on the pavement in front was a sea of Eastern European obsolescence. Each emporium duplicated the next's wares rather than specialise. We were looking for a pump to give to the household that had the well on the corner of the memorial site. In the dry season it would provide for the irrigation of the proposed garden, the Ben Hai being too saline for horticultural purposes. We pulled apart heaps of inferior power tools, fifties-styled upright vacuum cleaners, Romanian fans and liberated American appliances. Of the available range of pumps, it came down to a new Russian one, electric without intake or outtake fixtures, cable or plug, or a smart little American two-stroke Cushman, vintage early seventies, missing spark plug and tank cap. They had no petrol to try it anyway. Seventy dollars and another three days produced the latter machine in working condition, new plug and starter cord mounted to order on a wooden skid.

The reason for our search for a blue-flowered bush was that we wanted the garden to be planted in the colours of the Buddhist flag. The Vietnamese, being enthusiastic gardeners, got behind this one and came up quickly with the necessary white, red and orange plants. But blue in a bush is a rarity, though less so in a flower. The quest took us out of town to the strip of intensively cultivated land beneath the dyke of the Red River. From the road we could look down on classically organised villages, where each family farm is built around a small paved courtyard, the small fields radiating off beyond the home orchards into the tracts of paddy. Traditionally, this has been the market garden area for Hanoi. During the period before Tet, the small patches are ablaze with colour, flowers for the coming New Year festivities.

There was a bonsai master who would know where we could obtain the needed plant. To get his name and address we first had to visit the bonsai market behind the Defence Ministry, adjacent to the leaning-pillar pagoda. His daughter reputedly had a patch there. It was difficult not to come away from this research with a truckload of ridiculously cheap miniature bushes and trees; in a garden centre in Britain they were worth thousands. On the second trip we found the granddaughter, a fifty-year-old, who would guide us to the garden 10 kilometres away. She was mounted on a French-style ladies' bicycle of uncertain vintage; we were aboard a new Honda 90. She set a lively pace.

On the outskirts of Nghi Tan village she almost lost us, nimbly ducking down the tiny alleys, then over little bridges between paddies, past vine-covered arbours shielding young plants and tree nurseries. The family house had been newly whitewashed and the paths, bordered by upside-down implanted beer bottles, were freshly swept. The front yard, trellis-shaded, hosted the stock of bonsais. The art of miniaturisation of shrubs and trees is often thought to be uniquely Japanese, but the Vietnamese were also engaged in the same skills over a millennium ago. We were ushered inside and installed in heavy chairs in the family room to await the master's awakening from one of his naps.

Nguyen Cam was ninety-one, a hunched, frail old man with clear eyes and long piano-player fingers. He emerged in his striped cotton pyjamas, a great-grandchild attached to a finger. The granddaughter did the introduction and left for her flower stall. Cam left the small girl in Tien's happy hands to shuffle off, against our protests, to change into something more suitable for receiving visitors. He re-emerged in threadbare, flapping trousers, clean, patched shirt and holed, sleeveless pullover, clutching a large photo album, which was handed over for our perusal. Inside were faded clippings going back to the 1950s: letters, snaps, awards and citations. Any questions we had were answered by the much worn book, for he had been visited by people from dozens of countries. Tien was able to decipher the Cyrillic; I could handle the French, German (E-bloc) and Cuban Spanish. His oldest prizes dated from the thirties. He had kept on growing, pruning and training his mini-gardens and trees right through the various wars. During the North–South conflict, an anti-aircraft position of the Tu Liem district defence brigade had blazed away from an adjacent garden.

We were given a guided tour of his plot, gradually working the subject around to the blue-flower problem. Extended family members came and watched over the bougainvillea hedge as yet another foreigner was being entertained by Gramps.

Only on our second visit, three days later, did he agree to let us take away a prize bush just at the end of its flowering cycle. It had the tiniest of delicate blue blooms, almost alpine. Including the cost of the granddaughter cycling it downtown to the press centre twelve klicks away, it set the Indochina Medla Memorial Foundation back a total of $10. A phoenix-emblazoned planter was thrown in for the foundation's cause.

Finally we set off in the Soviet-made minibus. At sunset, way before the Khe Anh ferry, the electrics packed up. We were reduced to bump starts, all hands pushing, flashlights forwards as headlights. The planned, fairly comfortable 500-kilometre drive to Dong Hoi turned into an eighteen-hour jerky nightmare. At the end of it, we arrived too late to claim our rooms in the newly constructed barracks-like Bach Dong hotel.

The management and staff were all fast asleep, the latter in their mosquito nets over army camp beds in the darkened foyer. Our arrival caused much kerfuffle and scrabbling around to find the mislaid telex and our reservations. Our rooms were long gone and there were no spares, for an MIA team excavating two nearby sites had unexpectedly pitched up in three brand-new Cherokee Jeeps. The flustered staff now awoke other staff and, after consultation about who was least important, roused the residents of another downstairs chamber. It was suggested that I needed a separate room so they started making provisions to place me in the bathroom. A quick sweep of a flashlight beam disturbed a battalion of scurrying cockroaches making off across a swamped floor or into the raised squatter toilet, so I opted instead for one of the greasy, gritty, just vacated beds with holed mosquito curtain. Both the driver and Thanh, the poet, snored loudly. Hao and the girls had another evicted guest's monkey penned up in their bathroom to contend with. Before sunrise we were awoken anyway by a group of collegiate Americans chanting 'Happy Birthday' and 'For he's a jolly good fellow', followed by a chorus of hoorays.

There were no other inns or rooms in the 100,000-population town, which has only just started to rebuild itself from the rubble left over from the last shellings and bombings in 1972. It had attracted devastation, being the most southerly port in the North at the waist of the country close to the Ho trail; it had also hosted a naval base. In the centre of the city, the skeleton of the French-built cathedral towered above the remains of the godowns and warehouses now only a metre high, with locals pilfering bricks from the rubble to start an adjacent housing estate. The new breeze-block hotel squatted downstream from the centre, overlooking mud flats and mosquitoes. Across the riverside road, the ribs of assault craft and ferry pontoons still protruded from the shoals where they had stuck after being hit by US firepower two decades ago.

The Ben Hai is not visible from the ridges north or south; the tall flagpole still in situ on the south bank is. No flag flies today, though the rusting column has been declared by some a national monument. I had hoped the bloody thing would somehow have been removed, leaving the future memorial-garden site uncluttered. Breasting the last slope with Route One arrowing towards the river, clearly defined by its flanking planes and poplars, I realised that this had not transpired. As we hiccuped towards the river, I silently prayed the tree would still be alive.

The road mounts a ramp to approach the bridge and I had the Ruf stopped there to make a zooming photographic approach to the possible worst scenario. The daunting flag standard loomed out of its raised brick base, and next to it now stood a two-metre-high hedge of brown and green. Closing in revealed an interwoven bamboo picket fence surrounded by fast-growing prickly-pear cactus. The bo had grown strongly to shoulder height from the withered, two-leaved sapling we had left screened by a fighting-cock coop. The $50 bill John Sheppard had laid on the locals after the planting ceremony had been put marginally to work for maintenance, though a new corrugated roof and brick wing of the ramshackle *pho* shop represented the larger percentage.

The residents – the appointed IMMF site concierge and crew – were astounded to see someone return from the past; it had been the best part of a year. They would be delighted to install the *cuong*, they said. For the time being it was set up on some bricks beside the tree, which appeared to have actually flourished from twice being flooded, though the waters had risen above its current height and crested over the road, isolating the bridge, at the flood's worst.

The *cuong* temporarily installed, we bumped on south, Hao having arranged for a community meal to be served when we returned from Hoi An. We would bring back the neighbouring committee lads from Gio Linh for a feast, which turned out to be one of the most indigestible meals I have ever attempted to get down. The girls picked at the greased-over fried eggs with the three-day-old baguettes, the committee men drank only the beers we were double-charged for, while the one-eyed commune chief and his one-armed assistant, both North Vietnamese army veterans, scarfed up the swill. The owners of the café spent most of the meal computing the tab on a piece of grubby exercise book.

We were going to leave them another chunk of cash for maintenance but Hao opted not to when the bill for our party was passed over in the twilight; it was over a half a million dong, or about $50. The Gio Linh party people now promised to take over the site maintenance, seeing as it was attracting interest in the capital. Besides, road crews were busy at work improving the wretched highway to Dong Ha as well as south from Dong Hoi, so more VIPs could be expected. A spur road was also to be constructed from Route One straight inland to the largest war-graves cemetery next to the old US marine firebase at Con Thien. There lie the bits of remains of upwards of 22,000 men and women lost to the battles of the DMZ and nearby Ho Chi Minh Trail.

Before we headed north to the delights of Dong Hoi, our electrics now rejuvenated by southern mechanics, I lit a bundle of incense at the newly erected *cuong*. Afterwards some villagers touchingly approached Hao to ask whether they could also make offerings. Several came forward, leaving flowers, fruit and a bowl of rice to the Spirits. Looking back as we trundled over the bridge, I saw a circle of children and old people gathered around, quietly meditating. The sun was sinking in a post-monsoon brilliance of colour over the now peaceful former DMZ.

Madame Hao was docked a year's salary for rendering me

the above assistance, though I did not find that out until over a year later. The press centre perfidiously said nothing, stringing me along, when, three months later, I was back in Hanoi to discuss the whole memorial, faculty and fellowship programme. Now the stakes had been raised, I had to give a presentation of the overall project to a conglomerate of all the sundry branches of the Ministry of Ideology etc. There were to be a good dozen on the panel, the vice director of culture assured me. His sideline was a company that was creaming off state contracts to restore historical buildings and to build monuments and memorials. Our design was too biased, too Buddhist, too slanted towards one philosophy. He suggested that he become our sponsor in the machinations of pushing the concept through a newly created maze of business interests. He would help present our case to the panel. The problem was that we had nothing financial to offer, and the mean grubby paw of the ebbing command economy needed to rake in as much as possible before its demise. He was helpful in suggesting that the army corps of engineers should be involved; after all, their media personnel had been in uniform, so they officially qualified for veterans' and heroes' privileges. He was also on the board of the same engineering corps and could propose introductions.

He had been the only moderately important official of vice-ministerial rank available to approach, for suddenly all the other ones who had been big nodders were out of town or papered over in previous engagements. Somewhere deep inside the two-faced bureaucracy a big NIX had been red-lined across our endeavours. With hindsight, I realise that the result of the presentation to the humourless panel of associated subministry representatives was a foregone conclusion, though everyone at the press centre and the Ministry of Culture played to the hilt the illusion that the approvals would be ratified.

Someone had been slighted, at district, province or ministerial level. Taciturn Quang would normally have taken me out to dinner and explained things in his broken English. To announce our defeat, he chose to arrange an official meeting in the reception hall of the press centre, communicating via an interpreter in a voice usually reserved for testy members of the fourth estate who had not come to terms with the people's democracy. I was devastated and lost my cool with Quang for the first time in years. Luckily Denis Gray, the AP Bangkok bureau chief and one of the original trustees of the foundation, was on hand to temper my reactions. He turned Quang round so we could analyse the situation. Quang qualified the no. It was a question of sovereignty and perseverance.

Much later it was suggested we could help matters by getting a small bridge built in the Ben Hai district. But the pump still sits in the basement of the Hanoi press centre, and the blue bonsai adorns the outside stairs.

I took Denis's photographer Jeff up to watch the smuggling over the Klondike-like scarp north of Dong Dang on the Chinese border. Denis got on with his interviews in the prelude to the return of Prince Norodom Sihanouk to Phnom Penh and the application of the Paris peace accords.

Meanwhile, in the oily deserts of the Persian Gulf, the cavalry came to Joe's rescue in no less a guise than Storming Norman. Schwartzkopf, the commanding general of the allied expeditionary forces confronting the Iraqis in Kuwait and the Saudi desert, had been a captain, a company commander in one of the units sent to relieve the beleaguered 2/7 cavalry at LZ Albany, the second sector of the Ia Drang campaign. Joe's excellent piece commemorating the battle had been a cover feature in *US News and World Report*, much admired in military circles and becoming assigned homework for the new intake of officer candidates. On the eve of Desert Storm's air and land offensive, Joe had been requested to meet the general in his field-trailer home in Riyadh. In the ensuing tête-à-tête, Norman had guaranteed him a place on the lead tank, which he expected to gain the banks of the Euphrates within a matter of days. Meantime his personal chase ship, his back-up chopper, complete with SatFax line, was at Joe's disposal. That kept the covers coming and copies tumbling through the fast-improving Hanoi mail system to Phoung's and Giap's desks.

I caught four days of the return of Joe and the general. His Gulf War stuff had been passed to the top of the Defence Ministry, where that conflict had a confused audience. Vietnamese workers in Iraq had been expelled from Baghdad to Jordan, while Iraqi Airlines jets flew into Hanoi empty to pick up free fraternal freightloads of rice. The coalition victory illustrated the future side that the butter for their bread would come from, and the doors barred to the generals now swung open, the clique organising their audiences at a hectic schedule. Democracy had come shaped as Stealth.

The *US News* three-day assignment there compensated for the disappointment Hanoi had been. It involved a leisurely rattle in a down train to Saigon before going overland to Cambodia. We were expressly forbidden to deviate from our programme or try to get up to the Ben Hai. A now serious Mum was attached to the trip, assisted by a junior fresh out of foreign-language school. Thang got monikered Slow Lane, infuriating us by nodding enthusiastically when not a word had been understood. He was puppy-dog eager to please, with a goofy grin and a liking for Salem Lights. Probably he had never eaten or lived so well in his life.

After the downer in Hanoi it was terrific to travel at a fifties pace with an old friend, the frames of our nostalgias, slipping and clicking leisurely by, the very rhythm of the journey opening up the windows of exorcism. We had both graduated from Vietnam; Denis had been in army intelligence before joining the Associated Press and doing a two-year spell in war-torn Cambodia. This oriental steeping left him at Indochina's end in Thailand, married, happy to be an expatriate. The train journey was akin to a return to childhood, neither of us looking forward to the anti-climax of our arrival in Ga Saigon. To put it off we arranged to take day trains (breaking our voyage at Hue and Nha Trang), the better to relish the beauty we had so casually absorbed during the war.

An intimacy, a camaraderie, enveloped our descent, punctuated by Jeff's maddening Game Boy locked on a beeping golf game. Seemingly he was oblivious to the passage of such rich historical sights. By now the stations, stops and halts were as familiar as those on the line to London from my local station in Kent.

Three down trips earlier, a half-length as far as Hue with Tien, I had shared a top-category compartment with Ron Moreau and his Vietnamese wife Lac. Lac and Ron had been together since his Peace Corps days in the sixties on the banks of the Mekong. Express it might have been labelled, slow local it was, the traffic on parallel Route One overtaking our labouring brick-red and soot-smeared Soviet locomotive. We jerked to a standstill so often that peasants working the fields had time to down tools and come vend an assortment of nibbles to the stalled passengers. These oddities were identified with relish by Lac, who had come prepared with bags of strategic reserves. Paddy crabs, frog's legs, sugar cane, bitter-sweet yellow plum or greengage-like fruit, bugs and bananas. Our compartment started to resemble a market. The battered pump Thermos from the first train ride provided the hot water for instant coffee to wash down the somewhat indigestible. We were lucky to have it, for the restaurant car had now run out of all food and drink.

We parked in Nam Dinh for an hour, Ninh Binh for two, no explanation. We should have been way down past Vinh by this time, a mere 300 kilometres south. At a station called Duc Lac we ground to yet another halt. Here the trackside enterprises were brick kilns and firewood production among the partially filled scars left over from the bombing campaign. These we regarded morosely until late afternoon, and the chill came on with the mist off the fields.

We clanked on for a few more kilometres at bicycle pace, to pull up sedately in the partly rebuilt ruins of Ghenh, the last stop before the single track made its sweep into the hills that guarded the approaches to the Ham Rong, the Dragon's Jaw, bridge north of Thanh Hoa. The added trackside attraction of Ga Ghenh was the skeletons of burnt-out goods wagons and box cars. The train fell asleep. Ron went to practise his language on the idling diesel. His footplate diplomacy might elicit a morsel of railroad intelligence about our progress unavailable from any of the other fifty-odd train crew, the six security lads included, the trackside phone being inoperative.

Could this be the state railway's personalised test of our collective patience? Were we singled out in some test programme devised by an inner circle of the Politburo? Had there been some cataclysmic international incident or natural catastrophe? For a long time, we pondered these and other questions.

Ron's smudged face and five-o'clock shadow hauled itself back into our car. Hell, there was time to roll another combat spliff and ruminate upon life's track, toke a little Hanoi gold from the garden.

'Patience is a virtue,' he declared. 'The up express has yet again been derailed!'

*You want to find Peace.*
*When you are with others you just want to be alone.*
*When you are alone you miss your friends.*
*But Peace doesn't arrive through being alone or being with others.*
*True Peace arises from right understanding.*

# *Glossary*

| | |
|---|---|
| Anka | the central body of the regime of Pol Pot in Cambodia 1975–79. |
| *ao dai* | the Vietnamese national costume for women, consisting of a diaphanous tunic over pantaloons. |
| AP | Associated Press, a cooperative wire news service, the world's largest. |
| ARVN | Army of the Republic of Vietnam: the forces serving the US-supported regime of the South. |
| *bao chi* | a member of the press. |
| *bodhi* tree | a bo tree, or peepul tree, sacred in Buddhist countries. |
| *bo doi* | a soldier or veteran. |
| *café sua* | *café au lait* made with condensed milk. |
| *can sa* | marijuana |
| Charlie, Mr Charles | nickname for the Vietcong. |
| Cochin | the southern part of Vietnam. |
| *com pho* | rice and soup; inn serving this. |
| *cuong* | a spirit house, a small shrine, sometimes no bigger than a bird table, holding offerings and incense. |
| cyclo or *cyclo pousse* | a bicycle rickshaw. |

| | |
|---|---|
| *dau suc* | 'crazy smoke', opium. |
| DMZ | the demilitarised zone along the 17th parallel, dividing North and South Vietnam. It was established 1967. |
| *doi moi* | a policy of reform and opening-up, the Vietnamese equivalent of the Soviet Union's *perestroika*, introduced in the late 1980s. |
| FANK | Cambodian opposition to Lon Nol 1970–75. |
| *ga* | a railway station. |
| *gai phong* | liberation. |
| Ho Chi Minh Trail | the main supply route for the Vietcong from North to South Vietnam. |
| *huong* | an incense stick. |
| ICC | International Control Commission, set up 1954 to oversee the Geneva accords of 1954. |
| *kach san* | a guesthouse or hotel. |
| *krama* | a traditional Khmer piece of fabric serving as a scarf, loincloth, headwrap or sarong. |
| KIA | killed in action. |
| klick | a kilometre. |
| *liet si* | war graves, military cemetery. |
| MIA | missing in action. |
| Minf | Ministry for Information, or a representative thereof. In Vietnam a foreigner is expected to liaise with the local Minf in each town visited. |
| Mini-Tet | Vietcong offensive in May 1968, |

| | |
|---|---|
| | supplementary to the Tet Offensive of February–March the same year. |
| Nhan Dan | People's Army of present-day Vietnam; also the name of the largest newspaper. |
| *nuoc nam* | fish sauce. |
| *nuoc da* | ice. |
| NVA | North Vietnamese Army. |
| *phnom* | hill. |
| *pho* | broad noodles, or the place where they are served. |
| SAM | surface-to-air missile. |
| Tet Offensive | Vietcong offensive in February 1968 that took the fighting into Saigon. |
| Tonkin | the northern part of Vietnam. |
| TOW | (target on wire) a type of missile. |
| UPI | United Press International, a news service. |
| USMC | United States Marine Corps. |
| VC | Vietcong. |
| Vietcong | the guerrilla resistance to the South Vietnamese regime. |
| Vietminh | the nationalist army formed 1941 to oppose the Japanese occupation of Indochina. Led by Ho Chi Minh, it subsequently fought against French colonial control. |
| VNAF | Vietnamese Air Force: the air force of the South Vietnamese government. |
| WIA | wounded in action. |

# *Maps*

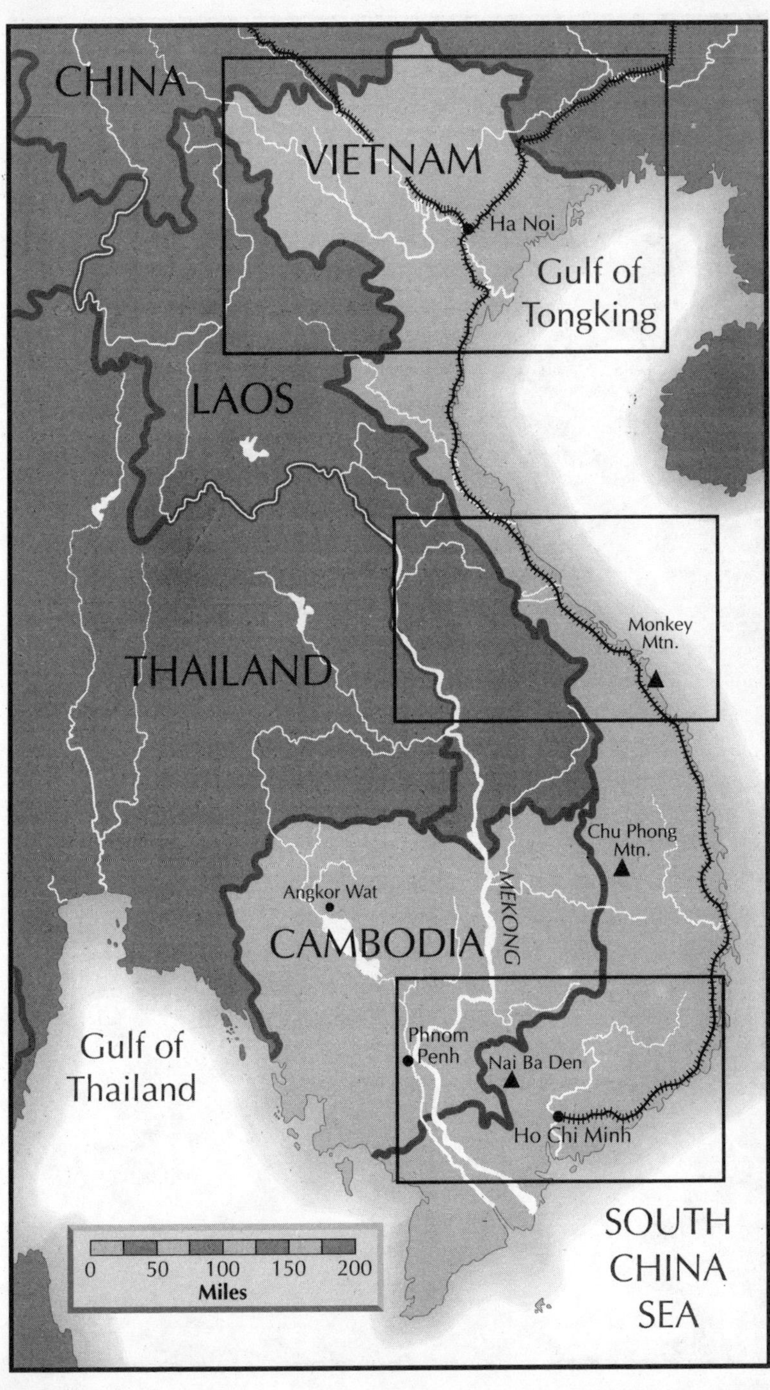
CHINA
VIETNAM
Ha Noi
Gulf of Tongking
LAOS
THAILAND
Monkey Mtn.
Chu Phong Mtn.
Angkor Wat
MEKONG
CAMBODIA
Phnom Penh
Nai Ba Den
Ho Chi Minh
Gulf of Thailand
SOUTH CHINA SEA
0 50 100 150 200
Miles

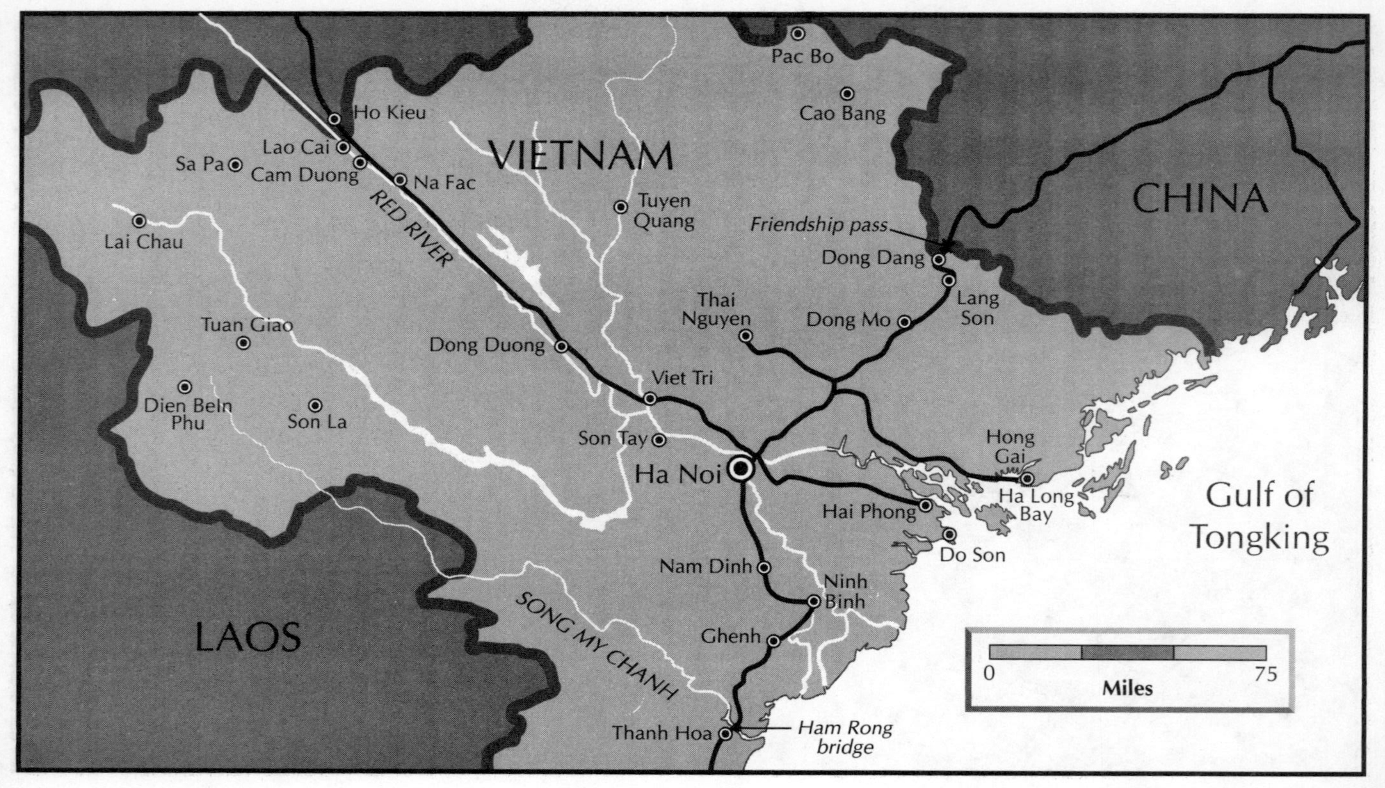
CHINA
VIETNAM
LAOS
Gulf of Tongking
Pac Bo
Cao Bang
Ho Kieu
Lao Cai
Sa Pa
Cam Duong
Na Fac
RED RIVER
Tuyen Quang
Friendship pass
Dong Dang
Lang Son
Lai Chau
Thai Nguyen
Dong Mo
Tuan Giao
Dong Duong
Viet Tri
Dien Beln Phu
Son La
Son Tay
Ha Noi
Hong Gai
Ha Long Bay
Hai Phong
Do Son
Nam Dinh
Ninh Binh
SONG MY CHANH
Ghenh
Thanh Hoa
Ham Rong bridge
0
75
Miles

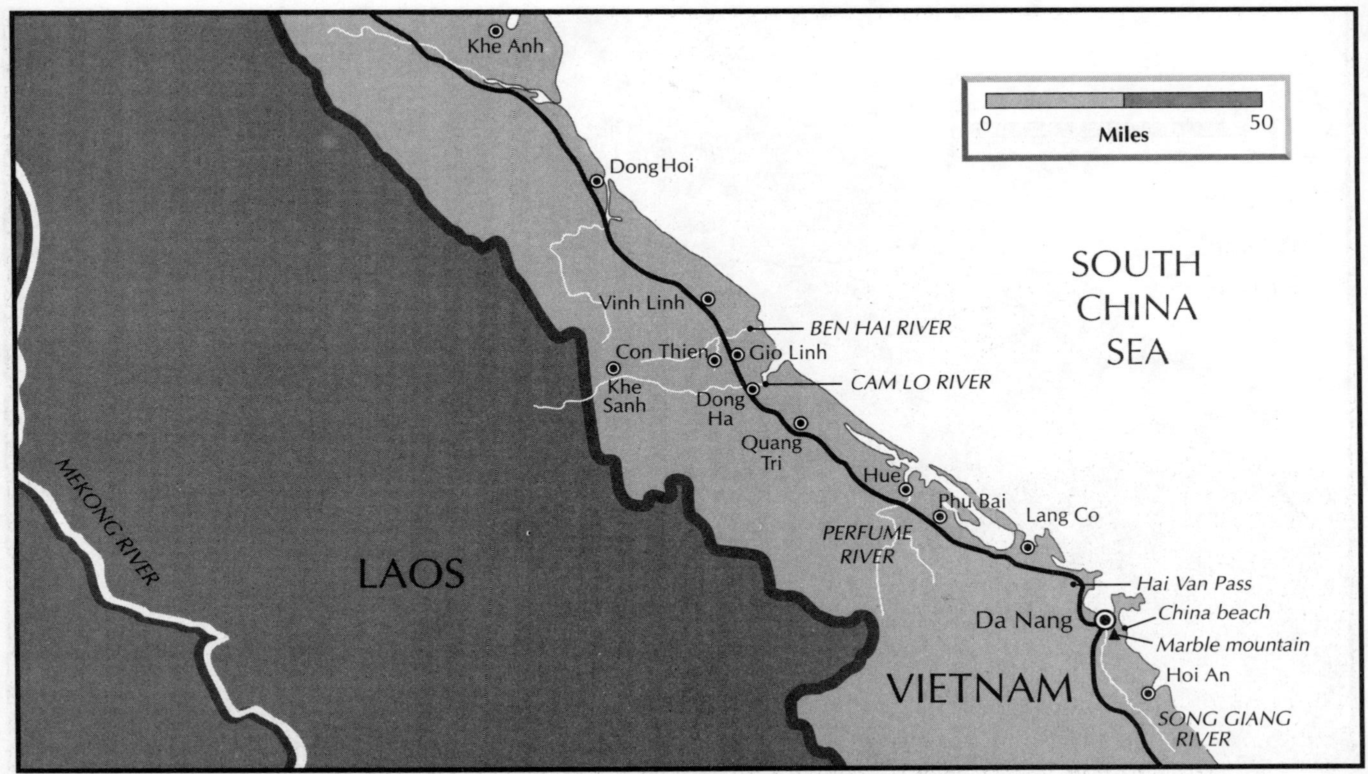
0
50
Miles
SOUTH CHINA SEA
Khe Anh
Dong Hoi
Vinh Linh
BEN HAI RIVER
Con Thien
Gio Linh
Khe Sanh
CAM LO RIVER
Dong Ha
Quang Tri
Hue
Phu Bai
Lang Co
PERFUME RIVER
Hai Van Pass
Da Nang
China beach
Marble mountain
Hoi An
SONG GIANG RIVER
VIETNAM
LAOS
MEKONG RIVER

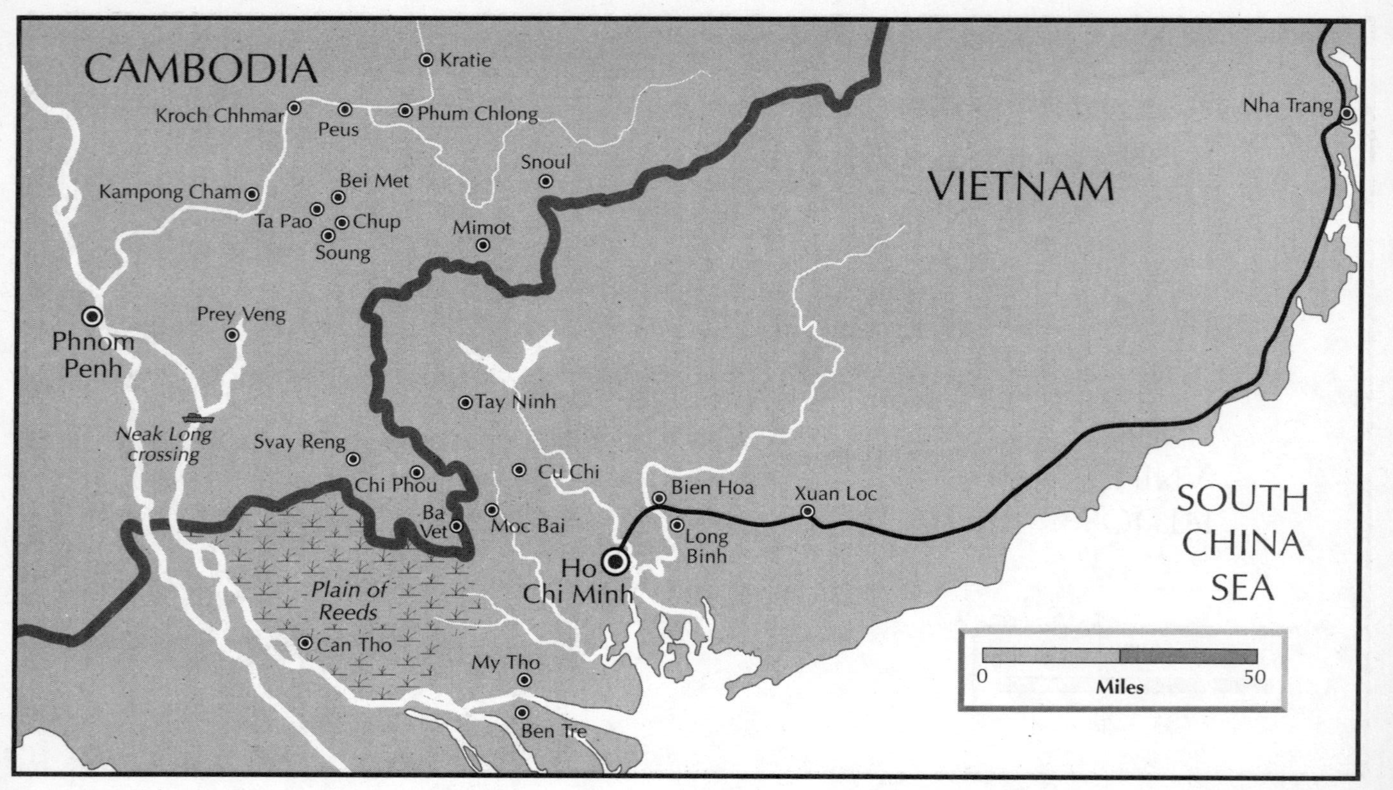
CAMBODIA
Kratie
Kroch Chhmar
Peus
Phum Chlong
Snoul
Kampong Cham
Bei Met
Ta Pao
Chup
Soung
Mimot
VIETNAM
Nha Trang
Phnom Penh
Prey Veng
Tay Ninh
Neak Long crossing
Svay Reng
Chi Phou
Cu Chi
Ba Vet
Moc Bai
Bien Hoa
Xuan Loc
Long Binh
Ho Chi Minh
Plain of Reeds
Can Tho
My Tho
Ben Tre
SOUTH CHINA SEA
0
Miles
50